MW01257269

EVENT MANAGEMENT SIMPLIFIED

Judy L. Anderson

authorHOUSE®

AuthorHouse™
1663 Liberty Drive
Bloomington, IN 47403
www.authorhouse.com
Phone: 1-800-839-8640

©2010 Judy L. Anderson. All Rights Reserved.

No part of this book may be reproduced, stored in a retrieval system, or transmitted by any means without the written permission of the author.

First published by AuthorHouse   03/16/2010

ISBN: 978-1-4490-7551-4

Library of Congress Control Number: 2010901080

Printed in the United States of America
Bloomington, Indiana

This book is printed on acid-free paper.

Introduction

"Let's Have An Event!"

These few words can be the start of an amazing adventure unlike any other. Each event is uniquely different, yet most contain common elements. Whether you are looking to create a new event or to revitalize a long-standing one, whether you are a novice or an experienced event planner, the systems, ideas and suggestions contained in *Event Management Simplified* are designed to help.

This book provides a systematic approach to event management for those wanting someone to "show them how to do it." The chapters are listed according to topic and most take no more than 15-20 minutes to read. Each chapter contains examples and worksheets to develop the detail required for nearly any kind of event.

These systems can be applied to festivals, galas, weddings, conventions, culinary and wine events, and many others. The exception to this is the management of charitable fundraising auctions which has been addressed in a separate book titled *Auction Management Simplified*. Many of the chapters are similar but the auction book contains alternate chapters with strategies regarding procurement of auction items, motivating bidders, and the writing of the auction catalog in addition to standard fundraising event elements.

Use this book as a reference tool to help create a customized management system that works for your event or to glean new ideas.

Event Management in General

Event management is an ever-changing landscape of new creative ideas, new ways to do things, new technology, new rewards, and new challenges. Part of the appeal of event management is that those who walk this path learn something new every day and on every event, and it never becomes boring.

While this book is a how-to manual about the techniques of event management, we did feel it important to address the characteristics of successful event managers and to provide tips as to where employment opportunities in the event industry may be found. Chapter One contains the core essence of being a credible, ethical event manager as well as other useful information.

Many of the examples given in the book are based on years of experience from the author and others to help share successes and pitfalls that event managers may encounter along the way.

Let Us Hear From You

We welcome your comments, ideas and suggestions. You can reach us via e-mail at powerproductions@comcast.net or check out our Website at www.eventsandauctions.com.

About The Author

Judy Anderson has more than 25 years of experience as an event producer in the public, private and nonprofit sectors. She specializes in large, complex events but helps events of all kinds and sizes. Her insights have a proven track record of incredible success in the fundraising arena where she has helped raise more than $12 million in the last ten years.

Anderson does event and auction management, consulting, and training work under the business name of Power Productions. She holds a Certificate in Festival and Event Management from the University of Oregon and frequently speaks at conferences and meetings about events, fundraising, and related topics.

Anderson is the author of two books. *Event Management Simplified* has been used as a course text by academic institutions including the University of Oregon's Festival and Event Management Certificate program and for Mt. Hood Community College's Hospitality and Tourism curriculum. Her second book, *Auction Management Simplified*, relates specifically to the elements of fundraising auctions and events held to benefit nonprofit organizations.

Credits

Kristin Anderson, Copy Editor
Heather Barta & Brenden Hyde, CircleTriangleSquare Graphic Design
Maria Corvallis, Peter Corvallis Productions
Gavin D'Avanther, Hollywood Lighting Services
Dona Eadus, Copy Editor
Patty Larkins, Copy Editor
Royce Mason III, Royce's Prop Shop
Tim Neill, Opus Solutions
Pascal Sauton, Carafe Bistro
Kim Seid, Metropolitan Printing Company
Becky Stroebel-Johnson, Sterling Talent Enterprises
Paul Vogel, Vogel Communications

Table of Contents

CHAPTER 4: COMMITEES

CHAPTER 5: SPONSORSHIP

CHAPTER 6: MARKETING & PROMOTIONS

CHAPTER 7: GRAPHIC DESIGN & PRINTING

CHAPTER 8: LIABILITY, PERMITS, & SECURITY

CHAPTER 9: VENUES

CHAPTER 10: FOOD & BEVERAGE

CHAPTER 14: VOLUNTEERS

CHAPTER 15: THE EVENT

CHAPTER 16: POST EVENT ACTIVITY

<u>Chapter 1 – Getting Started</u>

PLEASE NOTE: The systems outlined in this book work for both large and small scale events. Apply the systems to whatever degree is appropriate.

Event Management As A Career

Event management is currently one of the hottest careers out there. But a word to the wise… if you're going to be an event manager, be a good one! There are a lot of event managers (a.k.a. planners) doing celebrations of all kinds but it doesn't necessarily mean they are good at it. Just because someone coordinated their parents' anniversary party, their own wedding, or the office party doesn't make them a good event manager. It can take years to develop a reputation as a highly regarded event professional but it takes very little time to destroy your credibility.

A lot of people get into event management because it seems like "fun." They attend an event and say, "I can do that," but they only see the end result. Those of us who have been doing this awhile can say, "yes it is fun," but prior to that it's also a lot of hard work, long hours, heavy responsibility, stressful, and—if you're not careful—can turn out to be a big disaster. This is not to dissuade anyone from joining the ranks of event planners but if you're looking for an eight-to-five job with weekends off, this is probably not the career for you.

"Success is not about how fast you run, or how high you climb, but how well you bounce."

Malcom Forbes

Being an independent planner gives one the option to choose the events you want to work on and the clients you want to work with, and the sky is the limit on income. The downside is that you must do your own marketing and are taking all the risks and bearing all the costs of supporting a business.

There are some other things about the event industry that have mass appeal. A college degree isn't required, you don't need a fancy office space or you can work from home, start ups don't require a lot of capital, and it doesn't require much equipment or staff.

Industry standards have been developed by the International Special Events Society (ISES). This is the elite professional association for event planners and those in related services. In addition to a vast network of members, the association offers education and accreditation to become a Certified Special Events Professional (CSEP). This organization has local chapters in many states and countries. More information can be found on the Internet at www.ises.com.

Most event managers fall into two categories—in-house planner (directly employed by a corporation or nonprofit organization) or independent planner (self-employed). While corporate planners work hard, in some ways they have it easier than planners who work for nonprofit organizations because they have pre-established budgets and proceed to get things done.

Event managers in the nonprofit world not only have to coordinate the events, they often have to work with chairmen and management who may have opposing points of view. They must also interface with staff, coordinate committees, and essentially raise the money to pay their salaries through the charitable events they oversee.

Working for an established company or organization is a good way to gain experience before taking on the risks of starting your own business. The drawback is that the employer controls your income (usually at an "exempt employee" salary for which you will work many hours of unpaid overtime) and the employer controls your time with the exception of your annual vacation or paid holidays.

In economic downturn, corporate event planners are often the first positions to be cut. But those events they used to plan still need to go on, so this may be an opportunity for independent planners to contract for this work.

Many event managers start out as someone's employee before going it on their own. Choose whichever career path suits you best.

NOTES

Characteristics of Top Event Managers

- Well organized with attention to detail
  (event managers need to be organized people!)
- Ability to multi-task
  (the more you can do, the higher the level of responsibility)
- Honest and ethical
  (guard your integrity, it only takes a moment to destroy your credibility)
- Outgoing with social skills
  (don't have to be an extrovert, just able to carry on a conversation)
- Ability to meet people
  (we need to interact with many types of people)
- Listening skills
  (hear what they say and clarify what they are looking for)
- Communication skills
  (people want to know what's going on)
- Ability to motivate others
  (creates buy-in and willingness to help)
- Treating people with respect
  (ask others for their opinions and input)
- Ability to delegate
  ("manage" rather than "do" everything yourself)
- Hardworking
- Ability to handle stress
  (don't cry, yell or act unprofessional, work through it)
- A sense of humor
  (there's a point in every event where you just have to laugh)
- Resourceful and creative vision
  (find a way to make it happen, Plan A/B/C, Big Picture thinker)
- Knows their limits
  (when to ask for help, limits of physical and emotional endurance)
- Business knowledge
  (accounting/bookkeeping, writing, database, sales and marketing)
- Computer skills
  (word processing, Internet, spreadsheets, database, desktop publishing)

What Employers Look For

- On-the-job experience
- Proven track record of success
- Attention to detail
- Ability to work with people of varied backgrounds and cultures
- Computer skills
- Basic food & wine knowledge
- Flexibility
- Team player
- Sincerity and enthusiasm
- Ability to work independently and carry out directives
- Positive attitude
- Event related education

Where To Look For Jobs

Casinos	Networking groups
Caterers	Nonprofit organizations
Chambers of commerce	Park & recreation districts
Convention centers	Party rental companies
Convention/visitor bureaus	PR/marketing firms
Corporations	Professional associations
Country clubs	Municipalities
Cruise lines	Theme parks
Destination management	Trade associations
Event planning companies	Universities
Hotels	Venues
Incentive organizations	Wedding industry
Industry associations	Many more
Museums	

How To Begin

Every event has to start somewhere. Whether it is a new or a pre-existing event, the beginning steps are basically the same.

- ➢ Identify the Event Manager
- ➢ Select the Leadership
- ➢ Set Up the Tracking Systems
- ➢ Do Preliminary Research
- ➢ Develop Critical Strategy

Identify The Event Manager

Someone has to be in charge. The event manager can be a paid staff person, an independent contractor, or a high level volunteer. Professional event managers can often offset the cost of their services by knowing ways to save money and time. In many cases, and particularly in the nonprofit arena, the event manager has the opportunity to raise money to cover their salary and benefits. Independent event managers may be a good option for companies or organizations that don't wish to employ a full time events person.

The event manager has day-to-day responsibility, is the main contact, and tracks every single detail. He/she should be qualified, rather than someone who just wants to help out because it sounds like fun. The event manager doesn't need to know how to do *everything*, just where to look for information or to whom the task can be delegated.

In addition to the characters of a top event manager given in the previous section, here are some more to think about:

- Previous experience in events of similar size and/or scope
- Positive recommendations from previous event affiliations
- Ability to commit the time required for successful outcome
- Understanding of budget processes and cost control
- Contacts to leverage for sponsors, donors, etc.
- Problem solving and negotiating skills

"A goal without a plan is just a wish."

Antoinne de Saint Exupery

It is **not helpful** if the event manager thinks they have to control everything or is doing it for their own glory. This will not gain commitment on the part of others. Every person who comes in contact with the event should feel their ideas and opinions are valued. The core foundation of any event is building positive relationships for long-term success. Even critics have some truth to their opinions.

It's A Business

One of the best pieces of advice to remember is that even though it may be a party, treat the event like a business whether it's a charity event or for-profit. Businesses are in business to make and save money. Make every dollar you can, and save every dollar you can. That is how true professional event managers view events.

You'll want to have enthusiasm and put on a great event, but no one will take you seriously if you have a "party-all-the-time" mentality. This holds true whether you work for an employer or are self-employed. You want to gain a reputation as a serious, successful event manager.

NOTE: An example of an Event Manager job description appears at the end of this chapter.

Leadership Selection

In keeping with the business aspect, an event can be viewed as a specialized business requiring strong leaders and good employees to flourish. In applying this to the selection of event chairpersons, the higher the level of involvement by people who are successful in their own right, the better the event's chances for success. Careful selection of chairpersons and committee members will pay off in big dividends. Part of any business strategy is to leverage relationships that help the business to grow. Events are no different.

If the event has chairpersons, they should be carefully selected for their individual abilities to help build the event. Since the purpose of most events is to raise money or cover costs in some fashion, it is critical to have strong leaders who can provide focus and support. Key players have already built a community for themselves and can help extend your network.

Selection of chairpersons by the "take-whoever-is-available method" is counter-productive because the well-being of the event is partially dependent on their personal efforts. Others also take their cue from how much the chairs are doing. Another positive aspect is that business or community leaders who are acting as chairpersons want their name to be associated with events that are successful and they will work extra hard to ensure this outcome.

For small events with a minimal budget, the "power" level of chairpersons is not as critical as that of a multi-level, multi-day event that must raise substantial sponsorship revenue and motivate large numbers of people to attend or purchase products. Either way, the chairpersons need to be working partners that help make things happen and not just be acting as figureheads.

Setting Up The Tracking Systems

Master Notebook

For many event planners, especially beginners, a notebook system works well. With experience, you can operate from any method you choose. Task lists, notes and other materials are kept in their relevant sections and are moved out to regular file folders to relieve bulk as they are completed or no longer needed.

Use this notebook as your daily working tool. You'll need a 3" ring size and dividers to separate the notebook contents into the sections you desire.

NOTES

Use the following suggested divider sections or customize them for your event's activities and place the ones you'll use most to the front of the book. Some of these may even require their own separate notebook (e.g. exhibitors).

Board/Chairs	Printing
Committees	Production / Entertainment
Financial	Post Event
Exhibitors	Registration
Food / Beverage	Site Plans
Legal / Permits	Sponsors
Logistics Schedule	Volunteers
Marketing / PR	

If this isn't a new event, in the divided section, you would want to begin with *copies* of the previous year's materials that will need to be recreated for the current event cycle.

There are two reasons to use copies. One is that you don't want to be carrying around original documents (such as contracts) in case the notebook gets misplaced. The second is because you can jot notes directly onto the copies as you think of them. Use these to generate the new materials and put the new version in the notebook. Their either file or toss out the marked up copy. It's often helpful to retain these, if only for a short time, to remember what the original version said or looked like.

If you're one of those people who keep everything on a laptop computer, that's fine too but it's not quite as easy as flipping open the notebook.

For new events, use the same system, but you'll operate more from "timelines and work lists," inserting copies of documents into the notebook as they are created. In the beginning, a great many things will be "missing," but use sections lists to keep track. You can also put samples from other events into your notebook as resources.

Section Lists

NOTE: All items on section lists should be included on work lists as described in the next chapter.

For example, in the Sponsor section of the notebook, a limited version of your section list might read as follows. Tasks requiring creation of documents are indicated by an *asterisk.

*Create a list of potential cash sponsors and contacts
*Create a list of potential in-kind sponsors and contacts
*Develop benefits list based on sponsor levels
*Develop sponsor proposal packet and background information
*Develop confirmation forms
 Determine who will sign letters
 Determine who will personally contact each prospect
 Establish timeframe for follow up
 Determine sponsor gifts
 Sponsor logo or ad received (if in the program)
*Confirmation letter outlining sponsor's role with background
  information regarding parking, VIP privileges, etc.
*Post-event thank you letter accompanied by sponsor gift

As tasks are completed and documents are created, highlight them off the list and put copies in the notebook. Remember, this is your working tool, so set it up in the way that works best for you.

If you don't use a notebook system, you can create folders (like dividers) on your computer and in your file cabinet.

Computer Programs

You can track event progress and generate the materials and documents needed by using basic computer software like Word, Excel and Access. There is no need to spend thousands of dollars on a fancy program with multiple features you may never use if you're just doing basic functions.

A financial program is helpful or you can use Excel. It also helps to have a desktop publishing program like MS Publisher or similar software to create quick flyers or other printing needs.

Specialized software programs for events like auctions that require the maintenance of specific data, or for meeting or conference management that requires extensive registration, can pay for themselves in one use. If you plan to purchase any type of event management software, always ask for references of people who use it to ensure it will meet your needs and function as promised.

Preliminary Research

Prior to the Strategic Planning session, you'll want answers to some rudimentary questions. Do some research in advance. If not, include these kinds of questions in the creative planning process.

- What is our reason for considering this event?

  If the answer is "because it sounds like fun," you may want to reconsider because that's not a good enough reason. While events can be fun, they require substantial amounts of time, manpower and resources to be successful. They must also be feasible in order to attract sponsors, vendors and attendees.

  If the answer is "because we want to raise funds for a specific charity," "because there is nothing like it in our community," because we have a niche market," or a similar statement, then proceed with caution.

- What time of year might be our best chance for success?
- Are there other events like it in the community/region?
- When are they held?
- Are there open dates in the community's event calendar?

- Are there other things going on locally/regionally/nationally such as major sporting events, religious holidays, a major event at the convention center, a nationally televised event, or the like which might impact attendance?
- Based on the type or location of the event, are permits or insurance required and are there related fees?

The more unique you can make the event, the better its chance for success. If you're doing the same thing every other organization in town is doing, you may want to reconsider. Events that offer opportunities to see and experience new things have much better odds. If you're freshening up an older event, add some new twists to revitalize interest.

Event Categories

There are as many kinds of events as there are stars in the sky. Some are stand-alone events, but most a mixture of several kinds. For example, a dance is a simple concept. Make it a dinner dance, or a dance included as part of a convention's activities, and see how the concept changes based on the elements involved?

Generally, events fall into three categories—personal, special interest or community. These can, and do, cross over on a regular basis. A few examples are listed below:

Personal
Birthdays
Anniversaries
Weddings
Family reunions

Special Interest
Conferences, conventions
Trade shows
Auctions
Charitable fundraisers
Employee functions

Community Oriented
Fairs, festivals
Parades, runs, walks
Concerts, dances

Strategy Equals Success

Success in event management requires a great deal of strategy. This holds true regardless of the type of event being undertaken. Some call strategy the creative process, strategic planning, or other names. By employing strategy, it becomes more exciting than just "nuts and bolts" and adds a "thinking outside the box" perspective.

Creative strategy is critical to sustaining an event's longevity, attendance, and revenue producing power. Strategy is employed in all phases of event management. This includes the initial planning process, recruitment of chairpersons and committee members, development of the budget, venue selection, solicitation of sponsors, obtaining donations, food and beverage, invitations to guests, and more. Each of these strategies is discussed in related chapters in this book.

Regardless of whether the event is new or not, you'll want to hold a creative session to brainstorm ideas. If the event is new, there will be much to discuss and a substantial amount of time will be required to follow up on questions generated during the discussion (e.g. how much things cost, site or date availability, manpower requirements, etc.). If the event already has a history, creative planning is done annually to enhance the existing elements or to add new ones.

At the initial session, you'll want to:

- Determine the event and name (if new)
- Select a date or time of year
- Identify the event demographic (who is the audience?)
- Research several potential venues
- Identify potential chairpersons (if not in place)
- Set goals and measurable outcomes
- Clarify what you are and where you are going
- Discuss strategies to accomplish the desired outcomes

HERE'S AN EXAMPLE OF THINKING OUTSIDE THE BOX:
It was the job of the current co-chairs of a big charity fundraiser to recruit their successors and help them transition into their role. This was done on a rotation basis with a two-year commitment. One chairperson was always remaining, and one would drop off with a new person taking their place and being "trained up" to become the senior chairperson the following year.

The co-chairs went to the CEO of a big bakery chain and asked him to become an event chair. He said "Absolutely Not" for two years in a row, but the third year they first went to a large grocery chain and asked the CEO of that company to be a chairperson. He agreed. Then they went back to the CEO of the bakery and asked again. He said "yes" this time, and can you guess why? The rationale behind this strategy was that the big grocery chain was the bakery's main customer and if the CEO of that company had already agreed, the CEO of the bakery couldn't say no. It worked!

Remember that employing creative strategy is not only for the current event cycle. It will lay groundwork for the future as well. Think ahead and use this time to access the brainpower of others to build the framework of your event. Thinking "outside of the box" is a major key to success.

"As long as you're going to be thinking, think big."

Donald Trump

Who Should Attend The Meeting

Invite enough people (8-10 total is a good number) to have a lively, thorough discussion, but not so many as to be cumbersome. Too many people just bog down the system. The initial group involved often becomes the advisory committee as the event moves forward.

Be selective about who participates and keep the future in mind. Include persons of varying perspectives—those who are big picture thinkers as well as those who are more detail oriented. Don't forget those who may be able to significantly benefit the event as potential chairs or committee chairs, sponsors, key staff or volunteers.

If your event is not new, be sure to include at least a few key people who have been attendees, sponsors, former chairpersons, or high level volunteers. This can translate into renewed interest on their part, helps to keep things fresh and exciting, and maintains the "institutional memory" of the event. Try to avoid having the same people being part of this activity year after year. You need some new people with new ideas to keep the event from going stale.

The Strategy Session

Identify the facilitator in advance. This person should be a recognized leader who can keep things moving while being respectful of individual opinions. All ideas are equal during the creative process, no matter how outlandish they may seem. Sometimes the craziest ideas are what make your event unique and highly successful.

At the end of the session, there should be a fairly large list the group has produced. Pare it down to basic essentials that are realistic. As people commit to do things, write them down, assign a deadline, and hold them accountable (who, what, and by when).

Prior to the scheduled strategic planning session, distribute an agenda of the main topics for discussion (7-10 days is ideal). For the actual session, allocate specific blocks of time for discussing each agenda item. This avoids talking too much about the first items and never getting to the last items. Place the most important items at the beginning of the agenda.

Allow adequate time and avoid interruptions (no cell phones, emailing, or text messaging allowed!). Two or three hours are usually enough to get a good start if you stick to the agenda and have a good facilitator. People tend to lose their focus and creativity if the meeting runs too long. The point is to keep moving and not get bogged down on any one thing.

Once the initial session has been completed, the plan should be documented, then reviewed and revised at a later time, along with an accompanying budget. Don't expect the plan to remain exactly the same as when you began. Strategies will evolve and change as event components are clearly defined and things begin to move forward.

Setting Realistic Goals

Be sure the strategic planning agenda includes major goals to which measurable outcomes are attached. Think about the purpose of the event and create your goals around it. Keep it to five major goals that will encompass the essence of what you're trying to accomplish.

Remember that goals aren't always about money! They can be for purposes such as marketing, creating awareness, building membership, giving of awards of recognition, etc.

An example of a monetary goal:

GOAL: To raise $35,000 for the XYZ Charity
OUTCOME: A net profit of $10,000 or more after expenses

There is additional benefit in setting this measurable outcome. Once detailed expense projections are identified in the budget, you will know how much revenue in total the event must generate in order to cover all expenses and still net the $10,000 for the charity.

Keep detailed money discussions for another time. Strategic planning is to generate ideas and talking about money stops the creative process.

If you must identify revenue sources as part of the discussion, keep to a broad perspective such as "We will raise revenue through sponsorship, ticket sales" and so on rather than trying to specifically identify who will be sponsors, how many tickets need to be sold, and the like for each revenue or expense category.

NOTES

A detailed budget can be developed, discussed and adopted at a later date and will allow time to identify which ideas may prove too costly to implement.

An example of a marketing goal:

GOAL: To market an outdoor festival via the community newspaper, print ads, and direct mail to increase attendance

OUTCOME: Tabloid insert in the newspaper, accurate count at the entry gate, survey attendees as to how they learned about the event

The secondary outcome would be the identification of the marketing method/s that worked best in bringing attendees to the event.

Use the worksheet at the end of the chapter to help you get started. Then add your own ideas.

NOTES

Event Manager Job Description

Reports To: Board of Directors, CEO, Event Chairpersons
Supervises: Event Assistant, Volunteers

DUTIES & RESPONSIBILITIES

1. Implements and oversees all aspects of event with input from Board of Directors, event chairs, committee chairs and others
2. Provides support to Board, chairpersons and committees
3. Works to build strong relationships and encourage participation by individuals and businesses.
4. Creates and implements the event timeline
5. Responsible for venue, date, changes or additions to event lineup
6. Manages the event budget including revenues and expenses
7. Coordinates all legal, permit and insurance requirements with jurisdictions and venues
8. Oversees all activity for the main event, related events, and activities
9. Oversees contractors and their related services, including contract negotiation
10. Oversees entertainment, including contracts and related production requirements
11. Oversees public relations and marketing activities
12. Manages sponsor relations and communication
13. Manages media relations and media sponsors
14. Coordinates production of all printing and related processes
15. Oversees volunteer recruitment and activity
16. Supervises the event assistant, delegates on special projects, and monitors daily activity
17. Coordinates follow up activities, including post-event media, thank you letters and gifts
18. Responsible for final budget tabulation and report to Board of Directors or Executive Committee
19. Acts as the authorized representative of the Board on behalf of event

QUALIFICATIONS

1. B.A. or equivalent experience required
2. 3-5 years progressively responsible event management experience
3. Demonstrated accountability in event budget management
4. Proficiency in computerized word processing and spreadsheet software required
5. Database experience preferred
6. Ability to use desktop publishing software a plus

USE THIS JOB DESCRIPTION TO CREATE YOUR OWN, OR TO QUALIFY A CONSULTANT.

Organizational Chart Example

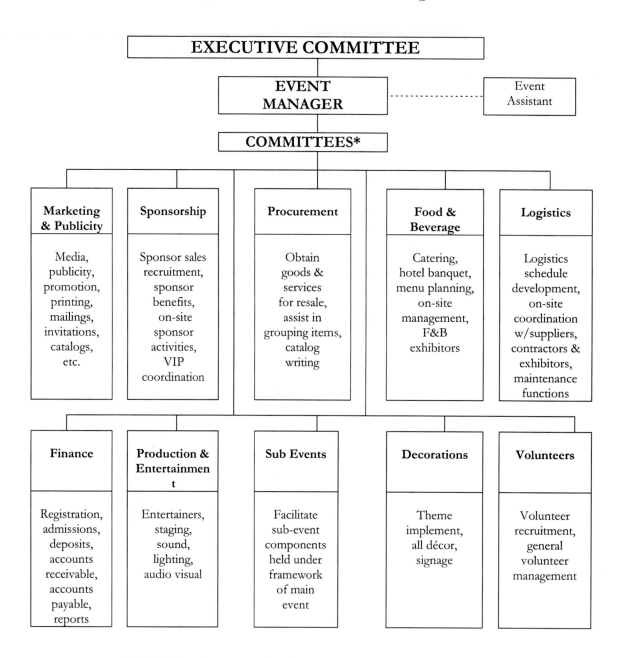

*NOTE: Not all events require all committees and some may require none.
The event manager may perform some of these roles as part of their job description.

Getting Started Worksheet

Filling the Leadership Roles

1. Has the event manager been designated? _____
2. Will there be a selection process? _____
3. What is the financial compensation, if any? _____
4. Does the event manager or consultant have the level of qualifications desired? _____
5. Does a detailed job description exist? _____
6. Have event chairpersons been designated? _____
7. Other _____

Setting Up the Systems

1. From what location will administration of the event be conducted? _____
2. Where will records be kept? _____
3. Is office equipment readily available (phone, fax, copier)? _____
4. Are there a computer and printer available with enough power/memory to handle the workload and software requirements? _____
5. Are recent versions of software like Microsoft Word/Excel/Access or a desktop publishing program installed and operational on the computer? _____
6. Will the event need email or Internet capability? _____
7. Will specialized software be required? _____
8. Anything else? _____

Preliminary Research

1. Will this be a general or special interest event? _____
2. What is the reason for doing the event? _____
3. What time of year might work and why? _____
4. Are there similar events in the community and when? _____
5. Are open dates available to hold this event? _____
6. Are other major events going on that may impact the ability to draw attendees or sponsors? _____
7. Are permits, fees, or special insurance required? _____
8. What are the approval channels? _____
9. Other? _____

The Strategists

1. Who might be invited to be part of the strategic planning process? _____
2. Is there a good cross-section of big picture thinkers, detail-oriented persons, and potential leaders or sponsors? _____
3. Other? _____

The Strategy Session

1. Was an agenda distributed outlining the expected outcomes? _____
2. Does the agenda contain set timeframes for each topic of discussion? _____
3. Have preliminary research questions been addressed? _____
4. What is the organizational structure? _____
5. Where will the event be held?_____ Is there a creative location? _____
6. How many attendees are expected? _____
7. What is the target demographic/audience? _____
8. Do the suggested activities fit the demographic? _____
9. What activities will be included? _____
10. What makes this event unique to draw attendance? _____
11. What are the main goals and outcomes targeted for success? _____
12. What is the measurement standard for each goal? _____
13. Is there a theme? _____
14. What resources are available (staff, equipment, volunteers, etc.)? _____
15. What other resources do we need? _____
16. What benefits will justify the sponsors' return on investment? _____
17. What kinds of committees are needed? _____
18. Have committee chairpersons been identified and recruited? _____
19. What charity will benefit and is it a good fit with the event? _____
20. What will the charity be required to do (recruit sponsors, provide volunteers, etc.)? _____
21. What resources does the charity have that can be tapped? _____
22. Are there any potential problems we can foresee? _____
23. _____
24. _____
25. _____

Chapter 2 – Timelines and Work Lists

Start At The End and Work Backward.

The process of creating the event timeline and work lists goes hand-in-hand with the budgeting process. You can't do one without the other. You will also need to incorporate information that was generated from the strategy session into these documents.

It's often easier to do a draft of the General Timeline and Work Lists first because you can see tasks, time commitments and other elements that will affect the budget. Then, as you create the budget, you will find things that weren't plugged into the timeline and work lists. Once the general timeline is completed, you may prefer to work on the budget before completing the work lists since you will have developed a conceptual view of the basics involved.

As you begin to develop the general timeline and work lists, you will most assuredly feel that it is a tedious and elementary thing to do. Events are extremely complex and, if done correctly, this process will take many hours to complete. It is by far the most time consuming part of your initial planning, but along with the budget, is *one of the most important things you can do to ensure success and keep everything on track.*

When finished, you will have completed the first draft of the timeline and work lists, plus a timeline for each element of the event. As the event progresses, you will continually add to this original list and cross off things as they are completed or found to be unnecessary.

In this chapter, you will find information about how to:

> ➢ Create a General Timeline
> ➢ Create Monthly and Weekly Work lists
> ➢ Use These Tools in Conjunction with the Budget

"Don't say you don't have enough time. You have exactly the same number of hours in a day that were given to Helen Keller, Louis Pasteur, Michaelangelo, Mother Teresa, Leonardo da Vinci, Thomas Jefferson, and Albert Einstein."

H. Jackson Brown

Before You Begin

Understand the Ripple Effect. Just like the ripples that radiate from a pebble thrown into the water, nearly everything in event management has an effect on something else, which in turn has an effect on something else, and so on.

FOR EXAMPLE: If a sponsor backs out, you may have to find a new one, increase revenue in other areas, or reduce expenses to offset the loss. You may need to change marketing materials or signage, or may need to revise the budget and work lists to reflect new financial figures and changes in related tasks.

Identify the event cycle. Based on the date of the event, the "event cycle" means the window of time from the day/month that planning begins to the day/month post-event activity wraps up. Most events are on an annual cycle, though some may happen more than once a year, or may be "one time only." *Keep in mind that an event cycle does not end the day after the event takes place!*

Using a 12-month (annual) cycle analogy, the actual event would ideally occur around the eleventh or twelfth month of the cycle. This does not necessarily mean, however, that planning for an event with a 12-month cycle would begin only ten months in advance. An event like an anniversary party has a very short lead time compared to the longer lead times that may be required for booking of some venues, soliciting high level sponsorships, etc.

Identify the budget cycle. Ideally, the budget cycle should align with the event cycle. This allows time in advance for generating revenues and enough time following the event for payment of bills, receipt of remaining revenues, final financial reports, etc.

Incorporate the identified goals. The event goals and the steps to their accomplishment need to be incorporated into the timeline and work lists.

The General Timeline

The general timeline is a broad concept that outlines the major elements of the event cycle and projected dates for their completion. The timeline should also include references as to what, when and who is responsible.

Creating the general timeline first gives a visual "overview" as to how the event will flow and where the bulk of the work will occur. It also establishes a foundation from which the budget and work lists can be developed. A side benefit is that it provides a reference point in establishing timelines for individual event elements and related activities.

The general timeline is used as a basic guide and is distributed to chairpersons, committee members, key volunteers and staff. It demonstrates the event progression and should include major elements as well as things that affect others (print deadlines, pre-determined meeting dates, major mailings, target dates, etc.). The identification of specific tasks is defined in the work list process.

Allow plenty of time to think through the general timeline and write it down. Don't underestimate the amount of time it will take. A good rule of thumb is 4-8 hours or more, depending on the size and complexity of the event. The timeline will change several times as you work through the subsequent processes of the budget and work lists.

Information to help you draft the timeline is located in the back of this chapter:

> ➢ Suggested timeframe list
> ➢ General timeline example

Novice event managers can use these tools as a starting point, or seasoned event planners can use them as a cross-reference.

The timeline can be produced in a table format or spreadsheet program that allows you to sort the information in different ways. Since we are dealing with "basic" event management concepts, the example shown at the back of the chapter shows a word processing format. Use the method that works best for you. It is sometimes helpful to produce the timeline manually and then enter the information into the computer, since physically writing it down often aids in remembering what needs to be accomplished.

Steps to the Timeline Process

- Start with the event date and work backward (except for items that occur after the event has taken place. Keep it simple and on a broad stroke basis. Remember, you'll define individual tasks in the work list process.

- Use a "by the month" system and enter each major element, activity or deadline into the month when it should occur. If you know the specific date, go ahead and use it. Otherwise, you can go back and enter it later.

For example, timeline listings for June might include:

JUNE

(WHAT)	(WHO)	(BY WHEN)
Executive committee mtg.	Event manager	June 5
Budget adoption	Finance chair	June 5
First press release	PR chair	June 15
Newsletter mailing	Event assistant	June 30
Venue contract signed	Event manager	June

- If something happens every month, enter it into each individual month's listings. For those things that happen more than once a month, just indicate how many times (e.g. Executive Committee x2) if you don't have the specific dates at the beginning.

Work Lists

Creating the work list is the process of implementing the timeline to ensure that no detail or task is overlooked as the event progresses. The work list includes all items on the general timeline, all deadlines, and the majority of tasks required for successful completion of the event. It converts the event tracking process into weekly—rather than monthly—segments. During the busiest times, you may even want to break the weekly work lists down into daily components.

The work list is the single most valuable tool (in addition to the budget) that you can create. It will keep everything on track. It will keep you organized. It leaves nothing to chance. It requires many hours to develop, but will pay off in ways you could never imagine. *One incentive is to remember that whatever you fail to plan for now will cost time and/or money to "fix" later.*

As the event cycle progresses, the work list will become your daily working tool. You'll add to it, and highlight off tasks as they are completed. Don't cross anything out with a black line unless it is a totally deleted task that is not going to happen. Allow space on every work list for notes and additions. By the time a work list gets filed, it should be marked up, highlighted, and look just like it sounds.

MAKE THE WORK FUN: If you use an assortment of colored highlighters to mark through completed tasks, you can still read them easily and your work list looks like a rainbow by the time it gets filed!

Don't underestimate how much time tasks take to complete. Seasoned event managers should have a fairly good concept of how much time tasks take to complete. Those who are new should allow more time for planning, as well as for the margin of trial and error. If you are new to event management, a good rule of thumb is to double the amount of time you think it will take. Some things will actually take 5 minutes and other things you thought would take 5 minutes will take 5 hours.

Due to the involvement of chairpersons and committees, things tend to change a lot during the ebb and flow of the event, sometimes to the point of doing things over several times because so many people are allowed to have input on various levels. If you can't be flexible in this regard, you probably should consider a different career.

Save your work lists. They will prove invaluable in planning for the next event. You'll find things that could have been done sooner or things that could have waited. Make notations directly on the work lists as soon as you think of them. You'll be too busy to remember them later.

HINT: Carry a pocket-sized notepad and jot down things you need to do or remember as soon as you think of them. Later, you can transfer them to the work list or put the notes in a file for future reference. You may even want to keep a notepad and pen on your bedside table for those times when you can't sleep because of all the things you are trying to remember to do. Writing it down takes just a few seconds, gets it off your mind, and allows you to relax.

Use the Work List example at the back of the chapter for ideas.

Steps to the Work List Process

- Break each month of the event cycle into weekly increments (Monday-Sunday) and list their dates
- Incorporate each major element listed in the general timeline into the work list according to the date/s specified
- Take all event elements and break them down into individual tasks placing them in their proper "week" based on your best estimate of when it needs to be done. You'll need to enter things pertinent to your role (and that of your assistant if you have one) that aren't included in the general timeline.
- In allocating time for the duration of tasks, remember that many of these will take longer than estimated. Delegate as much of the work as possible so your role is to "manage" rather than "do."

Here's what an example from the general timeline of what June might look like and also applying the "ripple effect."

The original items from general timeline are shown in bold type. Related tasks would appear in the proper "week" in the same month, or would be on a separate work list depending on the month. For the week of June 17, no specific items were carried over from the general timeline but there were tasks to be done.

WEEK OF JUNE 3-9	**RELATED TASKS INTO "WEEK OF"**
Executive meeting 6/5	Agenda out 2 weeks earlier (5/20)
	Confirm meeting space 30 days ahead (5/5)
	Place catering order 3 days before
	Meeting follow up 1 day after
Budget adoption	Budget developed 2 months earlier (4/3)
	Budget review 2 weeks earlier ((5/20)
WEEK OF JUNE 10-16	
First press release	Draft & finalize the release (6/10-13)
	Mailing prep 2 days before 6/13
	Press release mailing 6/15
	Minutes of 6/5 Executive Meeting*
WEEK OF JUNE 17-23	
Newsletter production	Write, edit newsletter copy 6/17-6/18
	Send newsletter to printer 6/19
	Disk prepared to mail house 6/20
	Postage deposit made for newsletter 6/23
	Notice out for July Executive meeting
WEEK OF JUNE 24-30	
Newsletter mailing 6/27	Printer deliver to mail house 6/26
	Mailing to recipients 6/27
Venue contract sign 6/28	Review final venue contract 6/27
	Sign & deliver venue contact 6/28

The **actual** work list would look like this:

WEEK OF JUNE 3-9
Place catering order 6/3
Budget adoption 6/4
Executive meeting 6/5
Meeting follow up

WEEK OF JUNE 10-16
Minutes of 6/5 Executive Meeting
Mailing prep for newsletter
Draft & finalize first press release (6/10-13)
Press release mailing 6/15

WEEK OF JUNE 17-23
Write, edit newsletter copy 6/17-6/18
Send newsletter to printer 6/19
Disk prepared to mail house 6/20
Postage deposit made for newsletter 6/23
Agenda and meeting packet for July Executive meeting

WEEK OF JUNE 24-30
Printer deliver newsletter to mail house 6/26
Newsletter mailing 6/27
Review final venue contract 6/27
Sign & deliver venue contact 6/28

Be Sure to Include

- Every single task during the event cycle
- Key dates for specific activities and flashpoints
- Checkpoints for budget status
- Last date contracts can be cancelled, plus dates for reminders
- Last date event can be cancelled
- Things that are not tasks, but could impact the event

Use the example at the back of the chapter to get started.

Suggested Timeline

*This suggested timeline is based on an annual event cycle with the event occurring in **Month 11**.*
Events vary in lead times depending on type and size. Not all of the tasks will apply to every event.
This timeline does not include daily activities.

Ten to Twelve Months+ in Advance

Identify staffing or consultant
Establish office location
Hold creative strategy session
Review critique from previous year's event
Develop event concept/activities
Define the demographic
Conduct research regarding other events
Prepare general timeline
Prepare work lists
Outline committee/s structure
Select/confirm event chairpersons
Establish preliminary budget
Open bank account/credit card services
Establish main goals and desired outcomes
Develop requirements for charities
Develop a logo
Order stationery, newsletter blanks
Choose a theme
Develop cash/in-kind sponsor prospect list
Negotiate/finalize contract for venue
Recruit committee chairpersons
Develop marketing and publicity calendar
Create a fact sheet for committees/staff
Develop mailing and contacts lists
Evaluate software programs
Post-event follow up from previous year

Nine to Ten Months+ in Advance

Define staff roles
Set up planning notebook
Finalize contract for venue
Outline committee structure
Create organizational chart
Determine sponsor levels/benefits
Determine ticket/admission prices
Develop exhibitor recruitment materials
Refine budget
Budget approval
Contract with professional services
Confirm committee chairs
Recruit committee members
Refine general timeline
Prepare committee booklet with timelines
Create timelines for individual activities
Contract speakers or entertainers
Develop list of printing needs
Obtain printing quotes
Research permit requirements
Determine meeting schedules
Expand sponsor prospect list
Post-event follow up from previous year

ALTER THIS TIMELINE TO SUIT YOUR EVENT REQUIREMENTS

Suggested Timeline

This suggested timeline is based on an annual event cycle with the event occurring in **Month 11**. *Events vary in lead times depending on type and size. Not all of the tasks will apply to every event.*
This timeline does not include daily activities.

Eight Months+ in Advance
Refine the general timeline
Refine the work lists
Refine organizational chart
Set schedule for executive meetings
Set schedule for committee meetings
Reserve space for meetings
Hold first committee meetings
Follow up work from committee meetings
Select participating charities
Finalize printing quotes
Refine budget
Refine sponsor prospect list
Draft sponsor recruitment materials*
Proposals out to long-lead sponsors/donors
Prepare sponsor packets for mailing
Mail out exhibitor recruitment materials
Develop marketing and publicity calendar
Develop advertising campaign
Develop mailing and contact lists
Develop invitation list, data entry
Research catering options
Contract speakers or entertainers
Research production – stage, sound, lights, video
Post-event follow up from previous year

*Corporations normally budget in August, September, October for the coming year, so plan accordingly

Seven Months+ in Advance
Refine the general timeline
Refine work lists
Hold committee meetings
Follow up work from meetings
Finalize printing quotes
Determine caterer/chef
Refine budget
Refine sponsor prospect list
Prepare sponsor packets for mailing*
Exhibitor recruitment materials
Develop invitation list
Print/mail Save the Date postcard
Refine marketing and PR timeline
Develop plan for décor
Contract with décor company
Contract production vendors
Identify raffle item

ALTER THIS TIMELINE TO SUIT YOUR EVENT REQUIREMENTS

Suggested Timeline

This suggested timeline is based on an annual event cycle with the event occurring in **Month 11***.*
Events vary in lead times depending on type and size. Not all of the tasks will apply to every event.
This timeline does not include daily activities.

Six Months+ in Advance
Refine the general timeline
Refine work lists
Hold committee meetings
Follow up work from committee meetings
Review of goals
Review budget status
Newsletter
Save the Date, if not done
Expend sponsor prospect list
Continue sponsor recruitment*
Process donations, acknowledgements
Develop invitation list
Determine media buys for advertising
Recruit, confirm exhibitors

Five Months+ in Advance
Refine work lists
Hold committee meetings
Follow up work from committee meetings
Review of budget status
Expand sponsor prospect list
Continue sponsor recruitment*
Process donations, acknowledgements
Process sponsorships, acknowledge
Expand invitation list
Press release
Recruit, confirm exhibitors

*Corporations normally budget in August,
September, October for the coming fiscal year,
so plan accordingly

Four Months+ in Advance
Refine work lists
Hold committee meetings
Follow up work from committee meetings
Review budget status
Refine sponsor prospect list
Continue sponsor recruitment
Process donations, acknowledgements
Process sponsorships, acknowledge
Expand invitation list
Press release
Recruit, confirm exhibitors

Three Months+ in Advance
Refine work lists
Hold committee meetings
Follow up work from committee meetings
Review budget status
Draft site plan
Draft logistics schedule
Draft invitation
Outline the event script
Registration begins
Begin to finalize exhibitors
Acknowledge donations, data entry
Prepare volunteer recruitment materials
Order awards
Purchase sponsor gifts
Raffle permit
Finalize other permits

ALTER THIS TIMELINE TO SUIT YOUR EVENT REQUIREMENTS

Suggested Timeline

*This suggested timeline is based on an annual event cycle with the event occurring in **Month 11**.*
Events vary in lead times depending on type and size. Not all of the tasks will apply to every event.
This timeline does not include daily activities.

Two Months+ in Advance
Refine work lists
Final committee meetings
Follow up work from committee meetings
Review budget status
Print/mail invitations
Registration
Volunteer recruitment materials sent out
Process donations, acknowledgements
Final sponsor lineup
Press release
Develop event program/catalog
Print raffle tickets
Secure final permits

One Month in Advance
Refine work lists
Distribute/sell raffle tickets
Final event program development
Finalize event script
Send out volunteer confirmation materials
Wrap sponsor/other gifts
Prepare thank you letters
Finalize site plan
Finalize audio and visual presentations
Finalize décor
Work on logistics schedule
Registration, confirmation
Process donations, acknowledgements
Collect any unpaid sponsor revenues

Three Weeks+ in Advance
Event program to printer
Review site plan
Review logistics schedule
Registration, confirmations
Tickets mailed to guests
Hold volunteer orientation
Conduct tasting for event menu
Conduct orientation with venue staff
Train financial/clerical volunteers

Two Weeks+ in Advance
Review/correct registration lists/info
Prepare volunteer supplies
Confirm entertainers/speakers
Print menus
Refine logistics schedule
Refine AV script
Refine speaker's remarks
Provide low estimate to caterer
Tickets mailed to guests
Request checks and petty cash
Prepare media advisory/press release

One Week in Advance
Review registration lists/data
Finalize seating arrangements
Finalize logistics schedule
Determine computers/equip for transport
Catering guarantee
Finalize AV/speaker scripts

ALTER THIS TIMELINE TO SUIT YOUR EVENT REQUIREMENTS

Suggested Timeline

This suggested timeline is based on an annual event cycle with the event occurring in **Month 11**. *Events vary in lead times depending on type and size. Not all of the tasks will apply to every event.* **This timeline does not include daily activities.**

Two Days+ in Advance
Finalize logistics schedule, distribute
Finalize guest lists
Finalize seating chart
VIP gifts ready
Prepare will-call tickets
Confirmations
Check on arrival of shipped goods
Final confirm with venue
Deliveries and set up, if possible

One Day in Advance
Review registration/cashiering procedure
Print out registration lists late in day
Review guest list for corrections
Make copies of guest lists for registrars
Begin event set up if possible
Meet with chairpersons/others to review
Final preparations
Final items ready for transport

Day of Event
Final set up of event elements
Final set up of catering elements
Final set up of production elements
Set up registration/cashiering functions
Final set up of volunteer area
Last minute seating adjustments
Corrections to guest names
Decorate venue, tables and other areas
Hold event
Clean up

Day After Event
Preliminary results review
Return supplies to office/storage
Delivery service to guests, if offered

Post-Event Activity
Financial matters—receipts, invoices, reports, accounts receivable/payable
Send out certificates
Thank you letters—chairpersons, sponsors, donors, committees, attendees, staff, volunteers
Debriefing meeting
Volunteer recognition
Revise timeline
Revise work lists
Clean up electronic and paper files
Clean up office, supplies, storage
Time off to recuperate!

ALTER THIS TIMELINE TO SUIT YOUR EVENT REQUIREMENTS

General Timeline Example – By Month

Create enough "months" to cover the event cycle. Insert month names in blank spaces.
Work backward from event date and allow at least one month after event for follow up activities.
The event should occur in Month 10 or Month 11. Month 1 is the start of the event cycle.
Month 12 is the minimal follow up period. List main elements only, then go back and
assign dates and who is responsible. Details will be developed in the Work Lists.
The general timeline does not include daily activities.

JUNE			AUGUST
Executive Meeting	Suzy*	June 5	
Budget adoption	Suzy	June 5	
First press release	Jim	June 15	
Newsletter mailing	Amy	June 28	
Hotel contract signed	Suzy	June 28	
Order stationery	Amy	June	
Research sponsors	Suzy	June	
Event Manager*			
SAMPLE ONLY			
Now refer to work list			
on following page			
JULY			**SEPTEMBER**

Work List Example – By Week

Work lists should cover a one month period with four to five weeks per month.
Insert month name at top. Insert tasks into the weeks they should be completed.
Some tasks do not have assigned dates for completion; they just need to be done that week.
The work list defines tasks for all event elements and is a list of daily activities.

JUNE

WEEK OF JUNE 3-9
Executive committee meeting 6/5
Pick up meeting supplies
Place catering order by 6/3
Meeting follow up
Final budget meeting 6/4
Budget adoption at Exec meeting 6/5
Call Bob re contract for stage
Copy of proposed budget to Sam on Monday
Weekly staff meeting 6/3
Volunteer recruitment packet developed
Follow up on sponsor calls
Volunteers on 6/3 for gift wrapping
Create copy for newsletter
Draft press release 6/3

WEEK OF JUNE 17-23
Write & edit newsletter copy 6/17-6/18
Send newsletter to printer 6/19
Disk prepared for mail house 6/19
Packets out for July Executive meeting
Weekly staff meeting 6/17
Final negotiations with hotel
Follow up on sponsor calls
Copy of adopted budget to Jim
Set appointment with caterer
*Dentist appointment 2:00 6/20
Postage deposit for newsletters 6/21

*You may want to include personal appointments on this list rather than keeping track separately

WEEK OF JUNE 10-16
Mailing prep 6/13-6/14
Mailing out by 6/15
Minutes 6/5 Executive meeting
Weekly staff meeting 6/10
Finalize copy for press release 6/14
Mail press release 6/15
Follow up on sponsor calls
Assistant's performance review 6/12
Return surplus supplies for refund

WEEK OF JUNE 24-30
Printer deliver newsletters to mail house 6/25
Newsletter mailed out 6/26
Weekly staff meeting 6/24
Review hotel contract 6/27
Sign and deliver hotel contract 6/28
Dinner meeting with Susan 6/25
Work on volunteer packet
Follow up on sponsor calls

Timeline & Work List Worksheet

Creating the Timeline

1. Has the event cycle been identified? _____
2. Does the event cycle coincide with the budget cycle? _____
3. Have you allocated enough time to create a thorough timeline sequence? _____
4. Do you have a timeline from the previous year to use as a reference? _____
5. Has the timeline been created to include all months of the event cycle, including post event activities? _____
6. Have all general elements of the event been addressed in the general timeline? _____
7. Have assignments been made as to what, who, by when? _____
8. Have flashpoints for critical review of the budget, sponsorship, and other critical outcomes been incorporated into the timeline? _____
9. Have identified goals been incorporated? _____
10. Do others need to have input into the timeline? _____
11. Has the timeline been distributed to event chairpersons and other key players? _____
12. Other _____

Creating the Work Lists

1. Have you allocated enough time to think through every aspect of the event and every task and related steps from beginning to end? _____
2. Do you have work lists from the previous year to use as a reference? _____
3. Do you have at least two pocket sized notepads to jot notes, or a small recorder to record notes for inclusion in timeline and/or work lists? _____
4. Have all components of the general timeline been incorporated into the work lists? _____
5. Have contract deadlines, advance reminder dates to review contracts or other critical elements been included?
6. Have you thought about things that could impact the event (weather, etc.) and set reminders to check on these in advance?
7. Have you moved tasks which can be done far in advance to weeks where the workload is not so heavy? _____
8. _____
9. _____
10. _____

Chapter 3 – Budgeting

Leverage Everything You Can For Everything You Can

Now that the event structure has been outlined, it's time to develop the budget—the second of the two main tools from which all other event components are generated.

Once developed, the budget gives a stark picture of where the event needs to increase revenue or alter expenses in order to meet the established goals. It must be constantly monitored for compliance and directly interfaces with the timeline and work lists to ensure that nothing is left to chance.

Information is provided in this chapter to help:

> ➢ Identify all revenue sources and expenditures
> ➢ Calculate projections based on established goals
> ➢ Cross-reference the budget against the timeline/work lists

A Word For the Wise

In many ways, budgeting is based on good common sense. Just like our own personal finances, unless the event is totally underwritten, it needs to make more money than it spends.

While we all anticipate that our events will be successful, setting revenue projections too high can result in over-expenditure and financial loss—or even worse, the demise of the event. In the beginning, you'll want to budget on the low side for revenue and the high side for expenses.

As the event manager, it is not only the event's reputation that's at stake, but yours as well. It's better to be lauded for starting small and having great success than to be criticized for having unrealistic expectations that resulted in a big disappointment for all concerned.

"Don't expect your ship to come in if you haven't built a dock."

Life's Little Instruction Calendar Volume VI

You'll want to budget carefully because executives, sponsors, donors, and others will be watching to ensure that the management of finances is above reproach. This is especially true if the event benefits a charitable cause or nonprofit organization.

It will be very difficult to obtain sponsors and major donations in the future if they feel event dollars aren't managed wisely. Sponsors want to be associated with a winner and charities count on events for financial support.

Include Flash Points!

Flash points are key dates and advance reminders that are inserted into the timeline and/or work lists.

Flash points should be established well in advance of large expenditures that require payment or deposits up front. Contracts with venues, suppliers, contractors, and others often contain clauses relating to cancellation dates or refunds that would impact the budget. Every event has a "no turning back" point, and it is best to determine where that point is and insert it (and an advance reminder it's coming up) into the timeline and work lists, rather than to be caught unawares when it is too late to cancel the event.

Revenue

It's easy to be unrealistic when it comes to how much revenue we think our event will raise. This isn't meant to dissuade anyone, but rather to provide the insight to cover all the bases when it comes to income sources. Careful scrutiny of any revenue-generating element should determine whether the money that will be generated outweighs the cost (staff time/wages, etc.) required to produce that income. For example, the time and effort required to sell raffle tickets may be better spent on recruiting a high level sponsor if the sponsorship would generate more than the raffle would bring in.

NOTES

Events typically generate revenue in the following ways:

- Sponsorships
- Cash donations
- Ticket sales or admission
- Exhibitor fees
- Auctions
- Miscellaneous sales (e.g. raffle, commemorative items, etc.)

Sponsorships: Businesses or individuals provide a cash contribution or in-kind donation of goods or services based on pre-determined benefit levels in return for recognition and/or special privileges not offered at the base level. In other words, the sponsor is receiving advertising or marketing recognition through the event.

Cash Donations: Direct contributions of cash for which the contributor receives no benefit, except as a charitable tax write off. Otherwise, it's a sponsorship.

Ticket Sales or Admissions: Revenue generated from sales of tickets prior to or during the event. Admission usually implies a ticket price or fee charged at an entry point.

Exhibitor Fees: Fees charged to exhibitors and/or vendors for the privilege of participating in the event and benefiting from the event's marketing efforts. Fees are based on a flat rate or on a sliding scale depending on the activity occurring in the exhibitor's booth, whether or not the exhibitor is allowed to sell products or services, or whether it is solely for promotion.

Auctions: Revenue generated from sales of items in live or silent auctions, or on-line auctions. Ticket sales, raffles, or other activities would be listed as separate categories.

Miscellaneous Sales: Revenue generated from a raffle, sales of event-related merchandise such as t-shirts, glassware, grab bags or other items. Any revenue that doesn't fit into a standard category.

You'll want to focus your main efforts on the revenue sources that will generate the most income for your event. As you document potential income sources, keep in mind where your event may be "financially vulnerable" and don't rely on only one source.

For instance, if the event is totally dependent on ticket sales as the sole source of revenue and ticket sales are poor, the bills are still going to need to be paid. Events held outdoors need to depend heavily on sponsorship, not just for income, but as a safety net in case admission revenue is down due to inclement weather.

Make sure that sponsors and clientele feel they are getting value, regardless of the price. You will build a loyal following if they feel they are getting the most for their investment.

Use common sense and look at all ways to cover your backside, and at the ripple effect of what the impact would be if one of your sources of revenue weren't available.

"Plan" To Make a Profit

Don't even consider "if we break even, we'll consider it a success." If you're just going to break even, why go to all that work and take all those risks? With good financial management, the event should strive to gross *at least two times* or more what it costs to produce. This ensures enough income to pay all the bills, provide start-up funds for the next event, and benefit the charity involved, if applicable.

One way to help stack the odds in the event's favor is to place major players in roles of leadership, such as chairpersons. These people have high level contacts and can "make it happen" in the areas of sponsorship or ticket sales. Having their name affiliated with the event has two benefits—they will work harder to ensure its success, and their involvement gives credibility and opens doors to opportunities that might not otherwise be available.

Partnering with nonprofit organizations provides an event with a ready-built support base. This partnership can result in leads for recruiting sponsors, can boost attendance, and can provide manpower in the form of volunteers.

Linking with a nonprofit may also allow your event to enjoy the benefit of nonprofit discounts on numerous expenses because the charity is receiving a portion of the event's net profits.

Tax Deductibility For Charitable Causes

When conducting charitable fundraisers, check the IRS guidelines regarding laws about giving tax deductible portions of sponsorship, ticket prices, or purchases. IRS regulations relating to charitable contributions are very clear. You may want to obtain a copy of these regulations for your records. They can be downloaded and printed from the IRS's Internet Website.

Be sure to check into legal requirements relating to statements such as "proceeds/partial proceeds benefit Nonprofit Name" presented in advertising or collateral materials.

In the case of charity auctions, you'll also print a disclaimer statement on donation forms for items and bid forms, such as "The XYZ Charity makes no representation as to the value given by donor. Please consult your tax advisor." Purchasers of items at charity auctions may only claim the amount of the difference between what they paid and the value of the item as the tax deductible portion.

Expenses

Covering the expenses is the same as paying the bills. Some things must be paid for in cold, hard cash but others can be bartered or discounted to keep costs down. Just as you did in the strategy session, "thinking outside the box" can help to reduce expenses. Every dollar saved reduces cash outlay and adds to the income side of the budget.

NOTES

Reduce expenses through donations and discounts. This is just common sense. And, this is another good reason for including respected business people in leadership roles for your event. Building relationships with the business community or individuals will do much to increase chances for financial success.

It may seem like extra work to offset expenses in this way, but many businesses who can't afford to be cash sponsors can help by providing goods or services instead.

Depending on the level of involvement, you might consider trading the value of the donation for an in-kind sponsorship and/or limited benefits such as seats at the event or a full-page ad in the program. This results in a win-win scenario for everyone.

Leverage your suppliers where possible. For example, if you rent tables and chairs, can the supplier also provide linens or other items you need? The more you obtain through any one supplier, the better the discount you should expect.

In other words, leverage everything you can for everything you can."

Nearly every day the businesses in your community are asked for a donation or discount on behalf of an event or a charitable cause. For significant requests—whether for sponsorships, donations, or discounts—using business leaders to do the "asking" often gains better results since they are relating "peer to peer." Gauge who should do the asking based on the level of the "ask."

The event manager may not be the best person to solicit large scale donations or discounts unless they are known to the business or individual being solicited. Staff members or volunteers can solicit smaller items, making sure to mention the connection to the event or the charity that may motivate the business to participate. Don't be shy! The worst that could happen is they will say "no" and you'll move on to the next prospect.

Avoid "After" Math

In developing the budget, you will certainly find more expense than originally anticipated. The good news is that you will also find additional sources of revenue. However, remember that what you fail to plan for now will cost money or time to "fix" later on.

Don't spend revenue you have received from advance ticket sales or sponsorships unless you are absolutely certain the event will occur. This is why it is imperative to build flash points into the timeline and work lists in advance of critical deadlines or contract cancellation dates.

Always leave yourself an "out" if possible. If the event is cancelled and revenues need to be refunded, it may be extremely difficult to come up with enough to cover the reimbursements if you have spent the income.

Contingencies. If your event has a history, you'll have a good idea of what the expenses will be. For new events, it's a good practice to factor an additional 20% of the total expense budget as a contingency to cover costs that weren't anticipated in the original planning process. It's a good practice to do this regardless since even the most well thought out events have unforeseen expenses.

This means if the overall expense budget totals $100,000 that another $20,000 will be added for unplanned expenses, totaling $120,000. If it's not needed, another $20,000 of net profit goes to the bottom line, but if you do need it, you've planned for it. It's better to delete an expense from the budget than to add a number of things you forgot

Committee budgets. We don't recommend that committees be given a budget because they invariably exceed their given limits. This is especially true when it comes to décor committees because they tend to lose control when looking at all the options available.

If you do provide budgets for committees, make sure they adhere to the amount specified. Make it clear the budget is not negotiable. Any expenditure should have approval of the event manager or other authority figure. If possible, it's always best to have the event manager purchase whatever goods or services are required in order to maintain control.

There are committees who do stay within given budget limits. You could also make it the responsibility of the committee chair to make sure that authorized expenses stay within the proper parameters.

It's normal for committee people to be excited and want to help, however, the more people who are purchasing event supplies or services, the more chance there is for overage in spending.

Helpful Hints On Budgeting

- Use the Budget Master List to help create the budget.
- Calculate income and expense projections based on established goals
- If you don't know how much something costs, call around and get quotes, then use the mid-to-high quote for the budget
- Factor in a contingency equal to 20% for unforeseen expenses
- Review the list of expenses for things that could be directly donated or underwritten by sponsors
- Review expenses again and eliminate things that aren't necessary because they can be added back later if funds are available
- Whittle the budget down to a point where those involved feel the income and expense projections are realistic

Budget Master List

Use the Budget Master List to determine which income and expense categories relate to your event, then itemize them on the Budget Worksheet or in a computer spreadsheet program.

Please Note: Not all categories apply to every event.

Income Categories	How To Calculate
Sponsorship	Each cash sponsor level amount times number of sponsors
In-kind sponsorship	Counts as sponsorship only if it eliminates an expense
Ticket sales	Price per ticket times number of tickets
Admissions	Price to enter times number of attendees
Registration fees	Price per person for conventions, seminars, etc.
Exhibitor fees	Fee per exhibitor space based on location desirability
Concessions	Income from event-run food & beverage concessions
Special activities	Price per person for activities not included in admission
Cash donations	Outright donations of cash, not considered as sponsorship
Parking fees	Fee per car in exchange for parking privilege
Auction	Sales from live auction, silent auction lots, etc.
Raffle tickets	Price per raffle ticket times number of tickets sold
Ad sales	Fee for advertising in event program or catalog
Pledges	Cash pledges to a charity via an event, 100% tax deductible
Seed money	Available cash for start up funding
Grants	Cash received from grants, as opposed to donations
Miscellaneous	Sales of commemorative merchandise, etc.

Expense Categories	How To Calculate
Administrative:	
Personnel	Salaries or hourly rate, benefits, payroll taxes
Part-time personnel	Hourly rate times number of hours times number of people
Administrative expenses	Space rent, utilities, telephone, equipment rental fees
Office supplies	Office supplies, postage, shipping, etc.
Professional services	Fees paid to accountants, lawyers, computer techs, etc.
Insurance	Costs for general, boards & officers, alcohol liability, etc.
Training	Educational training expense
Mileage	Use of personal vehicle, miles driven times rate per mile
Expense reimbursement	Reimbursement for travel, meals or other expense
Taxes	Sales or other taxes charged on auction income
Bank fees	Fees charged by banks for credit card processing, other
Petty cash	Available cash for small purchases, backed by receipts

45

Budget Master List

Use the Budget Master List to determine which income and expense categories relate to your event, then itemize them on the Budget Worksheet or in a computer spreadsheet program.
Please Note: Not all categories apply to every event.

Expense Categories	How To Calculate
Printing:	
Graphic design	Flat or hourly fee for design and layout of collateral materials
Commercial printing	Costs for press set up, paper, printing based on quantity
Name badges, I.D.	Costs of printing and preparing identification materials
Quick printing/photocopies	Costs for quick printing/copying not done by others
Advertising & Promotion:	
Print advertising	Cost of advertising space, usually by the column inch
Radio advertising	Cost of 15, 30, or 60 second ad based on number of times
Television advertising	Cost of 15, 30, or 60 second ad based on number of times
Signage	Cost to produce signs and banners
T-shirts	Cost of t-shirts based on quantity, size, colors, logo
Promotional merchandise	Cost of promotional merchandise printed with logo, etc.
Awards	Cost of awards, prizes, plaques, trophies, ribbons, etc.
Hospitality/VIP:	
Honorariums	A good-faith payment for services on which no price is set
Appearance fees	Cost of an appearance at the event, normally a celebrity
Travel expense	Cost of airfare or the like for VIPs, speakers, etc.
Lodging	Cost of lodging times number of nights per person, plus tax
Mileage	Use of personal vehicle for miles driven times rate per mile
Expense reimbursement	Reimburse for items such as meals, taxis, tips, etc.
Ground transportation	Cost of limousines, taxis, bus, light rail, or train
Hospitality suite	Cost of hotel suite for entertaining, meetings, or sales
Outside Services:	
Interpreters or translators	Fees for interpreter or translator services
Photography	Flat or hourly fee, cost of film processing, or by photo print

Budget Master List

Use the Budget Master List to determine which income and expense categories relate to your event, then itemize them on the Budget Worksheet or in a computer spreadsheet program.
Please Note: Not all categories apply to every event.

Expense Categories	How To Calculate
Food & Beverage:	
Meal costs	Cost per person times number of people each meal
Gratuity	Percentage (tip) applied to total cost of food & beverage
Corkage	A per-bottle charge applied when wine is served
Beverage	Cost for any individual beverage not included in meal cost
Outside catering	Per person charge for food, personnel, delivery, etc.
Wait staff / other personnel	Hourly rate per person times number of persons
Site Related:	
Permits	Fees for jurisdiction, site use, fire, liquor, noise, etc.
Site rental	Flat or hourly fee for use of venue or other site
Security	Cost of hourly rate times number of service personnel
Equipment rental	Fees for daily or hourly rental of equipment
Waste removal	Fees charged by waste management firms for disposal
Portable toilets	Fees charged for individual or trailer units, servicing
Construction	Hourly rate for construction services times number of hours
Electrical	Fees for hourly on-site electrician, cabling, hook up
Heating/air conditioning	Hourly fee for contractor services, rental of units
Maintenance	Hourly fee for maintenance (handyman) services
Parking	Fee per vehicle to use parking space
Valet parking	Hourly rate for parking personnel times number of workers
Ground transportation	Flat fee or hourly rate for shuttles, buses, drivers,
Tents	Daily rental for tents/sidewall, delivery, setup, tear down
First aid station	Fee for personnel/supplies (e.g. paramedics, ambulance)
Temporary office	Rental fee for temporary office space, usually a trailer
Utilities	Usage charges for electricity, water, etc.
Telephone	Usage and/or installation charges for cell phone rental
Fencing	Fee charge for temporary fence, by type and linear foot

Budget Master List

Use the Budget Master List to determine which income and expense categories relate to your event, then itemize them on the Budget Worksheet or in a computer spreadsheet program.
Please Note: Not all categories apply to every event.

Expense Categories	How To Calculate
Production, Entertainment:	
Decorations	Costs of goods and/or services for decorating purposes
Tables	Rental fee per tables times type and number of tables
Chairs	Rental fee per chair times type and number of chairs
Linens	Rental fee per linen times type and number of linens
Floral	Purchase or rental cost per item
Dance floor	Rental fee per section times number of sections required
Stage, skirting	Rental fee based on stage size, skirting by linear foot
Sound	Fee for sound equipment and technician/s
Lighting	Fee for lighting equipment and technician/s
Electronic media	Fee for video, PowerPoint, big screens, other production
Entertainers	Performance contract fee, including agency commissions
Entertainer travel	Travel provided as designated in entertainer's contract
Entertainer lodging	Lodging provided as designated in entertainer's contract
Entertainer ground transport	Limousines, taxis or rental cars designated in contract
Entertainer meals	Meals provided as designated in contract, or per diem
Entertainer miscellaneous	Cost for other items in contract rider
Contingency:	
Contingency	10%-20% of expense budget added for unforeseen costs

Budget Worksheet - Income

Under the Income or Expense heading, write the CATEGORY from the Master Lists,
then individual listings under it that apply. Under DESCRIPTION, write
"What" times "How Much" and/or "How Many." PROJECTED is the "Estimated Total"
for that line item. ACTUAL is the "Final Outcome Total" for that line item.
You may also wish to sub-total individual category groupings.

INCOME			
CATEGORY	DESCRIPTION	PROJECTED	ACTUAL

Budget Worksheet – Expense

Under the Income or Expense heading, write the CATEGORY from the Master Lists,
then individual listings under it that apply. Under DESCRIPTION, write
"What" times "How Much" and/or "How Many." PROJECTED is the "Estimated Total"
for that line item. ACTUAL is the "Final Outcome Total" for that line item.
You may also wish to sub-total individual category groupings.

EXPENSE			
CATEGORY	**DESCRIPTION**	**PROJECTED**	**ACTUAL**

Chapter 4 – Committees

Committees Need To Feel Valued for Their Work

Committees can be a tremendous asset when their involvement is carefully considered. Events provide a way to involve large numbers of people in support of the effort, and the knowledge and expertise of individuals within committees are a treasure that you can tap for the benefit of the event. If these volunteers feel valued and included they will work hard and produce incredible results.

Information in this chapter will help:

> ➢ Complete an organizational chart
> ➢ Create a general description and individual timeline for each committee that includes major milestones or deadlines
> ➢ Develop a job description for each committee chairperson and committee member outlining committee functions and expectations

Committee Member Selection

The strategy behind selection of event leadership and committee members was discussed in the Getting Started chapter. As you move through the process of working with committees, keep these strategies in mind and use the contacts of leaders and committee members to their best advantage.

Businesses hire employees to match the qualifications in a job description and this practice can be applied when selecting committee members. Establishing clearly defined committees and their related duties does much to eliminate confusion and focuses efforts in the desired direction.

It's a good practice to include the chairpersons of individual committees as members of the Executive/Advisory Committee so they can filter information down to their constituents.

"If you work for an organization that makes decisions by committee, make sure you're on the committee."

Life's Little Instruction Book Volume II

What Committees Does Your Event Need?

Determine which committees are necessary to the function of the event. <u>Less is best</u> when it comes to committees and they can sometimes be combined if their duties overlap. The event manager may elect to perform the function of a committee, especially if the event is small, or the "committee" may be comprised of only one, the chairperson.

Keep in mind that as the event manager, there is a good likelihood that you may be required to attend committee meetings to provide staff support, so the fewer committees the better.

Listed below are some of the most common event committees and their functions.

Executive/Advisory	Consists of event chairmen and committee chairmen having power to enact directives. Assist and advise at all levels of the event
Sponsorship	Recruitment of cash sponsors and patron tables based on a tier of pre-determined levels and benefits
Procurement	Obtain auction items to create auction lots (packages) for sale at the event. Assist in grouping items to best advantage. Provide information, assist in writing and/or editing of catalog copy
Marketing/Publicity	Marketing, promotions, and publicity including press releases, newsletters, special features, and working with media representatives
Food & Beverage	Oversee food and beverage activities including menu planning, on-site service coordination, and possibly pre-event contract negotiation

		NOTES
Production	Work with stage, sound, lighting, visual media, and other contractors in accomplishment of production elements	
Decorations	Develop and carry out theme and decor	
Special Activities	Oversee individual activities conducted under the framework of the overall event	
Exhibitors	Work with exhibitors during pre-event phase, oversee load in/tear down, and assist exhibitors during actual event	
Volunteers	Recruitment, communications, and on-site management of volunteers	
Finance	Handle accounting functions, including registration/cashiering and recording of bids if the event is an auction	

Give Them Tools for Success

It is the responsibility of the event manager to ensure that committees have the tools to do their jobs and operate within established parameters. Taking the time to do this at the outset will do much to eliminate questions or avoid misunderstandings later on.

Develop job descriptions for committee chairpersons. Each committee chairperson should have a job description containing an overview of their duties, a list of specific outcomes to be accomplished and timeframes for their completion.

Develop job descriptions for the committee members. All committee members should have a job description outlining what is expected of them, to whom they report, and a list of specific tasks or activities to accomplish within a set timeframe. This is usually a variation of the committee chairperson's job description. The format of job descriptions for committee chairpersons and committee members should be consistent.

Create a committee booklet and provide it to members of all committees. This helps committee members understand how what they do fits in with the event structure and how the various committees interact with one another.

The booklet should contain a cover page, table of contents, fact sheet about the event, an organizational chart, committee descriptions for all committees and their timelines, and the General Timeline for the entire event cycle. If the event benefits a non-profit, include a fact sheet about the organization that can be used by the committee member for reference.

It's also a nice touch to provide each committee member with a 3-ring binder so they can keep their committee materials all together as the event progresses. Make sure that any handouts are three-hole punched if possible.

General Notes About Committees

Recruit members based on the needs of each committee and the role they will perform. Obtain the highest level volunteers you can for each committee, preferably those with expertise or previous experience.

There is no "right" or "wrong" way to do things. Committee members often express varying opinions about how to accomplish things and they can be very headstrong. Regardless of personal preference, the event manager needs to remain objective and help those with differing opinions work toward a common solution. The ultimate goal is to do what is best for the event.

Sometimes committee members will make suggestions during meetings that event managers know won't work. If this situation occurs, be cautiously tactful in presenting an objection and back it up with facts or examples. Depending on the committee and its members, you may have to try it their way regardless.

Keep in mind that a vast majority of people who volunteer to serve on committees have not had the experience of actually running an event and don't realize that what they are suggesting is impractical, would cost a lot of money or time, or be impossible to achieve. The last thing we want to do is destroy their enthusiasm to help us or to dampen their joy in participating as a committee member.

Incorporate surprises and fun into committee meetings if possible. Don't wait until after the event to thank committees. Little things go a long way toward keeping committee members motivated. Occasionally surprise them with wrapped chocolates, hand-written thank you notes, a wine and cheese tasting, homemade cookies, small gifts relating to personal interests, and so on. You'll find they will be impressed with your thoughtfulness and feel you appreciate them.

Before Each Meeting

E-mail or send out meeting packets via regular mail approximately 7-10 business days in advance. Sending out agendas and meeting materials in advance serves as a gentle reminder if the person has forgotten to follow through and gives them time to get their "homework" done if this is the case.

These folks often have business or personal commitments that may interfere with meeting attendance or their ability to follow through with assignments. If they are consistently unable to honor their commitment, you may need to step in and offer to help them get back on track or find someone else to complete the tasks.

The meeting materials should include an agenda, minutes of the previous meeting, and any information that will be needed. A "start" and "stop" time with individual timeframes for each agenda item will keep the meeting moving along. The date/time/place of the next meeting should be the last item. Be sure to send packets to everyone, even if they weren't present at the last meeting.

NOTES

During The Meeting

Try to ensure that everyone has a chance to participate in the discussion and that one or two people don't dominate the entire meeting. When this happens, it is intimidating to new committee members who are excited about being part of the event, may be hesitant to speak up, and need to feel their participation is valued.

Take good notes and write down commitments as people agree to do things. Ask questions to clarify. It helps if a second person also takes notes for purposes of comparison following the meeting. You'll be surprised at how much you missed, especially if you participated in the discussion or were at the other end of a large group.

Food and beverages are always welcome. It doesn't need to be fancy. Choose simple food and beverages appropriate to the time of day or place where the meeting is being held. At a minimum, there should always be water available.

After The Meeting

Document who agreed to do what and by when in the minutes of the meeting. If in doubt, check with the person before sending out the minutes. The date, time and place of the next meeting should be the last item in the minutes. Insert your own assignments in to the Work Lists and make a note as to others that need follow up.

After every meeting, measure the committee's progress against the General Timeline.

Never Stop Saying Thank You

You can never say "thank you" enough. Say it often and be sincere. This applies from the highest level sponsor on down to the child who helps their parents stuff envelopes. Write notes, make calls, and say "Thanks."

Committee Description & Timeline

The following is an example of a page from the Committee Booklet.

According to this timeline, the event takes place the week of August 25.

Marketing & Publicity Committee

Joe Smith - ABC Advertising, Chair

- Focuses on marketing and promotion of Event Name on a local, regional or national level
- Works with the Event Manager in the development of marketing materials and/or promotions
- Develops the publicity timeline
- Creates or updates lists of key local, regional, and trade media
- Creates or oversees development of a media kit and its distribution
- Coordinates feature stories in the print media and interviews with broadcast media
- Assists in the recruitment of a television or radio sponsor
- Reviews materials developed by the Event Manager for content, makes suggestions or additions
- Other duties specific to your event

COMMITTEE TIMELINE

TASK	BY WHEN
Develop marketing/publicity timeline	February 20
Recruit broadcast sponsors, print media sponsors	February-March
Initial press release	March 15
Media kit distribution	June 15 (long lead) August 15 (short lead)
Follow up with local, regional, national media	July-August
Pitch for pre-event feature stories	July-August
Media alert, television and radio interviews	Week of August 25
Post-event press release	September 1
Post-event analysis meeting	September 15

Make sure to incorporate the individual committee timelines into the General Timeline

Job Description

Marketing & Publicity Committee Chair

REPORTS TO: Event Chairmen and Event Manager

Duties & Responsibilities

- Serves as a member of the Executive Committee
- Acts as team leader for the Marketing & Publicity Committee
- Develops the publicity timeline
- Sets meetings and agendas
- Oversees marketing and promotion of event on local, regional, national level
- Assists in the recruitment of a television and/or radio sponsor, and a print media sponsor
- Creates press releases and public service announcements
- Works with event manager in development of marketing materials and promotions
- Creates or updated lists of key local, regional, national, and trade media
- Reviews materials developed by the event manager for content, makes suggestions or additions
- Creates or oversees development of the media kit and its distribution
- Coordinates feature stories for the print and broadcast media
- Meets regularly with the event manager in the accomplishment of the marketing/PR timeline
- Provides input into the event newsletter

Job Description

Marketing & Publicity Committee Member

REPORTS TO: Marketing & Publicity Chair

Duties & Responsibilities

- Serves as a member of the Marketing & Publicity Committee
- Attends committee meetings as scheduled
- Assists in the marketing and promotion of event in specific capacities as designated
- Makes recommendations for marketing and publicity ideas
- Works with Marketing & Publicity chairperson in developing marketing/promotions
- Assists in development of the media kit and distribution
- Assists in coordination of feature stories for print media and broadcast media
- Works with volunteers or staff in distribution of marketing and promotion materials

Chapter 5 – Sponsorship

Sponsors Create Opportunities

Cash and in-kind sponsorships are one of the main revenue sources for events. Cash sponsors pay for special privileges and marketing exposure through the event. In-kind sponsors provide the cash value in goods or services rather than a direct cash payment.

Even in a bad economy, companies are still spending money, but not to as great a degree. They are operating on tighter timelines and are not making commitments as far in advance. Smart companies are continuing to use events and meetings to prospect for new clients and to showcase products and services. Even though the company may be rolling in dough, they still are going to want to maintain an image of frugality, rather than excess.

Just as important as the benefits they receive, the way a sponsor is treated and their perception of how the event is run are two major factors in their decision of whether to repeat the sponsorship.

This chapter covers ways to:

> ➤ Define cash sponsorship levels, sponsor prospects, and the number of sponsorships needed
> ➤ Inventory tangible and intangible benefits the event can offer
> ➤ Develop a sponsor packet that can be customized for each individual sponsor prospect
> ➤ Conduct confirmation and follow up with sponsors

Is It A Sponsorship or A Donation?

Sponsorships are usually very public, done for purposes of marketing or advertising, and are written off as a business expense through a marketing or advertising budget. The sponsor receives something of

"Every once in awhile, ask for the moon. You never know, someone just might give it to you."

Life's Little Instruction Calendar Volume VI

value in return (preferential treatment, marketing opportunities, etc.).
The event may, or may not, be associated with a charitable cause.

In the United States, sports-related events account for approximately
65% of sponsorship dollars with the remainder equally distributed
between entertainment, fairs and festivals, various causes, and arts.

True donations are 100% tax deductible with the corporation or
individual receiving nothing of tangible value in return. Make sure to
check with your tax advisor as to tax deductibility before quoting this
to any prospective donor.

In today's market, there is fierce competition among nonprofits for
every charitable dollar. Social services, health, and education receive
approximately 75% of corporate charitable giving budgets.

In addition, companies are looking to ensure that events align with
the company's mission and goals, and are not being held solely for
entertainment. This is known as Corporate Social Responsibility.
Events must not only cover expenses, but they must provide for
distribution of proceeds to benefit the good of the community.

Conduct An Inventory

Ideally, events should strive to cover all expenses through a
combination of sponsorship and ticket sales. If the event is a charity
auction, the auction proceeds should be pure profit. By conducting
an inventory of the event and what it has to offer, you will find
numerous ways for sponsors to participate at all levels.

Inventory the already-existing support base for sponsors.
Among your strongest supporters (and potential sponsors!) are the
business people who are serving as chairpersons of the event, or as
committee members. Several of them most likely could be cash or
in-kind sponsors, or have contacts they could leverage.

Conduct an inventory of tangible and intangible benefits the event can offer, and then add some twists! In addition to the more traditional benefits, the event should offer sponsors something they can't get in any other way. Think through every aspect and activity. The more unique or outlandish you can make it, the more attention it will get and the more appeal it will have.

Traditional benefits include preferred seating, a program ad, logos on signage, and so forth, but many perks don't cost money and have great appeal to sponsors. These may include things like opportunities to meet high profile persons or entertainers, early admission, personalized service at the event, or other exclusive privileges.

Don't forget that intangible benefits such as an event's importance or uniqueness have value to a sponsor. Things like prestige, exclusivity, or affiliation with a certain clientele the sponsor would like to reach are often just as important as the tangible benefits.

Review the list developed during the budgeting process to compare event needs with what sponsors can offer. Think about how sponsors would fit into the picture. Could a sponsor underwrite an entire activity such as an exclusive dinner, the entertainment, an award or something similar? Could a sponsor provide needed goods or services like printing or media exposure? If they can't underwrite an entire element, could they do part and another sponsor do part? An example of this would be one printer doing the color printing and the other doing the black and white pieces. *Don't assume they will be agreeable to do this, make sure to clear it with them beforehand.*

What's In It For The Sponsor?

Sponsors ask questions, so be prepared to answer them. Sponsorships are not easy sells, especially in a weak economy. You must have an answer when the sponsor asks, "What's in it for me?" These days, sponsors are more demanding and have higher expectations. The days of sponsors participating in events because it gives them a warm fuzzy feeling are over.

NOTES

NOTES

A key component in event marketing is *R.O.I.* which stands for *Return on Investment*. Since sponsorships are usually paid out of marketing budgets, the sponsor wants a return on their investment. In the case of corporations, the sponsor must be able to justify the sponsorship to the shareholders. The sponsor needs to be able to make a good case that the sponsorship not only benefits the event, but will pay off in other ways. This is the "what's in it for them."

Most corporations tend to fund certain types of events in keeping with their corporate philosophy. With a little research, you can find out what they are sponsoring now, or have sponsored in the past.

Cause-related marketing—a business strategy to link a nonprofit organization or cause to the sponsor's marketing efforts—continues to be a major factor in sponsorship deals. For those in the business of producing events for nonprofit organizations, this is good news.

So, what is in it for the sponsor? If it's a high-profile event, they may want to invite their top clients to attend. Sponsors traditionally receive preferential treatment, or are seated in a prominent location based on their level of sponsorship. The sponsor's name is listed in print and on signage at the event. They may have the opportunity to purchase special items through an auction or other means. And, they may be helping to benefit a charitable cause, which makes them look good in the community.

To provide sponsors with measurable R.O.I., you'll want to generate post-event reports that demonstrate financial accountability and demonstrate the value the sponsor received for their participation.

Dealing With Sponsors

Treat sponsors well and they respond favorably. It's not only about the sponsor having a presence at the event. It's about showing them how much the event appreciates their support.

Don't over-saturate the event with sponsors. Sponsors appreciate being in the "few" rather than in the "many" and will pay more to be in an exclusive group as opposed to being part of a crowd. Maintain the uniqueness of each sponsor level by carefully planning how many sponsors it will take to meet the financial goals. This is critical for high-level sponsors who receive premium benefits for premium dollars. The type and size of the event should drive the sponsorship structure.

Sponsors bring networking opportunities. These can translate into benefits for the event such as corporate volunteers, exposure to key patrons and new clientele, or through providing needed services. For example, a sponsor such as a bank could bring all three of the aforementioned benefits to your event *in addition to being a cash sponsor!*

Leverage sponsor resources. Encourage sponsors to tag the event in their advertising or promotions to expand the event's marketing reach. There are numerous ways to add exposure.

Is a big grocery chain or retailer one of the sponsors? They may be able to leverage the brands they represent to help underwrite the sponsorship. They might also help in obtaining needed supplies or other goods at reduced cost, or even donation.

Don't put all your eggs in one basket. If there is only one sponsor and the sponsor drops out, the event may not be able to recover, especially if the sponsor's name is strongly associated with the event. To keep the event financially sound, guard against being totally dependent on any one source by having a diverse group of sponsors at various financial levels.

Take a crash course or read a book about sales. Recruiting sponsors is basically "selling them" on the benefits of being associated with your event. Knowing how to overcome objections, read body language, or choose the right words will do much to increase the chances of "making the sale."

Coach your sponsors! Once a sponsor has come on board, you'll want to encourage them in ways they can help the event raise revenues and be successful through their involvement. For example, if your event contains a sales element (such as a charity auction), guests at sponsor tables tend to bid more than those who have purchased individual seats. For fundraisers, encourage the sponsor to invite guests who will come with the expectation of contributing in some form as opposed to merely having a nice dinner.

Don't give one sponsor the same benefits for less money than another sponsor. This is the kiss of death because sponsors talk to each other. Always keep everything above board and don't make "secret" deals, because they won't be secret for long.

First Time Events

Brand new events without a track record are difficult to sell to sponsors. Establishing credibility for a first-time event is critical since sponsors must feel comfortable that the leadership can deliver what is being promised.

Event and committee chairpersons who are strong business leaders can dramatically increase the "sponsorship odds" in the event's favor. The event will need to depend on a successful track record and the positive reputation of those involved. If a charitable beneficiary is included, make sure the organization has a good reputation in the community.

First-time events often raise less money from sponsorship than originally hoped. A good rule of thumb for new events is that one sponsorship commitment will come from every 10-15 solicitations.

Make use of strategic partners such as a benefiting charity, a venue, or professional associations to help recruit cash or in-kind sponsors. Every contact and every resource is valuable to achieving the goal.

NOTES

Media Sponsors

Media sponsors traditionally are in-kind sponsors who provide a service (public service announcement or 15, 30, or 60- second ad) rather than cash. They may want the event to purchase advertising which they will match as their contribution. Media sponsors include television, radio, transit, newspapers, and magazines. These sponsors help broaden marketing opportunities to provide exposure.

The media sponsorship should include pre-event promotion to help boost ticket sales and attendance. Media sponsors also may be willing to solicit their existing advertisers (which is handled through the media's account executives) to help underwrite the cost of their involvement. In this case, both the media and the advertiser would receive or share the sponsor benefits.

More information about media sponsors can be found in the Marketing and Promotions chapter.

Sponsor Levels & Benefits

It's always best to meet face-to-face with potential sponsors to discuss what they are looking for in the way of exposure and benefits, and then offer them a sponsorship package to meet that expectation. Not all sponsors will want the same benefits, and having some options for them to customize their sponsorship just makes sense.

Sponsor levels should be defined early in the budget and planning process. Avoid too many sponsor levels since it becomes confusing and it is difficult to justify jumps from one level to the next unless there is a substantial increase in benefits between them.

Use the Event Inventory List to develop the structure of sponsor benefits. Be sure to include both tangible and intangible benefits in what the sponsor receives. These should be listed in descending order from most to least important in each level of sponsorship.

"If you always do what you've always done, you'll get what you've always gotten."

Werner Erhard

If the sponsor wants to negotiate, play to win on behalf of the event. Try to remain firm on the tangible benefits and use the intangible benefits as bargaining chips. Having a "pick list" of benefits and their values in your memory will help in negotiations. DO NOT hand the sponsor a written list to choose from!

Would it be easier to sell sponsorship for individual event activities such as underwriting an important dinner, or is it better to divide sponsorships by monetary levels and factor sponsor revenue into the overall income? You may want to use a combination approach. Some quick calculations will show which approach is best.

The Sponsor Proposal

The sponsor proposal is a written document that clearly outlines the benefits of association with the event. It should be professional looking without being pretentious and address the kinds of questions that are typically raised by sponsors.

The most important information about the event should be right up front and presented in a way that will tantalize the sponsor to want to know more. Make sure the information is complete, but keep it to a minimum. Most potential sponsors won't take the time to wade through a ton of detail to find a couple of sentences worth of basic information. Being concise and to the point is much more likely to get your proposal read by a busy executive or decision maker.

Depending on the event, proposals can range from very simple to very sophisticated. For instance, a small local nonprofit organization would be best served by a subdued presentation as compared to a large, high profile event that would need a more sophisticated approach. If the small nonprofit had a slick-looking, expensive-to-print proposal, the potential sponsor would likely assume the nonprofit did not need the money—or worse, would not spend it wisely. On the other hand, an event like the Super Bowl would need the full-out slick marketing materials to attract sponsors.

NOTES

Sponsor proposals usually contain these basic elements:

Cover Letter	Introduces the event and invites participation in a way that creates excitement and interest. Use event or organization stationery. Make sure the contact name and company name are spelled correctly!
Fact Sheet	Basic information about the event—what, when, where, who, why, history
Levels & Benefits	A separate sheet/s outlining the levels of sponsorship and benefits of each, sponsor fees and payment deadlines
Confirmation/ Sponsor Agreement	Form filled out by sponsor indicating level of sponsorship selected, what benefits the sponsor receives, payment deadlines, signatory line, date
Background Info	Copies of information conducive to selling the sponsorship such as copies of press articles, but not too many. If the event is a benefit, include brief info or fact sheet about the charity

You may opt to send out the information in a nice, professional-looking portfolio. Another option is to present or mail it in a large colored manila envelope so it stands out in the sea of white paper (yellow is always good).

Follow Up

Don't expect sponsors to call you begging to participate. A potential sponsor should be contacted within 7-10 days after they receive the materials to discuss the proposal or set up an appointment. If they don't receive a contact within a short length of time, they will most likely disregard the request.

Benefits Inventory

WHY SPONSORS PARTICIPATE	
Affiliation with a successful event Branding Charitable support Client appreciation Corporate hospitality Creative ideas Customer incentives Employee incentives Exclusive rights or experiences High profile exposure Increase company awareness Increase sales Key client privileges	Marketing opportunities Media exposure Merchandising opportunities Product sampling Reaching a target market Public perception as community partner Unique concepts VIP privileges Others unique to your event

TANGIBLE & INTANGIBLE BENEFITS FOR SPONSORS	
Advance receipt of catalog or program Audio announcements Backstage passes Banners Branding Brochures Catalog ad Commemorative items Database info/guest lists/top bidder names Early admission E-marketing Exhibitor space Hospitality events Gifts for table guests Inside information Invitations Limousines	Media exposure Meet celebrities/entertainers Meet high profile patrons Pre-event activities Priority location Priority parking Priority seating Program ad Promotional sales Table tents Tickets or seats Signage Special privileges Stage banners VIP treatment What can you offer?

Benefits Inventory Worksheet

Inventory the Tangible and Intangible Benefits of the Event

Tangible Benefits	$ Value	Intangible Benefits – No $ Value

Sponsor Levels & Benefits – Example

Flat fee sponsorships can be offered in conjunction with activity-based sponsorships. Sponsors funding individual activities should be recognized on the level appropriate to the flat fee sponsorship amount.

SPONSORSHIP BASED ON FLAT FEE	
*Platinum Sponsor - $25,000 • Premier sponsor level • Highest visibility sponsorship • Two tables of 10 • Premier seating for you and your guests • Two limousines to/from event • Celebrity guest seated at your table • Exposure to affluent clientele • Personal sommelier/server for the evening • Hand-selected wines • Special gift for each guest at your table • Full page ad in event program • Company logo on designated signage • 10 tickets to the exclusive pre-event party • Opportunity for advance purchase of special activities tickets, subject to availability	***Bronze Level Sponsor - $5,000** Table for 10

* Name the sponsor levels something relevant like Winners Circle/Indy Level for an automotive themed event

SPONSORSHIP BASED ON ACTIVITY	
Gala Pre-Event Party on (Date) - $25,000 Host gala Pre-Event Party at (venue) Exclusive party limited to 150 guests 20 tickets for you and your guests Three-course dinner with wine Designated event signage including your logo Sponsor listing in newspaper ads Your logo on tickets to this event Entertainment & Decorations Souvenir glass with your logo No host bar Sponsor fee/benefits may be shared if you desire **Acknowledgement at Platinum Sponsor level*	**Printing - $5,000** Underwrite printing to include 1,000 invitations and 100 catalogs of 48 pages each Logo and tag line on invitation and catalog Full page ad in event catalog Listing in sponsor acknowledgements **Acknowledgement at Bronze Sponsor level*

The Language of Sponsorship

The following are common terms relating to sponsors and their roles.

Audience	The market segment as identified with the event that can be targeted by the sponsor
Branding	A readily identifiable image that embodies the event or company
Category Exclusivity	A sponsor is recognized as the sole company or product associated with a particular event activity
Cause Marketing	A business strategy that links the nonprofit organization or cause to the sponsor's marketing efforts
Co-Sponsors	Individual sponsors who are part of the overall sponsor lineup for the event; may or may not be directly partnered together
CPM	Cost per thousand used as a valuation measurement
Cross-Promotion	Two or more co-sponsors use the sponsorship as a joint promotion (e.g. a retailer and a soft drink company)
Database Building	Sponsor uses the event data to obtain demographic or purchasing information through guest lists or other means
E-Marketing	Online marketing featuring event catalog or other incentives and/or on-line payment options
Employee Relations	The sponsor's employees are involved in event activities to create enthusiasm and teamwork
Goodwill Marketing	Enhances the sponsor's perception in the community through involvement in the event
Hospitality/VIP Treatment	Sponsor receives special benefits (e.g. VIP tickets, parking, meet and greet) to host key clients, donors, employees
In-Kind Sponsorship	The providing of goods or services in lieu of cash in exchange for sponsorship recognition
Intangible Benefit	Benefits with no monetary value but that appeal to a sponsor (e.g. high-profile, exclusivity, prestigious, certain clientele, etc.)
Licensing	A right to use the event's logo or slogans in the sponsor's marketing efforts
Media Sponsorship	Providing cash or media services in exchange for the right of sponsorship designation (e.g. radio, television, newspaper)

The Language of Sponsorship

The following are common terms relating to sponsors and their roles.

Niche Marketing	A specific target market based on demographics or event type
One-to-One Marketing	Direct marketing by the sponsor to event attendees
Partnership Marketing	Companies sharing common business goals or interests partner together; may also be deemed co-sponsors
Perimeter Marketing	Signage or displays located on the outside perimeter of an event
Presenting Sponsor	A sponsor who is recognized by placing their name above or below the name of the event; not a title sponsorship
Promotional Items	Merchandise which is sold or handed out that may contain the event and/or sponsor's name
Right of First Refusal	A sponsor's right to negotiate or renew a sponsorship in advance of competitors
Sampling	Sponsor provides samples of products to attendees at the event (e.g. food, specialty advertising giveaways)
Segmented Marketing	Marketing directed at a specific demographic group or marketing segment
Signage	Designated items which contain the sponsor's logo (e.g. banners, flags, signs, scoreboards, posters, etc.); not necessarily all signage
Sole Sponsor	The only sponsor affiliated with the event and the sole recipient of sponsor benefits
Sponsorship	Negotiated partnering between a sponsor and the event in which a sponsorship is paid in cash, services, products, or a combination thereof in exchange for rights of exposure through the event
Tangible Benefit	A benefit based on price or cost (e.g. advertising, printing, entertainment, etc.)
Title Sponsor	The highest level sponsorship available; sometimes called the premier sponsor. Sponsor's name is placed above that of the event and implies ownership of the event
Trade Marketing	Marketing targeted to a specific trade or related group
Underwriting Sponsor	Sponsor underwrites a significant event activity or event expense

Sponsor Recruitment Letter

Date

Name
Company
Address
City/State/Zip

Dear Name,

We're gearing up for the 2008 Sagebrush Classic, one of the most prestigious golf and culinary events in the Northwest, and Central Oregon's Party of the Year. Set amidst one of Oregon's most spectacular scenic and recreational areas, the 2008 event is set for July 18-19 at the Broken Top Golf Club in Bend.

We've got some new surprises in store this year as well as our tried and true favorites. Friday offers a fierce and friendly best ball battle as 52 foursomes compete for cash prizes, trophies, and bragging rights on the private course at Broken Top. Saturday's Feast in the meadow for 1,000 guests presents the world-class culinary artistry of 20 national and international chefs, handcrafted ales from Deschutes Brewery, and cuisine-friendly wines courtesy of esteemed Oregon and Washington winemakers. Phenomenal rock violinist Aaron Meyer will open the show for Los Angeles based headliners Jack Mack and the Heart Attack. This is one you don't want to miss!

You can use the Sagebrush Classic to provide a high profile in- or out-of-town golf and gourmet culinary experience for special clients, management, family, or friends. You also have the opportunity to get your company on the radar screen of an affluent clientele through our event marketing channels. And, since this event is a charitable fundraiser, a portion of your sponsorship is tax deductible.

We encourage you to sign up now for this prestigious, perpetually sold-out event. This packet provides advance opportunity to review levels and benefits. We can also customize any of the upper sponsor levels to meet your needs.

Deschutes Children's Foundation annually oversees distribution of Sagebrush Classic proceeds to 15-20 charitable organizations serving children and families. In addition, the event provides support to the football programs of Bend, Summit, and Mt. View high schools. To date, more than $2.7 million in net proceeds has been distributed to benefit our communities.

Please don't hesitate to contact us at 503.332.5000 or by email at sagebrushclassic@comcast.net. We will be calling within the next ten days to follow up and answer any questions you may have.

Thank you for your consideration. Together, we can do more to help make a difference.

Best regards,

Name
Title

2004 Classic Wines Auction Fact Sheet

General Information

The Classic Wines Auction in Portland, Oregon is ranked as one of the top ten charity wine auctions in the United States by *Wine Spectator* magazine. Attended by an affluent clientele of 1000 bidders from around the country, the Saturday auction event includes pre-dinner wine tasting, a five-course culinary extravaganza prepared by top guest chefs, select wines from honorary ambassadors, silent and oral auctions. The exclusive Ambassadors Dinner is held Friday evening where wine ambassadors mingle with 150 guests and dine on an elegant meal prepared by a celebrity chef. A limited number of intimate winemaker-hosted dinners pairing top restaurants and wineries are held on Thursday evening.

Since its inception, the Classic Wines Auction has raised more than $15 million to benefit children, families and older adults in the Portland metropolitan area.

The wines to be auctioned are donated by private collectors, winemakers, retailers, and distributors. The quality and importance of the wines are superb and those donated from private collections are often not available to the public. A number of national and international travel packages are offered, including wine elements. Charitable tax deductions are allowed to the extent of the law.

Honorary Wine Ambassadors

Ambassadors for 2004 include Brand Name (International), Brand Name (Oregon), Brand Name (Washington), and Brand Name (California). The Classic Wines Auction and Ambassadors Dinner feature select wines.

Guest Chefs

The region's top executive chefs prepare dinner courses matched with wines of our ambassadors. Classic Wines Auction chefs for 2004 are (Chef Name) of (Restaurant Name), (Chef Name) of (Restaurant Name), (Chef Name) of (Restaurant Name), (Chef Name) of (Restaurant Name), and (Chef Name) of (Restaurant Name). (Chef Name) of (Restaurant Name) in Napa, California is the visiting celebrity chef for the Ambassadors Dinner.

MARK YOUR CALENDAR NOW!
Thursday, March 4 – Winemaker Dinners
Small groups hosted by winemakers at top restaurants
All dinners commence at 6:30 p.m.

Friday, March 5 – Ambassadors Dinner – (Location)
6:00 p.m. reception, 7:00 p.m. dinner

Saturday, March 6 – Classic Wines Auction – (Location)
5:00 p.m. registration, wine tasting, oral auction viewing, silent auctions
7:00 p.m. dinner, 7:30 p.m. oral auction

For More Information
Judy Anderson, Auction Director
Phone: 503.332.5000
Email: powerproductions@comcast.net

Ticket Prices Per Person
Classic Wines Auction Only	$XXX
Ambassadors' Dinner *and* CWA	$XXX
Winemaker Dinners	$XXX

SPONSOR CONFIRMATION

Spring Fling Gala Dinner

April 17, 2008

A benefit for Children's Hospital

COMPANY NAME	
CONTACT PERSON	
ADDRESS	

CITY/STATE/ZIP		**PHONE**	
EMAIL		**FAX**	

We are pleased to participate as a sponsor or patron at the following level:

❑ Presenting Sponsor - $20,000   ❑ Supporting Sponsor - $5,000

❑ Associate Sponsor - $10,000   ❑ Patron Table - $2,500

TABLE NAME	

AGREEMENT: In submitting this sponsor confirmation, sponsor or table purchaser agrees to payment in full according to the level of benefits selected and identified in the sponsor agreement. No sponsor benefits will be provided without advance payment.

Signature_____ Date_____

PAYMENT METHOD: ❑ Check   ❑ VISA   ❑ MC   ❑ AmEx

Card #_____ Expiration Date _____

Name on Card_____ Signature _____

COMPLETED FORM & PAYMENT MUST BE RECEIVED BY MARCH 1 TO RESERVE PLACEMENT

MAIL:	Spring Fling Gala Dinner	**CONTACT:**	Judy Anderson, Director
	Children's Hospital	**PHONE:**	503.332.5000
	PO Box 0000	**FAX:**	503.000.0000
	Portland OR 97000	**EMAIL:**	powerproductions@comcast.net

Thank you for your support!

Sponsor Confirmation Letter

Date

Name
Company
Address
City/State/Zip

Dear Name,

Thank you for your generosity in sponsoring the exclusive Gala Dinner Dance that is part of the Event Name. As you know, this high visibility event will take place on Friday evening, Date, at the Place, and is attended by business, civic, and social leaders.

Your company will be recognized as a Platinum Sponsor level. The benefits of your sponsorship are outlined in the attached Sponsorship Agreement. Please sign both copies, return one, and keep the other for your records.

Sponsor payments are due in full by Date. If you have not already done so, you may pay by check or credit card. A receipt will be provided upon payment.

On behalf of the many low-income children, families, and seniors in our community who are helped through Organization Name programs, we thank you for your support.

If you should have questions, please feel free to contact our Event Director, Name, by phone at Number, or Email at Address.

Kind regards,

Name   Name
Chairman   Event Director

Sponsorship Agreement

Fictitious Festival

This document will serve as an agreement between Sponsor's Name and the Fictitious Festival to be held on Event Date/s for Presenting Sponsor rights and benefits in the amount of $_____.

Fictitious Festival Agrees to Provide:

- Opportunity to mass market to 100,000 event attendees in pre-event publicity and on-site for duration of the festival (3 days)
- Company logo on all scheduled print advertising in newspapers and trade publications
- Company logo on event advertising on four major market television stations and two cable networks, including the television sponsor
- Company mention in event advertising on five major market radio stations, including the radio sponsors
- Company logo on transit ads
- Company logo on outdoor media
- Company logo on posters and flyers
- Company logo on daily event schedules
- Company logo on printed tickets
- Company logo on stage banners
- Company logo on event souvenir merchandise
- 20' x 20' exhibitor space at event
- Product sampling opportunities
- VIP parking for 20 vehicles
- Meet/greet with headlining entertainer
- Backstage passes for 10 persons
- 100 admission passes to the event
- 10 admission passes to the special activity of your choice (car races, concert, etc.)
- Opportunity to be affiliated with one of the state's most successful events
- Opportunity to host VIP clients or guests
- On-site sales/marketing opportunities

Sponsor's Name Agrees To:

- Pay 50% deposit of total sponsorship fee upon signing this agreement
- Pay remainder of sponsorship fee by Specified Date

Fictitious Festival agrees to indemnify, hold harmless and defend Sponsor from any and all claims which may be brought against Sponsor by any person or entity for any and all reasons, or for any damages which may arise from Fictitious Festival's conduct or activity under this agreement except property damage or personal injury caused by the negligent act(s) of the Sponsor.

Sponsor agrees to indemnify, hold harmless and defend Fictitious Festival, its directors, employees, agents, sponsors, subcontractors or volunteers from and against any and all losses, claims, suits, actions, payments, judgments, and any other liabilities including legal fees and expenses resulting either directly or indirectly to sponsor's participation.

Neither party shall be liable for failure to perform their obligations due to acts beyond their control including, without limitation, acts of God, acts of government, acts of the public enemy, civil disobedience, lock out freight embargoes or any other cause or condition beyond Fictitious Festival's or Sponsor's control.

Both parties agree not to disclose any proprietary information obtained about the other to any party without prior written consent of both Sponsor's Name and Fictitious Festival.

Sponsor's Name shall have the Right of First Refusal to act as Presenting Sponsor for the (next year) Fictitious Festival and sponsor's authorized representative shall notify the festival's authorized representative of intent no later than Specify Date.

If any controversy or breach should arise out of this agreement or its performance and the parties are unable to settle the dispute between themselves the dispute shall be submitted to arbitration in (county or state) in accordance with the Uniform Arbitration Act. The decision of the Arbitrator shall be binding on both parties.

The undersigned have the authority to execute this agreement on behalf of the respective parties.

Agreed and accepted:

_____   _____

For Sponsor   For Fictitious Festival

Print Name_____   Print Name_____

Date_____   Date_____

Chapter 6 – Marketing & Promotions

Build An Image and Make It Memorable

All events use marketing and promotions in some form. Marketing is simply defined as the art of buying and selling or motivating buying decisions. For events, this can include motivation to attend, sponsor, donate, purchase, or volunteer.

"Promotions" is the broader umbrella which encompasses not only marketing, but other activities such as advertising, publicity, and public relations.

Every time you speak, write, ask, show, tell, e-mail, phone, or do any form of communication with anyone in regard to the event, you are doing some form of marketing.

The Marketing and Promotions section of this chapter focuses on:

> ➢ Marketing
> ➢ Advertising
> ➢ Publicity and public relations
> ➢ Working with the media

"Marketing is everything— and everything is marketing."

Paul Vogel
Vogel Communications

In terms of sales, marketing and promoting an event is much like selling a product. In this case, the product is the event, or a part of the event that has an individual focus. Even sponsorship, which is selling a potential sponsor on the benefits of being part of the event, has marketing elements incorporated into the sales pitch.

Marketing provides exposure, gets the word out, creates excitement, and helps to generate attendance and dollars to support the event. So carefully craft your marketing plan with this end in mind.

Examples and work sheets for Marketing & Promotions are found at the end of the chapter.

Marketing & Promotions

You'll need to take a look at the event from the viewpoint of sponsors and attendees to develop a marketing strategy. Map your marketing effort to meet the needs of your constituency, as well as those of the event as a whole.

What will draw the audience in? How will marketing and promotion help to accomplish event goals? This is where the research you did to identify the event demographic during the creative planning process will play a significant role.

What makes your event special? Through marketing and promotion, the event will build an image. Remember that other events are also vying for the same market, so yours needs to stand out in the crowd. Leverage that "uniqueness" for all you can.

Marketing As A Strategy

Invite a professional in marketing, public relations, or advertising to be the marketing chairperson. The event manager can work closely with the marketing chair to create a dynamic marketing plan.

Working with a professional in one of these fields will result in a more polished production and a well-coordinated marketing effort. If the preference is to do the marketing in-house, at the very least ask a professional firm to do some pro-bono work in exchange for an in-kind sponsorship. Paying for these services should be a last resort because the event has a number of things to offer in trade.

Do some research about current trends in marketing practices. Avoid methods or statistics that are outdated. While they still have valid points, marketing methods that were used in the 1980s, 1990s, and even early 2000s, don't apply in today's world where the economic climate and expectations are different.

Develop a marketing plan. Spend time creating a strategy. Determine how various marketing and promotional activities can encourage, excite and motivate people to attend, support, sponsor or volunteer. By incorporating all these things into the plan, you'll create a viable roadmap to get to your goal.

Incorporate the activities and tools you'll need into a written marketing plan. The plan doesn't need to be a tome of epic proportions. It can be as simple as a list of topics with bullet points. The important thing is to have a planned strategy that can be changed if necessary. This written document should be shared with others working on the event to maximize marketing benefits.

Build relationships. Use existing relationships or build new ones to help market the event. Network constantly, use event chairmen or committee members, trade or barter, cross-promote, leverage sponsors, and maximize possibilities to use the media.

Once you've achieved attendance, the event itself is marketing. Guests need to enjoy themselves while being motivated to want to attend again or to spend money if it's a fundraiser.

Create An Image

The creation of an image is referred to as "branding" in marketing terms. Branding is a readily identifiable and consistent image of the event—such as a logo—that is used in marketing, promotions, and publicity materials. The brand should be on everything from letterhead to signage. This identity is established through graphic image, colors, type fonts, key messages or other means that capture attention and provide association with the event. In the marketing world, it has been said that branding "is about mindshare and market share." This applies to events as well.

There is a difference between "identity," which is the way we perceive ourselves, as opposed to "image" which is the way we are perceived by others. Branding is a melding of the two.

NOTES

81

Different Strokes For Different Folks

People are visual, audio, or kinesthetic learners—what they see, hear, and/or feel—so the marketing has to be developed to appeal to these methods by which individuals relate to the world. Each event needs to be examined for its own individual characteristics because a cookie cutter approach to marketing doesn't work. There are fundamentals that should always be executed, but shape them to your event and clientele. Those geared to a specific interest group, such as a trade association, would not be marketed in the same way as an event for the general public, like a festival.

Borrow Ideas From Others

It's perfectly all right to "borrow" ideas from other events as long as you don't exactly duplicate or plagiarize. They probably got the idea from somewhere else, too! If you borrow an idea, add a new twist to it and make it your own.

A good source of ideas is to attend other events to "see how they do it." There are great ideas to be had everywhere. Look at the signage, staging, décor, systems, food, you name it. You'll get ideas or see new ways to do things regardless of how sophisticated the event is.

HINT: Working a shift as a volunteer for other events is a good way to observe without having to pay the ticket price.

Advertising

One way to think of "advertising" as opposed to "publicity" is that advertising usually has an associated cost, while publicity is free. Most events don't have much advertising budget unless they're highly driven by mass media and this forces us to look at creative ways of getting the message out. This is why a marketing or advertising professional on your committee is an invaluable resource.

NOTES

Advertisement drives attendance, provides exposure for the event and the participating charity, informs, or gives thanks. It should be informative, sincere, easy to understand, and tell the who-what-when-where-why-how.

Some of the more traditional paid advertising mediums include radio, television, newspapers, magazines, and direct mail. Events are best served by forms of advertising familiar to the community such as local newspapers, radio or television stations. National publications normally do not offer much exposure, require substantial lead times, and are quite expensive in comparison.

If you spend money on advertising, spend it wisely. Don't make the mistake of spending lots of money on flashy forms of advertising that in truth will draw only a few people. If the event has a media sponsor who is willing to do a major marketing blitz, by all means go for it. If you don't have that luxury, careful consideration should be given to obtaining maximum impact for minimum (or no) dollars.

The implementation of any advertising campaign should be weighed by a realistic look at how much attendance, sponsorship, or other revenue will be gained versus how much time and money will be spent. Do your homework. Some advertising costs a great deal for a very small return, while other methods cost very little and attract many paying customers.

In a down economy, decreased advertising spending means there is a lot more open advertising space because the media has a lot more inventory. Go to media partners and come up with a marketing plan that benefits you both.

Pay Attention! Look for event advertisements in entertainment sections of local newspapers. Which ones grab your attention and why? Clip out the ad and make notes about what you like or don't like about it. You can keep these in a file and use them for reference in developing your own ads.

Media Advertising

Standard forms of advertising are electronic media and print media. Radio and television are forms of electronic media while newspapers and magazines are print media. All have rate cards that outline the costs for their services. On-line media is growing in popularity with the Internet becoming the main news source for many people.

Television Advertising

Television provides a visual means of promotion and gives the audience instant identification with the event. Television ads are priced according to the time slots in which they are aired and duration of time (typically 15, 30, or 60 seconds) for which they run. Prices are per station rates and can be paid in cash, underwritten through sponsorship, or done on a buy-one get one match if the station wants to be an in-kind sponsor.

The television station will produce the "spot" or it can be done by an ad agency and submitted according to certain standards. The production of the spot may or may not be included in the buy. The event manager should be present during studio production since mistakes are costly to repair if the ad is not done correctly the first time. The best possible solution would be to have an advertising agency donate these services in conjunction with a media sponsor.

A CD or DVD copy of the advertisement or promotional piece can also be used as a great tool to recruit potential sponsors. If the event has a television sponsor and the station tag is on the disk, this shows a potential sponsor that a highly visual advertising medium supports the event.

NOTE: Media sponsors can produce your event promotion without the station tag. Copies of this can be used by other stations as public service announcements.

Local stations for major network affiliates (ABC, NBC, CBS, Fox) are always great to have as sponsors. But don't forget about cable service providers who can insert your ad into local programming for nationally televised shows on the Food Network, HGTV, and others whose viewers may match your event demographic.

Another way to use a local television station is to promote the event on a live "morning show." These shows usually allow a designated number of people to attend as audience members and you may be able to verbally plug the event on the air (usually around 30 seconds). Come prepared with notes so you don't forget to mention something critical. It's great fun to do this, and as a side benefit you'll learn something about television production!

Radio Advertising

Radio provides an audio means of telling the listening audience about the details. Since this form of advertising is not visual, the radio spot must have vivid language that enables the listener to clearly understand the message and "picture" it in their mind.

Radio ads are priced similarly to television ads (15-30-60 seconds). The station will assist in studio production using a professional announcer and copy written with the help of the station's promotions personnel. The event manager will need to approve the commercial prior to the time it is aired.

It is especially significant if the radio station is a media sponsor and the spot includes in the message that they are a sponsor or a mention that station personalities will be present.

A radio station can give the event free publicity as well. They often conduct phone or live interviews with the event manager or spokesperson that is either broadcast live or taped for later use.

Print Advertising

Newspaper and magazine ads provide visual information. These can offer more details about the event schedule, admission price, and so on than are radio and television ads. There is not a professional announcer to hype the event, so the print ad must motivate by creating energy through words, pictures and/or graphics. Less is best and white space is a good thing. Keep the information clear and as concise as possible. It needs to be easily read and understood.

Print ads are sold by column width and number of vertical inches. Prices will vary considerably depending on the publication, its circulation and the time period during which the ad will appear. There is normally an extra charge for layout services if the ad is not submitted in its final form. Ads should be "familied" with the event's branding, image and message.

Other Advertising & Marketing Methods

Web Site. There is significant use of the Internet as an informational resource. Having a Web site where people can find details or photos is an invaluable tool. You can also have a "fill in" form on-line where people can register and purchase tickets via credit card.

Social Networks. Use free marketing tools like Facebook, Twitter, LinkedIn, blogs, and other social media to expand marketing reach.

Banner Ads. You can also purchase banner advertising for Internet Web sites where your ad "pops" up when a specific page appears on the screen. These ads are relatively inexpensive depending on where the ad will appear and market share.

Direct Mail. Printed materials like brochures or invitations can be mailed directly to homes and businesses. There are a number of ways to generate mailing lists. Some of the more common forms are to use the database of previous attendees, a list from the benefiting charity, or you can purchase lists from mail houses that are targeted by zip code or for your specific demographic.

Publicity & Public Relations

Publicity is free as opposed to advertising. Publicity and public relations are powerful tools to create awareness, build image, motivate or educate, generate attendance, recruit volunteers, recognize sponsors, etc. Use publicity to forge relationships with the media and others who can assist in promoting the event.

Public relations also ensure that sponsors, committees, volunteers, participants, the media, and the general public are kept informed throughout the course of the event cycle.

Publicity is free media coverage so use it as a golden opportunity. Once a story appears in one media outlet, it often gets noticed by other media and they provide coverage as well. This expands the base of publicity and can save money.

Difference Between Advertising and Public Relations

In advertising, you:

- Pay for print space or air time
- Control the content of the ad's message and design
- Designate when and where the ad will appear in print, radio, TV

In publicity, you:

- Don't pay for the placement of a news article
- Identify newsworthy events and request that reporters cover them
- Have minimal or no control over what the media say
- Have no guaranteed placement as to when a story may appear
- Have an efficient, no-cost method for gaining visibility
- Establish credibility through third-party endorsements versus paid advertising

NOTE: Interestingly, a news story is estimated to be 3-5 times more credible than advertising!

Other Publicity Vehicles

Special Features. These provide in-depth human interest stories about specific persons or unique aspects of the event. They are worth pursuing because they create extra attention. It also provides an opportunity to establish a connection with the reporter, assignment editor, or news editor for future contacts.

Copies of news articles are great additions to sponsor packets!

Newsletters. Publicity regarding the event can be incorporated into an organization's existing informational systems or can be presented as an event-specific newsletter. These are sent to contacts generated from a database list of supporters and/or for internal distribution.

Other Organizations. Help the word get out through local chambers of commerce, convention and visitors bureaus, benefiting charities, associations, service clubs, and the like.

Event Calendars. Event calendars are used to generate pre-event publicity where information is presented in just a few words. Event calendars are especially good for print publications but listings can also be submitted to broadcast media (e.g. television and radio) for inclusion in community calendars.

Many print publications have long lead times for their event calendars (6-12 months out). Send a compelling photo along with the event listing, and include who should receive photo credit.

E-Mail. Compile an e-mail list from your data base to send out regular communication about upcoming events and information.

Volunteers and Committees. Those directly involved with the event are some of the most ardent communicators. Through their individual networks, they can help publicize and promote by word-of-mouth, distribute invitations or newsletters, etc.

Working With The Media

The media is a powerful communications tool. Most people read a newspaper, use the Internet, watch television, or listen to the radio at some point during the day.

These days, a great deal of the media is held by huge conglomerates who own many stations within a market. This is especially true of radio and television, and can also be true of newspaper chains.

Establishing a working relationship with individual members of the media is still the best bet for long-term coverage. Events with a history have the benefit of knowing who to contact. New events will need to build these affiliations. Talk to media representatives or meet with them before crunch time on the event. The downside is that in today's working climate, media people move around in their jobs or can be gone at a moment's notice.

To effectively work with the media, you need to know what the various departments of the media do. You'll want to provide accurate and timely information, know how they prefer to receive and process the information, and be respectful of their deadlines. Allow the required lead time and be sure to follow up.

Due to increased use of electronic communications, media people tend to respond better to email than to telephone calls. Find out the preferred method of communication, because the easier it is for them to process the information, the better chance for coverage.

Editorial Calendars

Most media outlets, especially newspapers and tabloid sections, have editorial calendars which show a major topic that will be covered each month for the coming year. Pay attention to these and get your information to the editor well in advance of the publication date that relates to your subject because it dramatically increases your odds of being included.

Be prepared if you are interviewed! Whatever you do, <u>don't wing it</u>. Remember that everything you say to a reporter is "on the record" so don't say anything you wouldn't want to see in the news. If you don't know the answer to a question, tell them you'll get back to them, and then follow up.

Speak in sound bites (short sentences). Never say, "no comment." If you don't want to answer a question, respond by refocusing on your message and maintain your composure. Volunteers should also be coached about speaking with reporters. Volunteers often don't know the answers and will make something up that may or may not be true. The best bet is to have volunteers direct media folks to the event manager.

Build A Media List

Decide which media outlets will best reach your target audience. Based on this information, you'll want to develop a media list that includes contacts and information for local radio and television stations, local newspapers and magazines, on-line media, corporate or trade publications, and even regional or national publications. Don't forget to include local cable television stations, since they are a community resource.

Check the newspaper or watch the news to learn which reporters cover events. Many media outlets have Web sites with contact information. Chambers of commerce or convention bureaus often maintain media lists, or the information can be gathered the old-fashioned way, by calling. Regardless of method, this may be a good project for a trusted volunteer to take on.

Create the media list in a spreadsheet or table format with columns for contact name, title, media outlet, address, city, state, zip and email information. You can also add columns to indicate deadlines, desired format, or other requirements. Further refine the list into long and short lead media. Long lead media typically need the information at least six months or more in advance.

NOTES

For a small event, about 20-30 contacts are sufficient. For larger events, the list should contain at least 50 names between television, radio, magazines, newspapers, and specialty publications. Since media personnel change often, make sure to keep the list updated.

Preparing A Media Kit

Media kits, also known as press kits, need to be sent out or delivered based on publishing dates or deadlines. The kits provide basic information about the event and are used for reference by media representatives in writing articles or creating news stories.

Standard elements of a media kit include:

- A brief cover letter
- Most current press release
- Fact sheet
- Select copies of the most recent news articles
- CD with photos of the last event or other pertinent subjects
- Examples of current or previous collateral materials (optional)

Other items of interest could include the event schedule, biographies of key participants or speakers, or information about charities.

NOTE: The cover letter should contain the "pitch." Give it a hook. Most media people won't read past the cover letter unless it catches their interest.

The information can be placed in a portfolio that includes a business card. A simple way to get added attention is to mail the media kit in a colored envelope and to hand write the name and address. It stands out in the crowd and shows personal attention.

Another way to get attention is to include a personal note referring to your knowledge of the reporter's work or to express appreciation for a story they covered (e.g. "I saw your recent story on XYZ and feel you may be interested in an event that we're working on."

NOTES

Press Releases

Press releases are produced at regular intervals throughout the event cycle, including a post-event wrap up. Each should have a different focus or the media will only cover them once. Use a "hook" to get attention with a catchy (not cute) headline. Incorporate a human interest element if possible. Most events have stories to tell and it increases the odds of the release being used.

Submit information in standard press release format using Associated Press style. The media receive numerous press releases daily, so present your information in the format they prefer (Associated Press standards). Place crucial information at the beginning. Use short sentences. Write conversationally and use action words. Use a hook, but don't try to be cute or you'll lose credibility. Include margins of at least one inch and one and one-half to double line spacing, and stay to one page if possible.

Make sure your message is compelling, is concise and relates to the media's audience. News assignment editors may get as many as 100 press releases a day, so you really need to make your press release look professional and have your story stand out from the crowd.

Event information including contact name, title, phone number, fax number, email and/or Web address should be placed in the upper left or upper right corner of the page.

Slightly below the contact information is placed the release date. This is normally shown as "FOR IMMEDIATE RELEASE" rather than a specific date that narrows the window it can be used.

The headline should be a strong message (the hook) that attracts attention and should be centered on the page. Sub-headings should be in a smaller font size and/or be italicized. Keep the body text of the release concise since "less is more" when it comes to whether the event will receive column space or air time.

NOTES

The first paragraph should begin with your city, state, and the date (called the "dateline"). Place crucial information in the first paragraph following the dateline which should answer the questions of who-what-when-where-why-and how. Subsequent paragraphs should be in order of declining importance as they may be cut from the copy.

Add your "boilerplate" statement at the very end of the release. The boilerplate is standard language at the end of most releases that describes your organization/event history, unique positioning, or motto-like statements.

If the release carries over to a second page, the word "-more-" should be centered at the bottom of the first page. The end is signified by using three # # # (pound sign) characters or the word "END" centered on the page.

Media Advisories

Media advisories, or media alerts, are used to tantalize media interest to be present on-site at some time during the event. They also include the "who-what-when-where-why-how" information and highlight interview or visual opportunities. These should be sent to news assignment editors at radio or print outlets a week or so in advance, and to arrive at television outlets two to three days in advance. Be sure to make follow up calls after sending an advisory to verbally highlight visuals or offer to schedule advance interviews with key speakers or others.

Fact Sheets

Some reporters prefer to use fact sheets to build their own stories. These contain basic, detailed information in a concise format and can include information on benefiting charities, if any. Fact sheets apply for a longer length of time than do individual press releases It is helpful to include both a press release and a fact sheet in the media kit since there are often things in a fact sheet that a reporter might like to cover at a later time.

Public Service Announcements (PSAs)

Public service announcements are not to exceed 30 seconds in length and are written as if they were being spoken (in other words, a script). They are used by individual stations as time permits. If you're fortunate enough to have a media sponsor, audio or video CDs or DVDs without the station tag can be produced and sent out to other media. The format for public service announcements is similar to that of a press release.

Photographs

Use professionally taken photographs. Action photos or those with a visual appeal are more interesting than "talking head" pictures. Keep them simple. Busy or complicated photos do not produce well.

Send photos in a digital format of at least 300 dpi (dots per inch) which are needed to reproduce well. Be sure to label each photo with a caption and to identify the photographer for photo credits.

Obtain a signed release from individuals in a photo, especially if it is being used for publicity purposes. The release allows use of the photo and is a form of legal protection for the event.

Photo credit is given as a means of identifying the photographer and/or copyright date in a photo caption. Some media do not give photo credit and will publish the photo without identia.

In Summary

Take a look around. There are opportunities everywhere to market, promote, and get your message out. Use them to your advantage!

Marketing Terms in Relation to Events

The following are common terms used in marketing and by the media.

Advertising	The action of calling something to the attention of the public especially by paid notice or broadcast
Audience	The market segment identified to be the best demographic fit
Branding	A readily identifiable image or slogan
Cause Marketing	A business strategy to link a nonprofit organization or cause to the marketing efforts
Collateral Materials	Written promotional materials such as invitations, catalogs, and other image pieces
Cross-Promotion	Two or more co-advertisers join together for promotional purposes (e.g. retailer and soft drink company), or this could mean cross-promotion between a sponsor and the event
E-Marketing	On-line marketing or ticket sales
Licensing	Right to use the event logo/slogan to market an affiliation
Marketing	The act of buying and selling products and services
Media	Agencies of mass communication
Niche Marketing	A specific target market based on demographics or market territory
Positioning	Rank, status, or advantage between you and the competition
Promotions	An umbrella term that encompasses marketing, advertising, publicity, and public relations
Publicity	Media mention of the event, affiliated persons, or activities
Public Relations	On-going activities to ensure a strong public image through marketing, publicity, or promotions
Sponsorship	Cash, goods, or services provided in exchange for sponsorship recognition
Target Market	Those likely to attend or support the event
Trade Marketing	Marketing targeted to a specific trade or association group

Sample Press Release

Contact Information
Judy Anderson, President
Power Productions
503.332.5000
powerproductions@comcast.net

FOR IMMEDIATE RELEASE

Unique Concept in Event Training Featured at October Workshop

Portland, Oregon – October 10, 2006—Learn how to manage or improve special events at the exciting Event Camp seminar! The training features two full days of intensive, hands-on, how-to on October 28-29 at the Oregon Convention Center, 777 NE Martin Luther King Jr. Blvd.

"The idea was to do something fun and unique as well as educational," states Judy Anderson, Event Camp creator and owner of Power Productions, a local event management and consulting firm. "Participants will use a proven system to learn how to successfully manage every element of an event."

Anderson knows of what she speaks. She is the current director of two large high-profile fundraising events—The Sagebrush Classic, a celebrity chef and golf event in Bend, and Portland State University's signature event honoring philanthropy, the Simon Benson Awards Dinner. For six years, she was director of the Classic Wines Auction, one of the top ten charity wine auctions in the United States raising more than $1 million annually for local charities. A veteran of more than 20 years in event management, Anderson has written a 300-page book titled *Event Management Simplified*, that is used as the class text.

To enhance the educational aspect, Event Camp is held in a state-of-the-art event setting complete with décor, electronic visual media, sound, and lighting. Guest speakers include sponsors, service providers, and media professionals. The workshop is for anyone interested in special events, for novice or experienced event managers, or for those in event related services. The $XXX registration fee covers both days of training, class materials, Anderson's book, lunch, break refreshments, and special surprises.

Event Camp is sponsored by Power Productions, the Oregon Convention Center, Aramark, The Prop Shop, Spirit Media, Hollywood Lighting, CircleTriangleSquare Graphic Design, Peter Corvallis Productions, and Metropolitan Printing Company.

For more information or to register, call 503.332.5000 or email powerproductions@comcast.net.

Event Camp Fact Sheet

This is another version of a fact sheet than can be used by the media.

WHAT: Event Camp

WHEN: October 28-29, 2006

WHERE: Oregon Convention Center
777 NE Martin Luther King Jr. Blvd.
Portland, Oregon

WHO: Persons interested in learning about event management
Novice or experienced event managers
Development/event directors, board members of nonprofit organizations
Persons in event related services

DESCRIPTION: Two days of specialized training in all elements of event management

Immersion in an event environment complete with décor, electronic visual media, sound, lighting

Class Text: *Event Management Simplified*, a 300-page workbook authored by class facilitator, Judy Anderson

Guest speakers including sponsors, service providers, and representatives from the media

An assortment of activities, surprises, and insights

Sponsored by: Power Productions, Oregon Convention Center, Aramark, Hollywood Lighting, The Prop Shop, Spirit Media, Peter Corvallis Productions, Spectrum Acoustics, CircleTriangleSquare Graphic Design, and Metropolitan Printing Company

COST: $XXX covers training, class text, all materials

CONTACT: Judy Anderson, President/Owner
Power Productions
503.332.5000
powerproductions@comcast.net
www.eventsandauctions.com

Marketing Worksheet

Use this worksheet to outline the various methods and tools to be used in marketing and promotions.

Research

1. What makes the event unique? _____
2. What marketing strategies are needed to accomplish goals? _____
3. What are the prime motivators for the audience? _____
4. Are there other similar events that could be attended for ideas? _____

Marketing

1. Are you familiar with current event trends? _____
2. What publicity methods will be used to promote the event? _____
3. How much lead time is required? _____

Creating A Brand

1. Is there a logo or other identifiable image? _____
2. Does the marketing strategy appeal to different interests? _____
3. What are the main promotional methods for the event? _____

Advertising

1. Will you use paid advertising and if so, what is the cost? _____
2. What is the ratio of benefit to cost? _____
3. What form of advertising will be the main "driver" and what is the purpose? _____

Media Advertising

1. If the event has a media sponsor, what are they contributing? _____
2. Will the event pay for television ads? _____ How many? _____ Cost _____
3. Will the event pay for radio ads? _____ How many? _____ Cost _____
4. Will the event pay for print ads? _____ How many? _____ Cost _____
5. Can you leverage existing media advertisers to be event sponsors? _____

Working With The Media

1. Are there existing media contacts that provide advertising or publicity? _____
2. Do you have a current media list? _____
3. Have you prepared a media kit containing comprehensive information? _____
4. Are press releases, PSAs, and fact sheets written in traditional media formats? _____
5. What unique angles could be pitched for media attention? _____

Chapter 7 – Graphic Design & Printing

Graphic Design Is An Art; Print Is Its Canvas

Graphic design and printing are critical in conveying the look and feel of the event to the audience. Graphic design plays an important role because it communicates a visual identity. Good graphic design is essential to creating the eye catching and memorable collateral materials most events require. Equally important is using a reliable printer who provides quality at a reasonable price.

Graphic Design

If you want "image with impact," a graphic designer is the answer. Many of us can create newsletters or other materials using desktop publishing programs, but for real power in your image you need a professional to give it extra polish.

"Everything you can imagine is real."

Pablo Picasso

The cost of graphic design services could very well turn out to be one of the best investments the event can make. A great logo prominently used on event materials and promotional items for several years actually turns out to be a real bargain. A digital version of the logo could also be inserted into proposals, newsletters, flyers, email, or do-it-yourself layouts.

Inviting a graphic designer to be on the event's marketing committee can go a long way toward reducing, or even eliminating, these costs.

If you opt to do it yourself, a number of computer software programs have pre-formatted templates or allow freehand capabilities for layout and design. Smaller events may not need a highly professional image and using your own layout for printed materials may work just fine. Present the most businesslike image possible, no matter which method you use.

Principles and Elements of Design

There are no hard and fast rules for graphic design, but most professionals operate under certain principles and incorporate a number of elemental aspects into the process. Graphic design is purposeful, informational, and creates a visual language.

Standardized principles of design include the following:

Balance	Even distribution of the "weight" of the design elements
Proportion	Size relationship between elements
Contrast	Variety created through size, shape, color, texture, typography, etc.
Emphasis	Elements within the design contain a hierarchy of visual importance
Rhythm	Repetition of one or more elements to create harmony within the design
Direction	Movement created through use of lines, contrast, white space, graphics, etc. as a way to lead the eyes to follow
Unity	All parts of the design work together to create the message

Think about how these various principles and elements of design apply to invitations, catalogs or programs, signage, promotional items, newsletters, and the like, and you begin to see what an impact strong graphic design can make. The creation of a Web site would also use this process.

If the designed piece will be mailed, check with the post office before it is printed. Small design errors that could cost big dollars in extra postage fees can be resolved in advance by using this practice. This especially applies to the size of finished pieces because if they are outside the norm, the postage is much more costly for each piece.

Printing

Establishing a good working relationship with a reliable printer results in both time and cost savings. At the outset, you'll want to identify and compile of list of everything that will need to be printed (e.g. stationery, invitations, response cards, response envelopes, save the date postcards, newsletters, catalogs, and so on).

These can then be grouped by category—commercial printing, quick printing, screen printing---so that a printer can bid for all items within a particular group. This save money because most printers offer a better deal in exchange for the opportunity to do most or all of the printing rather than just one print job. If you bid each printed piece separately, you'll pay top dollar and the quality won't be consistent. You'll also get a better deal in regard to price, deadlines, and scheduling if you work with a printer on a consistent basis.

Other ways to save money. Combining colored ink jobs and printing them at the same time can save substantial dollars since the printing press will only need to be used once. Each time ink colors or printing plates have to be changed it costs money to set them up. Another way to save is to use standardized Pantone Matching System (PMS) ink colors, and metallic inks are more economical than using foil processes.

Specifications. The specifications that printers need in order to provide an accurate bid include quantity, size, paper type, black and white or color process, binding requirements, etc. Graphic designers typically provide these when working with a printer. If doing it yourself, work directly with the printer to identify specifications.

Timelines. You'll need to develop a timeline for each printed piece, working backward from the completion date, in order to know the dates when written copy, layouts, and final proofs are due.

By establishing timelines at the beginning of the process, the printer knows when to expect the print jobs and can reserve time on the press. An added benefit is that you know when the job will be complete for purposes of distribution or to schedule volunteers if they are needed to process large mailings.

Other Considerations

Paper costs. These are continually on the rise and these costs are passed on to you, so carefully consider each printed piece. Two or more pieces can often be combined into one thereby saving time and money on the printing, graphic design, or postage.

You may want to reconsider the quantity needed or the frequency of pieces such as newsletters. On the other hand, it ultimately costs less to print more of something the first time rather than having to do a second press run because you underestimated the quantity.

Consistency is important. Try to use the same "paper family" for things like letterhead, envelopes, newsletters, and the like to create consistency. This also applies to design elements such as logos, typefaces, colors, etc. A good printer will lead you in this direction.

Check the size requirements! If the printed piece needs to be mailed, it should be of a standard size and/or fit into a #10 business envelope. Irregular sized pieces cost extra to mail. You can obtain a reference template from the local post office to check sizes. Another way to save money is by using postcards. Make sure the card doesn't exceed the post office standard of 6" wide by 4 ¼" high or it won't qualify for the postcard rate.

CAUTION: Of critical attention is the area scanned by the automated mail reader at the post office. Since the scanner reads the bottom line, if the last line on the return address on your envelope is lower than the last line on the mailing address, you'll get your entire mailing back and will have wasted the costs of printing and postage!

NOTES

NOTES

Mail houses. Check with a mail house about the cost of large mailings. You may find that this method is actually cheaper and saves time since addresses and bar codes can be directly imprinted onto the mailing piece. You may also receive a discounted rate on postage since the mail house can presort by zip code from the disk data or electronic file.

Bulk mail. For high volume mailings, or if timing is not critical because delivery is slow, bulk mail may save money. A bulk mail permit is required. You'll need to print bulk mail identia including the permit number on the envelope or use bulk mail stamps. Once the initial mailing is done, a first class postage stamp will need to be affixed to any printed pieces sent out after the fact.

Bulk mail used to be a common way to save money, but it is very time consuming and labor intensive. The staff time involved for a bulk mail project could actually end up costing more than if a mailing house were to handle it when you factor in wages and benefits. If you opt to do it yourself, the post office offers training and has printed information available.

Address Correction Requested. Incorrectly addressed mail (especially bulk mail) will not be returned to you unless the piece has been printed with an "address correction requested" tag near the return address. Using this statement will ensure that mailed pieces with incorrect addresses or expired forwarding addresses will be returned. You'll have to pay a small fee (about the cost of a stamp) for each returned piece, but it's a cheap and effective way to keep the mailing list updated.

Collect photos and statistics as you go or ahead of time if possible. you'll need a photo for next year, make sure to take several this year or stage something ahead of time to create an illusion. Entertainers, venues, and service providers all have promotional photos. Photos need to be at least 300 dots per inch to produce well.

There's nothing wrong with taking a photo somewhere else, as long as there is no identifiable reference in the picture as to where it is. If you need a photo of a carnival booth, get a friend to pose in front of one at another event and crop out anything that would identify where it is. You can also find copyright-free photos of places, services, or objects without brand names on the Internet. Use your imagination, maintain ethical standards, and don't publish anything misleading.

Shipping printed materials. If the event is being held in a city other than your own, compare the cost of shipping heavy printed materials against the cost of using a printer at the site location. Another option might be to ship part of the printing and do the rest at the event location. You'll want to allow extra time either way to make sure the printing is available when you need it and of good quality.

Examples of Printed Materials

Printed materials in the following groups have been based on category—commercial printing, quick printing, and screen printing—as a means to understand different ways to use print providers. Use these examples as a basis to develop your own list of printing needs.

Commercial Printing

Commercial printing covers a broad range of both color and black and white work. Commercial printers may use a printing press or digital copiers, whereas quick printers use copy machines. Use a commercial printer where higher levels of quality and service are needed, and don't hesitate to ask for samples of the printer's work.

Letterhead, envelopes and business cards. These are among the first things an event needs. Since they used throughout the duration of the event cycle, be sure the quantity ordered will cover all uses, plus some for unforeseen needs.

NOTES

Save the Date and invitations. These are traditional printed materials used as marketing tools for events. Save the Date postcards should be sent out approximately six months or more in advance of the event date. Invitations are typically mailed 6-8 weeks in advance, or less depending on the event.

The information should be presented in an attractive and easily readable format that will grab the reader's attention. Use action words and be concise. Don't make the recipient wade through excessive copy. Blank space on printed materials is a good thing!

When deciding on the shape or size of these printed pieces, think about how much it will cost to mail, either as a self-mailer or in an envelope, and make sure that it conforms to postal standards.

Catalogs or programs. Depending on how sophisticated the catalog or program needs to be, either a commercial printer or a quick copy printer can be used. If the catalog or program requires great quality, has photos, requires four-color printing, die cuts, or special handling, it's best to use a commercial printer for printing and binding services.

Quick Printing

If you're looking for convenience and fast turnaround, a quick printer may be the answer. Keep in mind that "quick" doesn't necessarily mean "cheap." You may want to weigh the cost of convenience against the price.

Newsletters and annual reports. Quick printing usually works well for newsletters unless they contain photographs that need to be half-toned (screened) to produce the dots that printing requires.

In some cases, it's helpful to use a commercial printer to produce newsletter "blanks" at the same time letterhead and envelopes are printed. These blanks are printed with standard information such as the logo, masthead, address, and contact information. The paper blanks are later sent to the quick printer as client paper stock and the text layout is submitted separately on white paper, disk or via digital file which is then copied onto the blank newsletter format.

Screen Printing

Screen printing has been around a long time but was brought to creative prominence by Andy Warhol during the 1960s. This form allows printing on a wide variety of materials such as plastic, glass, metal, textiles, and more. Everything from the smallest button, to banners, to billboards can be printed using this method.

The most basic method consists of stretching fine nylon mesh (originally silk, hence the name silk screening) over a wooden or aluminum frame. A special photographic process creates a "stencil" through which ink is. The screen is placed on the press and is then raised or lowered onto the object being printed. Computerization of this process has greatly speeded up production.

Some of the more common event materials produced by screen printers include t-shirts, banners, signs, flags, pins, buttons, awards, glassware, billboards and just about anything!

Writing Copy

Written messages can be powerful marketing tools, so *always ask someone to proofread your work*. After you've written copy, set it down and wait awhile before revising or rewriting. Read it out loud. If it's hard to say out loud, it's probably hard to read or comprehend.

Use a cohesive style and provide a clear message. Pay attention to spelling and grammar. Keep a dictionary and thesaurus handy. Know your target audience and write like you are speaking to them. Use simple, strong statements and delete words and phrases that do not add meaning. Keep sentences short and don't ramble on. Use action words for energy. Delete commas where possible.

NOTES

Present information in a logical order beginning with the most important. Use bulleted lists to communicate complex messages. They are easier to read and create visual breaks in blocks of copy.

Avoid these common errors. "Its" shows possession, while "it's" is a contraction of "it is." The number of the subject determines which verb to use—a horse runs (singular) and horses run (plural). Form the possessive singular of a noun by adding "'s." Form the possessive plural of a noun by adding "s'." An example is "Joe Smith's house" (singular) and "The Smiths' house" (plural).

Watch the words you choose in writing copy. Here's an actual example regarding a hotel's annual client appreciation party. A signature social event held at the hotel every year was a large, high profile gala. There was a big budget for décor and production, and the event was visually amazing. Imagine the client's and décor company's surprise upon arriving at the party to see a huge framed photo of their event hanging outside the hotel's catering office. In essence this was a lovely gesture by the hotel to pay homage to the client, but the words in the caption at the bottom of the picture, "Let Us Plan Your Next Event," were a big surprise.

Why do you think this is? The implication by the use of the word "plan" is that this was an event that the hotel produced and it made the client and the contractor feel like the hotel was taking credit for their work and their event. The hotel did not plan the event, was not responsible for the theme, décor and other production elements, the food was provided by guest chefs, the wine was donated, and so on. Had the picture caption read, "Let Us Host Your Next Event," the whole scenario would have had a totally different meaning.

Do you see how just one word, taken out of context, can change the whole meaning of a message?

Use the worksheet and tools at the end of the chapter to help build your printed materials.

Graphic Design & Printing Terms

The following are common terms used in graphic design and printing.

Alignment	Placement of an item creating a visual connection to another item
Balance	Even distribution of the "weight" of the design elements
Collateral Materials	Promotional materials such as letterhead, invitations, postcards, business cards, catalogs, etc.
Contrast	Using size, shape, color, texture, typography, etc. to create variety
Direction	Creating movement in a design that leads the eyes to follow through use of lines, contrast, white space, graphics, etc.
Duo-Tone	The use of two colors of ink to add depth to a photograph
Emphasis	Elements in a design containing a hierarchy of importance
Half-Tone	Overlaying a dot screen on a photograph to increase reprographic capabilities
Headlines	Call out messages placed at the top of a page
Layout	An arrangement of typography and/or images on a page
PMS Colors	Pantone Matching System is the industry standard covering all the solid color ink systems and process color systems published or sold by Pantone, Inc.
Proportion	The size relationship between design elements
Proximity	Grouping related items together to form a visual unit
Repetition	Repeating some aspect of a design through the entire piece (graphics, lines, typefaces, headline fonts, etc.)
Rhythm	Repetition of elements within a design to create harmony
Sans Serif	Typeface without little "tails" on the letters (Arial)
Serif	Typeface with little "tails" on the letters (Times Roman)
Sub-Head	Call out messages placed intermittently in the text to indicate a change in subject
White Space	Blank space not occupied by any text or graphic
Unity	All design parts work together to create the message

Writing Terms

The following are common terms used in writing copy for print.

Acronyms	Abbreviated forms of business names that use the first initial in each word of the name (e.g. Public Broadcast System - PBS)
Boiler Plate Text	Standardized text used as a document template and adjusted as necessary (e.g. contract, legal paper, etc.)
Bullet	Use of a solid dot or other symbol at the beginning of a sentence or message point to create emphasis
En Dash	A dash symbol indicating a duration of time (June-July, 5:00-6:00) and approximately the width of a capital letter N
Em Dash	A dash used similar to a colon or parenthesis or to signal an abrupt change in thought. Twice as long as an en dash and approximately the width of a capital letter M
Kerning	Process of removing small units of space between lines of type
Leading	Refers to the amount of space between lines of type
Orphans	One line at the bottom of a page that did not fit at the end of the paragraph and moved to the next page or column
Subscript	Type moved below the line of text (e.g. H_2O)
Superscript	Type moved above the line of text (e.g. 2nd)
Syntax	Similar elements in a sentence are phrased in a similar structure or grammatical form
Tracking	Tightness of spacing within type
Widows	Seven or fewer characters in the last line of body text

Graphic Design & Printing Worksheet

Use this worksheet to outline graphic design and printing needs.

Graphic Design

1. Will the event use graphic design services? _____
2. Is the graphic designer willing to donate services? _____
3. Have you seen examples of the designer's work? _____
4. Does the designer have a clear understanding of the image/s desired? _____
5. Does the designer willingly suggest ways to save money? _____
6. Is there a qualified person to perform in-house graphic design services? _____

Printing

1. What printed materials will be required? _____
2. Is there an existing relationship with a commercial printer? _____
3. Is there an existing relationship with a quick printer? _____
4. Will the event use screen printing or specialty advertising? _____
5. Have timeframes and deadlines been set for each printed piece? _____
6. Are specifications provided for each printed piece? _____
7. Will the printing be bid out? _____
8. Has the printer suggested ways to save money? _____
9. Will photographs be needed or used in printed materials? _____

Distribution Methods

1. How will each printed piece be distributed? _____
2. If to be mailed, does the design layout comply with postal regulations? _____

Writing Considerations

1. Who will write the copy? _____ Who will proofread? _____
2. Are reference books or other resource materials available? _____
3. Is there too much text for the printed piece? _____
4. Does the written copy have impact? _____
5. Is the message clear, concise, and presented in a logical manner? _____
6. Has the copy been thoroughly checked for grammar, spelling, and punctuation? _____

Chapter 8 – Liability, Permits, & Security

Cover your backside

Special events have always carried an element of risk, but in today's world the stakes are higher than ever before. Since events involve large numbers of people, a risk of potential liability exists in many areas—permits, contracts, alcohol service, safety, volunteer management, automobiles, or outright emergencies. Incidents regarding terrorists or crime are less likely to happen at local events than at an event such as the Super Bowl or the Olympic Games, but we should still be prepared.

"The best offense is a good defense" applies to events as well as to sports. Think through all aspects of the event—every day, every activity, every job. Much of this brainstorming can be done during other planning phases (e.g. identifying volunteer jobs, contracting, and so on).

This chapter covers information to:

> ➤ Identify potential liability areas
> ➤ Negotiate and review contracts
> ➤ Determine which permits are needed
> ➤ Evaluate security needs
> ➤ Develop a security / emergency plan

Examples and a worksheet are located at the back of the chapter.

Liability

Liability may result from a situation where we inadvertently find ourselves in a whole heap of trouble if we're not careful. It may not be today or tomorrow, but by embracing some risk management practices, we can protect ourselves to the degree we are able.

"When you need professional advice, get it from professionals, not from your friends."

Life's Little Instruction Book, Volume II

Don't assume everything will be just fine. You're not just risking the budget here. Murphy's Law prevails when it comes to events, so it's better to be ready for a "worst case scenario" than to be caught unprepared if something happens. The more things that are left to chance, the greater the risk for liability.

You obviously can't think of every possible thing that could go wrong or control the behavior of others. You can do research and talk with contractors, insurance providers, security personnel, and others who can help visualize where risk factors may be present.

It's not meant to cause panic, but rather to safeguard the event, and yourself, against possible negative scenarios.

Items of General Note

Apparent Authority. By definition, apparent authority occurs when an event manager or other person, acting on behalf of the group or event, signs a contract without official authorization. Though it rarely happens because the expectation is that the event manager will sign contracts on the event's behalf, you need to be aware of this possibility.

An example would be a hotel that was holding space for an event that cancelled and the hotel was then unable to rebook the space for another group. In instances of cancellation, the contract may call for some form of payment in damages to recoup lost revenue. Since the facility signed the contract in good faith, the event manager or other representative who signed the contract made the group liable, authorized or not.

One way to avoid this issue is to have an authority figure (executive director, event manager, board president, financial officer, etc.) sign any contractual documents, or sign a form authorizing the event manager to be the signatory. A statement to this effect should also be included in the event manager's job description.

NOTES

Contracts

Negotiating contracts is similar to playing poker and everyone should come out with some winnings. Entering into contracts is a necessary function. Without a contract, an event can find itself without a venue, service providers, entertainment, equipment, food, beverage, or any number of other things that allow for its operation or success.

Review contract documents very, very carefully. Read every single word in every single line, especially the small print, and understand it before signing. Clarify the meaning of any words or items you don't understand, correct it on the contract, and initial it. If you don't agree with something cross it out completely and initial it. **Don't sign anything you haven't read at least three times with a break in between. And never sign a contract with blank spaces.**

A contract should be straightforward and contain simple language. Pay special attention to cancellation clauses to be aware of the "escape window" and any penalties that may be incurred. Build the final escape date, as well as a target date for review, into your timeline and work lists.

If a contractor is pressuring you to sign right away without a good reason (like it's only two weeks until the event and they need to schedule equipment/personnel), proceed cautiously. If your instincts tell you do some research, wait awhile before proceeding and get references as to the contractor's reliability.

NOTE: A good practice is to make a copy of the contract when you receive it and temporarily set the original aside. Mark up the copy with your changes, have someone else review it in addition to yourself, and make their own changes on the copy. Once you are satisfied with the changes, mark them onto the original document. Make a copy of the original corrected document and date it before sending it back to the contractor for signature. This way if several changes go back and forth, you'll always have a copy of the most recent version, won't get confused, and can cross-check to be sure the changes you wanted have been made.

Lost Profit versus Lost Revenue. One thing you can do is to negotiate "lost profit (your word) versus lost revenue (their word)" in your contracts. This can be done in the cancellation clause section where it typically says something like "if you cancel within 90 days out, you owe nothing; within 60 days out, you owe 50% of expected revenue; 30 days out, you have to pay the whole thing anyway."

What it means by negotiating lost profit is that essentially, the venue (or other contractor) didn't lose the entire revenue amount because they didn't have to hire the staff, order the food or equipment for your event, and so on. They only lost the profit they would have made, not the whole thing.

More information about profit margins on food and beverage functions is found in the Food & Beverage chapter.

Liability (Hold Harmless) Statements. Contracts usually contain some form of language whereby the event is asked to indemnify another party (contractor, entertainer, etc.) against claims, damages, loss, and such resulting from their participation in the event.

The event, in turn, can require contractors, entertainers, volunteers, and others to sign a liability statement releasing the event from any claims resulting from the person's or group's participation.

If the person signing the statement will be performing a specific function requiring them to be at a location other than the actual event site (e.g. acting as a driver for VIPs), that should be noted in the statement.

Insurance

Insurance is essential for protecting the event. Don't think of insurance as an extra expense, think of it as a beneficial safeguard. It will pay for itself many times over if you ever need to use it.

114

Commercial General Liability (CGL). This is the industry standard and many contracts require proof of this coverage which protects the event and/or related parties if a claim of negligence is filed by someone arising from damage to their property or bodily injury to themselves. This coverage may include protection against liability in regard to contracts, personal injury, products, advertising, fire damage, or operations.

A standard CGL policy typically includes a $2 million aggregate limit ($2 million total in coverage); $1 million each on products or completed operations, $1 million each occurrence personal and advertising injury; and $50,000 fire damage. You'll want to verify the deductible amount applicable to each category of the policy.

Additional Insured. What's NOT covered in the standard CGL policy needs to be covered separately. Sometimes what's not covered in the policy is just as important as what is. Separate policies need to be written for items excluded from the main policy. Liquor liability, pyrotechnics, rental equipment, entertainment limitations, non-owned or hired automobiles, accident insurance for volunteers, errors and omissions, directors and officers, and others are not normally part of a standard special event insurance policy unless as addendums.

For a nominal charge volunteers, employees, venues, subcontractors, and others can be covered under the CGL insurance. This is typically an endorsement added to the main policy. The event should also require subcontractors and others to list the event as additional insured on their individual policies (a.k.a. an insurance binder).

Work with reliable companies who deal in special event insurance. If you don't know who to contact, ask other event managers, check the local phone book, or the Internet for agencies that handle this kind of insurance coverage.

Permits

Nearly all events require a permit of some form— use permit, liquor permit, noise permit, fire permit, health department permit, lottery game permit, and so on. Failure to obtain a required permit could cause a complete shut down of the event. Get to know permit issuers and ask for their help. It makes a difference on approvals!

Use permits. These usually relate to the location like a hotel, park, or other facility. These are sometimes called special event permits and are most often obtained through local jurisdictions such as a city or county, parks department, liquor commission, or property owner.

In addition to a specified fee, standard information required includes event name, date/s, time/s, estimated attendance, responsible parties, event description, proof of insurance, hold harmless agreement, and similar questions. Approval signatures from local law enforcement, the liquor control commission, fire marshal, noise ordinance officer, health department, venue, or others are required.

Liquor permits. Serving alcohol is a serious matter. Make it your business to know who assumes liability for the service of alcoholic beverages. The caterer or venue may carry liquor liability insurance but that doesn't preclude the possibility of the event being held liable for an alcohol-related incident. This is why it is important to check into liquor liability coverage and ensure that proper procedure has been followed in regard to state liquor laws. Special event licenses for alcohol service typically require approvals by local law enforcement, the venue, and the state liquor control commission.

Whether a permit is required depends on the state in which the event is held, the type of event, the kind of alcohol being served, and the method of alcohol service. This can be further broken down into public and private functions and hosted or non-hosted bars. The state has specific requirements and deadlines for applications that must be met to obtain the permit.

The best bet for any event is to hire professional beverage servers who have completed alcohol server training through the State Liquor Control Board. Restaurants, hotels, and catering companies all have professional trained staff that can provide alcohol service in accordance with the law. They are trained to handle various situations, those who have over-imbibed, or those who are underage. Using trained servers is well worth the peace of mind.

If your state allows the use of volunteers for alcohol service, they must adhere to state law. Some states mandate that volunteers complete alcohol server training while others do not. Volunteer servers should be required to sign a statement that they understand the law. Under no circumstances should volunteers be allowed to drink while on duty. If in doubt about using volunteers, always take the safe road with state-approved beverage servers.

NOTE: Under no circumstances should you place bottles of wine or other alcoholic beverages on the table and let guests serve themselves. This leaves both the venue (if under their license) and the event open to potential liability if an alcohol related incident should occur because no one was monitoring the alcohol consumption. This is not a good practice even though many events do this!

Noise Permits. If the event will use amplified sound, a noise permit may be required. This is especially true of outdoor events that feature amplified stage entertainment or announcements, as well as activities that generate substantial amounts of noise such as car races. The permit mandates that the noise factor must not exceed a designated decibel level or a fine and/or event shutdown can result.

Fire Marshal. When it comes to capacity limits, fire regulations, and related matters a Fire Marshal will have no qualms about shutting down the event or fining the violator. Take special care to ensure that décor, equipment, capacity limits, fire lanes, aisle widths, emergency exits, and other items of concern are addressed in advance rather than at the event. Venues often work directly with the Fire Marshal on the event's behalf.

NOTES

Lottery games. Bingo, raffles, and the like are considered to be games of chance and may require a license from the State Department of Justice. Strict regulations governing the conduct of lottery games are outlined and a fairly lengthy (though not difficult) application must be submitted with the license fee. Post-event reports are required. Contact the authorities to obtain information or download the rules and application from the Internet Web site.

Security

Webster's defines security as a feeling of safety and contentment. It used to be that people didn't worry about their safety at an event, and barring a major catastrophe, most problems were easily handled. This still holds true today but the people who come to our events depend on us to make their experience a safe one. Since events can generate attendance that varies from relatively few people to many thousands, the odds greatly increase for accidents, injuries, or legal liability. Huge events like the Olympic Games or the Super Bowl have a much higher risk for terrorism or some kind of a disaster than do fairs, festivals or social events.

Regardless of the type of event, communication in regard to safety measures is paramount. Make sure everyone understands the procedures to be followed if they need to be implemented. Take enough precautions for security but not to the extent that the event feels like an armed camp.

Security personnel should be readily identifiable—whether law enforcement, private security, or volunteers—through uniforms or by wearing shirts with "Security" on the back.

If using a private security company, the cheapest option may not be the best if the company is not properly insured, personnel are poorly trained, or have faulty equipment. The price the event could pay for economizing could be very high.

NOTES

The Security Plan

By working with others to develop a security and emergency plan, key players get to know one another and become familiar with event activities. These are the people who will implement the plan if needed. The security plan can be simple, or very detailed, based on the level of security required. Most venues have existing security or emergency plans that can be adapted for your event.

Emergencies

The truth is that emergencies can and do happen, so adopt the Boy Scouts of America motto and "Be Prepared." Build on the security plan to include measures for scenarios such as medical emergencies, fire, bomb scares, and others that require immediate action. The plan should provide for escape routes if it becomes necessary to evacuate the site, as well as criteria to determine when it is safe to re-enter.

Be sure the site plan indicates emergency access routes, triage areas, first aid stations, command post location, etc.

The amount of time it takes to develop a simple security and emergency plan could very well turn out to be critical if you ever need to implement it.

A worksheet and example of a security/emergency plan follow.

Liability, Permits & Security Worksheet

Liability

1. Have potential liability areas been identified? _____
2. Have contracts and other documents been reviewed by more than one person? _____

Contracts

1. Does the contract contain simple, easily understood language? _____
2. Is there a cancellation clause, and if so, what are the terms? _____
3. Have cancellation deadlines and review dates been added to work lists? _____
4. Have liability or hold harmless clauses in contracts been reviewed? _____
5. Have you read the contract at least three separate times? _____
6. Are changes marked and initialed? _____
7. Have you kept copies of all contracts, including those in process? _____

Insurance

1. What are the insurance requirements for the event? _____
2. Is existing Comprehensive General Liability (CGL) insurance adequate? _____
3. Have you double checked about items which may not be covered? _____
4. Do contractors/others provide insurance and include the event as additional insured? ___
5. Are volunteers, employees, or others covered under the insurance policy? _____

Permits

1. What permits does the event require and from whom? _____
2. If serving alcohol, who will handle alcohol service and are they licensed? _____
3. If volunteers will be used, have they complied with state regulations? _____
4. Has the Fire Marshal reviewed the plan or been included in the process? _____
5. Is a bingo, raffle, or lottery game part of the event? _____
6. Has the appropriate paperwork and fee been submitted to the authorities? _____

Security/Emergency Plan

1. Have the event's security needs been evaluated and by whom? _____
2. Is an existing security/emergency plan available? _____
3. Do all appropriate parties have a copy of the final version of the plan? _____

EMERGENCY CONTINGENCY PLAN

Big Bucks Auction

Continental Hotel
1111 Imaginary Street – Anytown, USA

HOURS IN EFFECT:

Friday – March 4, 2005 8 am – 10 pm
Saturday – March 5, 2005 8 am – 1 am
Sunday – March 6, 2005 10 am – 2 pm

I. **General Responsibilities**

II. **Emergency Vehicle Access**

III. **Medical Emergency Procedure**

IV. **Site Plan**

NOTE: The purpose of this plan is to provide guidance for security and emergency response personnel in case of an incident resulting in injury to persons attending, or connected to, the Big Bucks Auction in Anytown. The Incident Commander is responsible for direction and control of an incident and has the authority to use or alter the contents of this plan as appropriate.

I. General Responsibilities

Power Productions

Contracts with the Nonprofit Agency Name to produce the Big Bucks Auction. Responsible for overall event direction and control of activities at the Continental Hotel (auction site), as well as both pre- and post-event.

The on-site office is located in a small meeting room on the ballroom level just off the foyer at the Continental Hotel. The cell phone number is 503.332.5000. Power Productions will have portable radio communication that will be monitored by security, hotel staff, and volunteer leaders. Judy Anderson is the auction director and event producer.

XYZ Security

Responsible for: General Crowd Control
Security at entry and exit points
Security of jewelry located in the live auction display area near the stage
Security of the Ferrari on display in the ballroom foyer

Volunteer Services

Volunteer Services will provide security to monitor alcoholic beverage service and consumption throughout the event area. Personnel will also be stationed at strategic points near valuable memorabilia items on display in the Silent Auction area located in the parlor rooms to the side of the ballroom at the Continental Hotel. Volunteer team leaders are equipped with radios.

City of Anytown Police Department / Fire & Rescue

Responsible for providing police, fire support, rescue and medical services, if needed. Contact through 9-1-1. Fire rescue units will be provided through the fire department channels. Fire Station 222 is located within a six block radius of the Continental Hotel.

II. Emergency Vehicle Access

Emergency vehicles should approach the Continental Hotel from the primary access on Wide Street, if at all possible.

Primary Access: Wide Street   Secondary Access: Main Street or Narrow Street

The primary access is through the front lobby and up the elevator or escalator to the ballroom level. There is also a stairwell on the left side of the lobby near the elevators, however, clearance is limited due to the narrow stairwell. Access from Narrow Street is off a cul-de-sac.

Public parking for the event is on city streets and at parking garages surrounding the Continental Hotel.

III.   Medical Plan

Routine first aid will be provided by Continental Hotel personnel, located on the ballroom level. In case of a medical emergency that exceeds first aid capabilities, hotel or event personnel will immediately contact 9-1-1 via cellular telephone or by radio. Fire Station 222 will be the first responder dispatched.

The first arriving Fire Rescue/Advanced Life Support unit will advise 9-1-1 Communications of the situation. The designated triage area is the northbound lane of Wide Street.

<u>Command</u>: The Incident Command Post will be established in the Big Bucks Auction office area.

<u>Ambulance and Fire Apparatus Staging</u>: Located on Wide Street outside the main hotel entry. Wide Street will be blocked off to traffic from Main Street and Narrow Street. Alternate location for staging is Tree Filled Park across Wide Street from the Continental Hotel.

<u>Life Flight Landing Zone</u>: Located off Wide Street and Main. Traffic control needed at Main Street, Narrow Street, and Wall Street.

Medical Emergency Procedures

Should a situation exceed first aid capabilities, the Anytown Fire and Rescue should be contacted immediately.

<u>Response Procedures:</u>

Power Productions (Big Bucks Auction Office)	Immediately call 9-1-1 for Police and Fire assistance
	Notify Security to clear emergency vehicle access
	Assist Police and Fire Personnel, as directed
Anytown Fire Department	Establish Command, direct and control fire suppression, rescue and emergency medical activities
Anytown Police Department	Regulate traffic control into and out of area; at direction of Incident Commander, assist with clearing an area for medical triage, if needed
	If requested by Incident Commander, provide traffic control to utilize Wide Street for LifeFlight landing zone at intersection of Wide and Main.
XYZ Security Services	If activated, assign representative to Incident Command Post
	Assist Fire and Police personnel as directed

Big Bucks Auction Site Plan

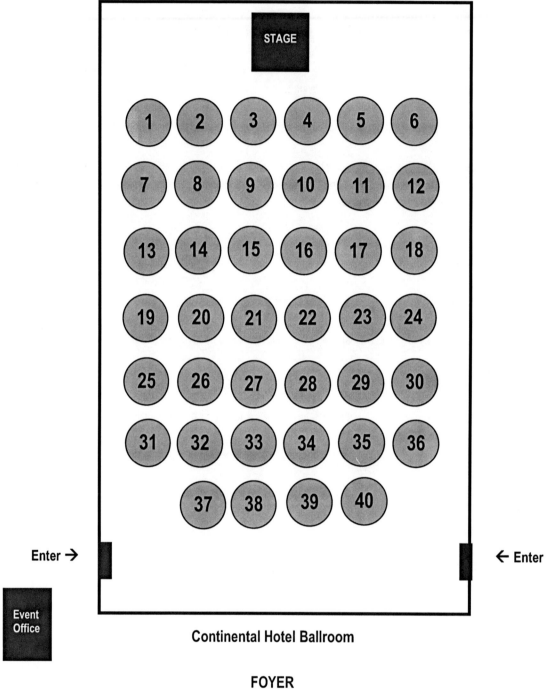

Enter →

← Enter

Event
Office

Continental Hotel Ballroom

FOYER

To Elevators / Escalator
↓ ↓

124

Chapter 9 – Venues

Location, location, location

Selecting the best venue (event location) should be based on a number of factors. Take into consideration how the venue can help to create ambience or save time, not only how the venue can accommodate the logistical needs of your event.

Don't hesitate to shop around. Look for something unique. You don't have to take the first location that will work. Compare more traditional venues to non-traditional ones. Just because your event has always been held in one location doesn't mean it would do just as well (or better) in a different place provided that the new location is a step in the right direction.

This chapter provides information covering how to:

> ➤ Create a venue profile
> ➤ Identify potential venues
> ➤ Narrow the number of choices
> ➤ Conduct site inspections
> ➤ Negotiate and contract for the final venue choice

Examples and a venue profile worksheet are located at the back of the chapter. Details on site planning are found in the Site Planning and Logistics chapter.

Create A Venue Profile

A venue profile is basically a standardized "shopping list" of desirable features a site should offer to accommodate the needs of your event. Obviously no venue will be perfect, but creating a profile will be of great assistance when comparing amenities, costs, and convenience.

"The world is round and the place which may seem like the end may also be only the beginning."

Ivy Baker

Geographic location, square footage, meeting rooms, sleeping rooms, access for disabled patrons, food and beverage, contractor requirements, and amenities are but a few considerations. Creating a profile for each venue based on standardized information allows you to compare "apples to apples" so to speak.

Once you've created the venue profile, use it to search for that ideal location. As you investigate various sites, you'll find things that need to be added to the shopping list. Knowing requirements in advance helps to identify items you may wish to negotiate in the contract.

An Amazing Array of Choices

Whether the event is held indoors or outdoors, you are limited only by your imagination. Don't be afraid to think outside the box! Be creative in considering an event location and think about the kinds of ambience and energy to be gained through imaginative selection.

Change may be good for an existing event looking for a new twist. For new events, there's a canvas upon which to create a masterpiece.

Every city has traditional and non-traditional options:

Airports	Lodges/granges
Art/film studios or schools	Lofts
Atriums	Mansions
Ballrooms	Marinas
Boats/ships	Museums
Breweries	Parks
Campuses	Parking garages/parking lots
Community centers	Performance centers
Convention/expo centers	Planetariums
Country clubs	Private clubs
Estates	Tents
Fairgrounds	Theatres
Farms	Warehouses
Hotels	Wineries
Libraries	Zoo

Selecting the Site

Begin the site selection process at least 12 months in advance if possible. Even then, you may find many of your top choices have already been booked up to two years in advance.

Know what your needs are before conducting the screening process. Venue representatives can easily tell the difference between someone who knows what they are looking for as opposed to one who is "fishing" for information to figure out what they want.

Start with a list of five possible locations. If you initially have a big list, use the Internet to do research on each one, and then hone it down to the top five. Then, conduct the preliminary screening.

Based on information gathered, narrow your choices down to the top three. Conduct a site inspection of each venue before making a final choice. You may have to compromise on some points because very rarely does a venue have everything you want.

Set priorities as to which event elements are most important. This will influence the final decision. If the event includes dinner and dancing, make sure the venue has plenty of space to accommodate the stage, dance floors, guest and/or banquet tables, chairs, décor, and other elements. The dinner would need to include such things as great food, service staff, and an adequate kitchen. If you plan to serve wine, you'll need a venue that allows alcohol.

Multiple Days, Multiple Sites. The event may have different activities on different days in different locations. In this case, the event manager should develop a "best use" scenario of all sites to make the best use of resources and/or contractors to save money.

Venues and Children. Be sure that the site is practical from both use and safety aspects. Private areas for diaper changing, breast feeding or quiet space may be needed.

Other Considerations

Fit the venue to the size of the event. Successful events may outgrow a venue every few years. If the event is new, you'll need to estimate the size requirement. Too large a site can make it look like nobody's there event with a crowd. A site that is too small makes people feel cramped.

For existing events, one way to forecast is to factor the average annual rate of growth. This can predict approximately when the event will outgrow its current venue and can provide lead time to locate and contract another venue if necessary.

For new events, the space needs to accommodate all activities and attendance, plus or minus 15-25%. This allows the event to expand but won't look overly large should attendance not meet projections. An ideal scenario would be a venue where the event could use part of the space and have the option to expand as growth occurs.

The venue should lend itself to the ambience. Does the venue have an ambience of its own or will you have to supplement it with décor, lighting, or rental equipment to get the look and feel desired?

Be sure to check for obstacles in the way of sight lines to the stage or other things that would be in contradiction to the site layout. An event like an auction would need an open space for guests to be able to see the auctioneer on the stage in order to bid, and a venue with support posts blocking the view would not work. On the other hand, an event where people wander around looking at things, like a trade show, might work all right in this kind of space.

A venue that needs a little help may cost less and the savings can be used for décor or equipment rentals. Venues with spectacular views, elegant furnishings, beautiful gardens, and great ambience tend to cost more to obtain as event sites, but the savings on décor or other supplements may offset the cost. Shop and compare.

Site Inspection

Once you have determined the top three venue choices are available on the date desired, it's time to conduct site inspections. If possible, put a hold on all three sites for approximately two weeks. This should allow enough time to visit them, evaluate their potential, and make a decision. You might want to check out various kinds of sites unless you're absolutely certain the event has to take place in a specific type of location. Be open to possibilities. You might come up with a dynamite location by using a little imagination!

Conduct the site inspections and make a choice as quickly as possible. This avoids the possibility of the venue being booked out from under you by someone else who is ready and willing to sign a contract. *After you've made sure your final choice meets your needs, release the hold on venues that are not selected.* Failure to do so may cause them to lose a potential client because they are still under the assumption that you are considering their site.

Be aware of rules, restrictions, and their ramifications! Don't sign a contract until you know what is allowed and what isn't. Different venues have different requirements. Some may not allow food to be brought in from the outside. Some allow only authorized vendors or service providers. Others may require the use of unionized labor. Still other may impose limitations on lighting, electricity, signage, décor, floral arrangements, or any number of other things. If a venue has too many rules and restrictions, or charges for every deviation of the rules, you may want to take your business elsewhere.

What About . . .?

Accommodations. If a substantial amount of attendees will need sleeping rooms, a hotel may be the best bet for the event location, especially if alcoholic beverages are served.

Transportation and Parking. If the majority of attendees will be driving to the event, you'll need to ensure there is parking at the event site or communicate the availability of parking in the surrounding area. It's always a good idea to provide transportation such as limousines, town cars, or private vehicles for VIPs, dignitaries, entertainers, and others who require special treatment.

Outdoor Venues

Outdoor venues can provide beautiful settings and lend themselves well to activity-based events. Depending on the property, they can bring their own unique set of challenges, as well as rewards. Many of the amenities we take for granted with indoor venues (restrooms, drinking water, waste disposal, etc.) may not be readily available for outdoor sites and will need to be brought in.

The number of permits required for outdoor venues usually is greater than for those held indoors. In addition to the use permit for the event site, you may be required to obtain other permits through local jurisdictions.

The use of private property (such as wineries) may have greater potential for negotiable terms but may be restricted by size or terrain, or have limited amenities. The use of outdoor venues may require additional insurance coverage as well.

Contract Negotiation

Unless the event has a built-in location, you'll need to negotiate a contract for use of the venue, staff, a pick list of services, or other needs. Negotiating a contract should be a win-win scenario.

Price should not be the only consideration. Look at the overall package of price and quality of services offered. Which venue will better help achieve the event goals? If the goal is to provide a high profile event to an affluent audience, you need a high class venue, which in turn costs more but will better meet the goals.

NOTES

Make sure you understand exactly what is contained in the price quoted. Determine which amenities and services are included in the basic price. Some sites include taxes and/or service charges (gratuity) in the pricing while others do not. Different venues have different price structures, even within a specific venue group (like hotels). Often the quote that looks like the higher price may actually be the better bargain because more is included in the package price.

For example: Hotels typically calculate event pricing based on dates and space requested, and the projected number (block) of hotel rooms likely to be used. Other factors may include estimated food and beverage sales, the number of other events taking place in the hotel at that time, or the like.

Watch out for extra charges for kitchen use, facilities manager or service staff, electricity, heating, air conditioning, set up or tear down labor, and the like. Volunteers can often perform services like setting up tables and chairs, thereby saving money on labor costs.

The event may be able to create its own price package based on negotiable items. It certainly doesn't hurt to be creative in bartering what the event needs or offers against what the venue wants. Don't get bogged down on one item because there are plenty of things to negotiate.

Understand that venues have sales quotas they must meet in order to stay in business. Even though the event may be for a charity and is trying to save money, the venue still needs to make a profit. It's highly unlikely the venue will agree to provide the space at a loss, nor should we expect them to. Remember the saying, "Leverage everything you can for everything you can."

Pay attention to attrition clauses. Carefully read the conditions pertaining to cancellation and understand the repercussions which may result. This is especially true if the event cancels and the venue is unable to rebook the space for another client.

After the Contract is Negotiated

The contract is a legally binding document. Always have more than one set of eyes review the contract before signing. Each person may find something someone else missed.

Read the contract at least three times before signing. Take a break in between readings, clarify anything you don't understand, and don't sign the contract unless you agree with what it says.

Keep a current copy of the contract in the files. You'll be surprised at how many times you'll need to refer to the contract during the event cycle. In addition, you'll always be aware of what the event needs to do to comply with the agreed upon terms and conditions. And if the contract is in transition, you'll always have a copy of the most recent version.

NOTE: Be sure to incorporate the contract deadlines into the overall event timeline and work lists.

Work with a designated venue representative throughout the process. If one isn't automatically assigned, ask to work with the same venue representative for the duration. This person becomes familiar with you and the event and knows how to efficiently work to obtain the desired results. It's frustrating to everyone if the communication is poor or we have to continually change partners.

Common courtesy will go far toward making the experience a positive one for both parties. Prepare a list of several questions in advance when contacting the venue representative so you can make the best use of the time. You wouldn't want them to call you every single time they had a question, so give them the same courtesy.

Event related terms and worksheets follow.

Venue Related Terms

The following are common terms in regard to venues as well as some which relate to food and beverage

Acoustics	Relating to elements of sound and how it is absorbed by various materials
Ambience	Mood or atmosphere
Audio Visual	Equipment or materials to aid in learning through sight or sound
Banquet Event Order/BEO	A written document outlining specific details for catered functions including, timing, menus, service ratios, etc.
Blocked Rooms	A reserved number of hotel rooms or meeting space
Capacity	Maximum number that can be accommodated either due to structural limitations or to conform with jurisdictional regulations
Cash Bar	A bar where guests pay for their own drinks; no-host bar
Change Order	A written document altering previously agreed upon terms of a contract or agreement
Complimentary Room	A sleeping or meeting room provided free of charge; usually based on the total amount of space/rooms being used by the event
Cutoff Date	The last date the client can make changes in regard to the number of guests expected or space to be used
Décor	Ornamental elements or materials used for decorative purposes
Drayage	Usually refers to bringing freight or supplies in and out of a facility or other location
Exhibit Hall	Facility space where vendors and/or others demonstrate or sell products or services
Flat Rate	A price that the event and venue have agreed upon in advance
Floor Plan	A scale drawing of the facility or specific room/s used for plotting the placement of tables, booths, chairs, stage, equipment, etc.
Freight/Service Elevator	Designated elevator used for hauling freight or supplies into a facility as opposed to a passenger elevator
Gratuity	Normally a percentage of food and beverage or other sales added to the bill as a service charge; the "tip"
Guarantee	Final number of guests and/or meals on which event will be charged; guarantee may be raised, but not lowered, once given
In-House	Services provided through a facility rather than by outside sources

133

Venue Related Terms

The following are common terms in regard to venues as well as some which relate to food and beverage

Letter of Agreement	Legally binding written agreement signed between the event and venue or others in acceptance of terms & conditions
Loading Dock	A designated entry area where contractors or suppliers load and unload, usually at the rear or non-public side of the facility
Master Account	General financial account to which charges for the event are billed; typically broken out by sub-categories (e.g. meals, rooms, etc.)
Option Date	The date on which a commitment must be made to use a venue or date it will be released for rental to others
Pickup	Actual number of rooms used from the block originally reserved
Pipe and Drape	Metal rods form a frame upon which curtaining is hung
Potable Water	Water which is suitable for drinking
Preset	Placing food on tables before seating guests; standard practice is to preset salad or bread, condiments, etc.
Property	The facility or site at which the event is held
Refresh	Clean up or replenish supplies between meetings
Room Nights	Number of sleeping rooms reserved at a hotel multiplied by the number of nights of occupancy
Room Rental	A charge for use of meeting or event space
Scale	The proportional relationship between the event site and other elements such as staging, props, signage, etc.
Self-Catering	Food products and service provided by the client as opposed to the venue or an outside catering company
Set Up	The pre-event process of setting up event elements
Shipping/Receiving	The location at which equipment or supplies arrive and depart from an event site; usually near the loading dock
Site Inspection	Viewing a location for potential use; may also apply to inspections conducted during execution of the event (e.g. Fire Marshal)
Site Plan	A scale drawing of the event site that is used for plotting the placement of event elements; may or may not include a floor plan
Tear Down	The post-event process of dismantling and clean up

Event Profile / Site Inspection Worksheet

Use this worksheet for evaluating venues and related services.

Not all items will apply to event venue; some of this information may be used for the site plan.

Event Profile

Event name _____

Event dates/time _____

Type of activities _____

Food and beverage service/type _____

Alcohol service/type _____

Staging/décor/production _____

Permits required _____

Contractor requirements _____

Special needs _____

Other _____

Site Information

Venue name _____

Contact name _____

Venue address _____

City/State/Zip _____

Phone _____ Fax _____ Email _____

Availability on date/s needed _____

Site Inspection

Easy to find/easily accessed _____

Facility or site clean and well-kept _____

Public or private access _____

Ambience/atmosphere, why _____

Grounds or landscaping _____

Restrooms (check both men's and women's) _____

ADA compliance _____

Capacity limits _____

Lends itself to décor or staging _____

Acoustics (loud or muffled) _____

Event Profile / Site Inspection Worksheet

Use this worksheet for evaluating venues and related services.

Not all items will apply to event venue; some of this information may be used for the site plan.

Site Inspection (cont'd)

Traffic flow _____

Service personnel/appearance _____

Recreational facilities (pool, play equipment, etc.) _____

Security procedures/emergency plan _____

Sleeping rooms accommodations/type _____

Extra space availability if needed _____

Business services available (phone, fax, copier, Internet) _____

Outdoor venues (dry, level, shade, shelter) _____

Floor space/seating chart/site diagrams available _____

Parking/parking fees _____

Display space (size, capacity, etc.) _____

Storage available _____

Availability for early set up / late tear down _____

Shipping/receiving capability _____

Food & Beverage

Guarantees required by when _____

Catering (in-house only, preferred, outside, self-catering) _____

Menus (standardized, negotiable) _____

Beverage service _____

Service ratio (staff-to-guests) _____

Kitchen adequate/equipment working _____

Refrigeration availability _____

Food storage space _____

Sinks/counter space _____

Rules for kitchen use _____

Glassware/dishes/flatware/linen _____

Other _____

Event Profile / Site Inspection Worksheet

Use this worksheet for evaluating venues and related services.

Not all items will apply to event venue; some of this information may be used for the site plan.

Logistics
Adequate restroom facilities (1-2 stalls per 100 people) _____

Utilities (electricity, gas, water, etc.) _____

Stage/size _____

Sound system _____

Lighting (regular, stage, ambience) _____

Audio visual needs _____

Décor/props _____

Floral _____

Coat check _____

Registration area _____

Shipping/receiving _____

Elevators (freight, passenger) _____

Stairs/access _____

Ceiling height (affects lighting/décor/sound) _____

Rental or other equipment needed _____

Outdoor Venue Specific
Excessive evidence of insects (flies/mosquitoes/ants/beetles) _____

Utilities (on site or bring in) _____

Potable water available _____

Curb/gutter/street hazards _____

Fencing requirements _____

Tents and rental equipment _____

Sprinkler system/sprinkler head locations _____

Turf damage/repair _____

Signage restrictions _____

Trash removal/dumpster location _____

Tax-supported services (police, fire, public works) _____

Refrigeration _____

Service providers (authorized only or outside contractors) _____

Event Profile / Site Inspection Worksheet

Use this worksheet for evaluating venues and related services.

Not all items will apply to event venue; some of this information may be used for the site plan.

Contractors

Check in/check out procedure _____

Service providers for exhibit construction/décor _____

Set up date/time _____

Tear down date/time _____

Labor rates for electricians/carpenters _____

Signage _____

Venue regulations for contractors _____

Financial/Legal

Pricing structure _____

Terms of payment/deposits _____

Option date _____

Cutoff date _____

Insurance requirements _____

Additional charges (utilities, etc.) _____

Labor rates if applicable _____

References _____

Other _____

Miscellaneous

Who/what/when is the group preceding yours _____

Who/what/when is the group following yours _____

Sales or promotions by client or outside vendors allowed _____

Set up/drop off day before event _____

Tear down / clean up morning after event _____

Other _____

Chapter 10 – Food & Beverage

Eat, Drink, and Be Merry

Rare is the event without a food or beverage element. Food is one of the major motivators for people to attend events—unless, of course, it's an event built around beverages. Because of this, we want the food and/or beverage to make an impression on our guests.

The food is often what people remember most and is limited only by the budget and your imagination. Look at food as an entertainment element and how it can be incorporated into the theme.

This chapter covers many aspects of food, beverage, and catering including:

- ➢ Determining the food and beverage budget
- ➢ Ways to save money
- ➢ Negotiating food and beverage contracts
- ➢ Developing menus
- ➢ Determining portion sizes
- ➢ Service styles
- ➢ Working with caterers or banquet staff
- ➢ Do-it-yourself catering

A Food & Beverage worksheet is located at the end of the chapter.

Items of General Note

Keep the audience in mind. Be realistic about the type of foods and beverages that are served. Consider the demographic. Are they a meat and potatoes crowd or do they appreciate more trendy foods? Just as it's unrealistic to plan a four-course gourmet dinner when the budget is $5 per person, you wouldn't want to serve champagne to a mostly beer drinking crowd.

"I've learned there are two words that will always draw a crowd --free food."

Live and Learn and Pass It On Volume VI

Men seem to prefer more substantial foods, and young men tend to eat more than anyone. Women like lighter foods or more vegetables. Young adults will likely choose beer or wine over hard liquor. Older people appreciate foods that aren't rich or spicy and are more easily chewed and digested. Teenagers like finger-type foods, while children like simple foods that aren't fussy to serve or eat. Vegetarian options should always be made available.

Use common sense in selecting the menu. Don't serve alcohol or give wine as gifts for an event benefiting a rehab center. Don't serve several meat courses if much of the crowd is vegetarian or vegan. An entrée of chicken with wine sauce would probably go untouched if served to a group of children. You get the idea!

Ethnic, religious, or group considerations are also important. The last thing an event needs is for the guests to be mortified over the menu. Some cultures or religions don't eat red meat while most do eat fish. If the group is predominantly from another culture and you aren't familiar with the cuisine, do some research and make sure to include dishes they will enjoy. You should also avoid scheduling your event on a major religious holiday.

Adapt the food to the circumstances. Events held indoors make it easier to serve a variety of foods than outdoor venues do. Will people sit down for the meal, or will they need to carry the food around with them? If it's hot weather, you'll need to provide more water, soft drinks, or juice. Beer consumption at outdoor events is always greater in hot weather than cool.

For events that last all day or into the evening, you may need to offer more than one meal. Having a brunch may be more cost effective than serving breakfast and lunch. Serving lunch-size portions for dinner can lighten up a meal, though you may be charged the "dinner" price. Meals are also priced differently depending on the day of the week or the time of day. Many places will charge a higher price after 3:00 p.m. for exactly the same menu item.

Be health conscious about the menu. Greasy foods are expected at fairs or festivals, not at upscale events. Serve lighter fare so that guests remain alert. Food should be colorful and pleasing to the eye as well as taste good.

Don't forget about food for volunteers! This can be accomplished by making food available at a volunteer "headquarters" location or by giving volunteers "meal tickets." They appreciate the added benefit of a meal, even if it's only a sandwich and a soft drink.

Start planning early. Start at least three months in advance if possible. This allows time for researching options, choosing menus, taste testing, making decisions, and identifying catering requirements.

Make use of available resources. Talk to the chef or caterer. Look at menus from other events, or invent your own.

Outside or In-House Catering

Catering services are often available as a part of a facility rental package (in-house) or you may need to hire an outside caterer. Either way, there are a number of points to consider. Do-it-yourself catering is discussed later in this chapter.

Choosing An Outside Caterer

Finding a suitable caterer works much like the venue selection process. You'll start with a larger group of possibilities, then screen them down to just a few.

Not all caterers are the same! You can find catering companies through friends, business associates, or in the phone book. If you attend a function where the food impresses you, get a business card. Make notations on the card as to when/where you obtained the caterer's name, and remarks about the food, presentation, or comments made by guests. It's always nice to have this information in the files even if you don't use it immediately.

NOTES

141

Full service caterers work with the event manager to prepare and serve the meal and may be able to provide other things such as dishes, linens, décor, etc. *Drop-off caterers* prepare the food in their own facility and deliver it to the event site (or it can be picked up at their location.) *Partial caterers* will perform meal preparation at the event site but normally do not include shopping or service staff.

Develop a list of potential candidates. Make a list of potential caterers (no more than five) and conduct a preliminary screening. Call around and check on availability for the dates of your event, the types of events they cater, etc. Or you may be able to find out much of this information from the caterer's Web site. Based on this information, narrow it down to three choices.

Ask to visit an event they are catering. You'll get a good idea about the quality of the food and service provided. It may also afford an opportunity to speak with the host about their working relationship with the catering company.

Ask the caterer for references that you can call to gauge customer satisfaction. Trust your instincts. If something seems amiss, hire someone else.

Menus and the budget. Most caterers operate from a "cost per person" perspective. To calculate this for one-time meals such as dinners, divide the preliminary budget you have allocated for the meal by the number of persons expected to attend. This gives you the "per person" amount and should include the gratuity percentage.

Be sure to ask whether the per person amount includes the gratuity and/or tax. Most caterers will assume it does not unless you have specified this in advance. Keep in mind that the catering company must factor its costs for food, equipment, and staff into the budget you are working with.

NOTES

Don't be afraid to ask questions! You have a right to know exactly what is being provided for the price quoted. Based on the per person cost, choose from standardized menus or ask the caterer to create a customized menu for the event. Given adequate lead time, most catering companies or chefs appreciate an opportunity to create special menus and will allow a "tasting" prior to final selection.

Does the caterer offer other services? Events often can obtain package deals through caterers that include items such as linens, decorations, centerpieces, candles, party favors, or other needs.

Since there is normally a mark up by the caterer, you'll want to compare whether it is less costly to obtain these things through other sources. The time saved in shopping or carting supplies to and from the event may be well worth having the caterer do it.

Make final selection based on a combination of menu and service. Contract details should include information about the menu, beverage, guarantee dates, number of service personnel, taxes, gratuity, and payment schedule. Be sure to specify other items to be provided by the caterer in the contract.

Do not sign the contract until all details have been agreed upon and do not pay the entire amount up front. Make an agreement to pay any balance the date of the event and bring a check. Otherwise, you have no recourse if you aren't happy with the food or service.

Make it very clear that you will not pay for any charges that were not outlined in the contract, unless they have been separately discussed and agreed upon (such as things that are added at the actual event).

A fun thing that you might ask the caterer about if you are doing a fundraising event such as an auction is to ask if they would be willing to donate a cooking class for 8-10 people. You will not only make money on the auction lot, you'll make up some of what you spent on the catering this way.

NOTES

In-House Catering

Larger venues such as hotel or convention centers have their own in-house catering or banquet services, or they contract with authorized food service providers which you may be required to use. Options for standard or customized menus are also available.

The advantage of using in-house catering is that it can be included in the package deal for the use of the facility. There is usually no need to bring in basic dishes, linens, and the like (unless you want something different) because they are owned by the venue and are included in the pricing. Another way to look at it is "one stop shopping." For a busy event manager, the opportunity to combine facility use and catering services at one location can save a great deal of time and coordination.

Most facilities with their own in-house catering stipulate that the food service only be provided by their facility due to liability issues. To bring in outside chefs, or vary the standard services, check with the venue.

Serving Styles

The way the food is served should be in keeping with the theme and the desired atmosphere. Just as you choose the menu, you can also select from a number of standard serving styles—plated, preset, buffets, food stations, cafeteria style, family style, or receptions. Some events may use a combination of several styles. More elegant affairs may use high level Russian or French service styles.

Plated style. Normally used for seated dinners, plated service means that food is assembled on the plate in the kitchen, then brought to the table by the server and placed before the diner. An advantage of plated service is that it allows for portion control and may result in less cost per person than serve-yourself options.

NOTES

Preset style. This is just as it sounds. Either all or a portion of the food (such as a salad) is placed on the table prior to guests being seated. Items such as salt, pepper, water, bread, butter, cream, salad dressing, and others are standard preset items.

Buffet style. Guests proceed along a line of tables serving themselves from a number of foods, thereby reducing the number of service personnel required. Potlucks are a form of buffet style. A partial preset (such as the salad and dessert) can do much to save time, especially if the group is large.

To reduce the amount of time it takes for large groups to go through a buffet line, it helps if guests can serve themselves from both sides of the buffet tables, or to have a separate buffet service in another part of the room. A good rule of thumb is one double-sided buffet service for every 100 people.

Drawbacks to buffet service are that since guests serve themselves, they may take larger portions or have extra helpings which can result in higher food costs than portion-controlled service. People also tend to move slowly through a buffet line because they are talking to others or considering their choices among the food offered.

Food station style. A variation of buffet style service where food is placed on smaller tables in various locations in the room. Service personnel may stand at these stations to provide foods (e.g. meat carving or omelets) at the request of the guest. This cuts down on the buffet lines and attendees are able to socialize more freely.

Cafeteria style. Like a buffet line except the service staff may or may not dish the food onto the plate according to choices made by the guest. The guest then takes the plate to their table.

Family style. Seated guests serve themselves from common dishes that are placed on the table by wait staff.

Receptions. Receptions (also known as passed hors d'oeuvres) often replace traditional sit-down dinners because they offer guests a chance to mingle and carry on conversations while sampling a variety of individually portioned foods. Hors d'oeuvres and champagne are traditionally served in this manner.

Cocktail receptions generally refer to the serving of alcoholic beverages and light hors d'oeuvres. *Dinner receptions* usually serve heavier hors d'oeuvres or slightly larger portions. Hors d'oeuvres should be able to be eaten in two bites.

Russian style. More elegant sit-down dinners may use this form of service that features diners helping themselves to food presented by wait staff. Extra room must be allowed for wait staff to operate and this practice is often used by smaller specialty restaurants.

French style. Small, exclusive restaurants or VIP dinners sometimes use this service style in which wait staff place each individual food item on every diner's plate. Very formal service.

Service Ratios

Clarify the ratio of service personnel to guests up front. For buffets, the desired ratio is 1-to-35 for breakfast and 1-to-30 for lunch or dinner. At a sit-down meal, there should be at least one wait staff for every 20-25 guests. High profile events may require a 1-to-10 ratio for multi-course dinners. Otherwise, you will need to pay for any increased staffing levels above the standard service.

Seating

Industry standards for table seating are based on "rounds" (round tables) seating from 2-12 people depending on size, or at "banquet tables" (rectangular shaped 6-8' tables) providing seating on both sides and the ability to seat from 6-8 people. Don't try to squeeze too many people at a table. Add more tables rather than overcrowding.

NOTES

Head table. Head tables are usually set on an elevated platform or placed at the front and center of the room. If you opt to use a head table on a dais or stage, be sure the table is skirted for privacy's sake. Many events do not have a formal head table unless they have keynote speakers or guests of honor.

Use of seating charts and floor plans. These are mini-versions of a site plan that serves a multitude of uses for food functions. Larger venues like hotels and convention centers have computer software programs to create seating charts showing various ways tables can be arranged in the room. This software has been pre-programmed to factor requirements stipulated by the fire marshal or others regarding aisleways, number of people at a table, etc.

If you don't have the luxury of a specialized computer program, you can create a scale drawing of the room on which to plot the seating chart using a desktop publishing program or just plain old graph paper. Aisleways between tables need to be a minimum of 4' wide (6' is better) because it allows space for seated guests to push their chairs back a little and for servers to pass through. At the table, a minimum of 2' per person is required (3' is better because it allows for more "elbow room").

Number the tables, especially for large groups. Seating assignments can then be made by table number. Most event planning software has this feature and allows information to be changed or sorted in a number of ways.

No shows. For a nearly full table that is missing guests, you might wish to remove place settings and the additional chairs to allow more room (just make sure the missing guests will not be arriving later). If you planned for a table of eight and six of them don't show or cancel, move the remaining two people to another table that has empty chairs so they aren't sitting by themselves.

The Importance of Presentation

Ask any chef about presentation of the food and they will tell you it is critical to the dining experience. The way food looks affects the way it tastes. When you are presented with a beautiful plate of food combining color, texture and artful arrangement, don't you anticipate that it is going to taste great? Presentation is important because it shows guests that someone has taken the time to ensure that the food is pleasing to the eye.

Table linens, dishes, flatware, glassware, decorations, and other ambience enhancers should lend themselves to the presentation. Candlelight is flattering to food as well as people. There's no excuse for guests to have a boring dining experience when so much can be done with so little effort.

Presentation is a little harder to achieve for a buffet, but strive to showcase the food in the best manner possible. Even buffets find creative ways to decorate tables and present the food.

Menus

When it comes to creating menus, the sky's the limit. Just because a caterer or banquet manager may present a standardized menu doesn't mean you have to use it. Base your food choices on the type of event, who will attend, and the per-person cost. This frees you to be creative in the menu selection.

Menu Development

There's nothing wrong with using standardized menus for those who want a no-hassle way to make a selection. The information is often listed according to price per person based on various entrees and accompanying side dishes. You may be able to mix and match the side dishes, change sauces and the like within the established price structure for entrees. Desserts are often priced separately.

Another method of menu development is to state the established per person budget with a few guidelines (e.g. "I'd like chicken, fish, and pasta entrée choices and a chocolate dessert for $30 per person). This allows creativity in developing a specialized menu while operating within the parameters you have established.

Portion Size. For entrees, a good rule of thumb is to plan on 4-6 ounce portions. This includes boneless meat, poultry or fish as well as pasta or meat substitutes. If serving bone-in meats, allow for increased ounces in the portion. Buffets require smaller portions than do sit-down meals.

Think about the entire meal in regard to portion size. What is a reasonable portion size for a menu of salad, bread, entrée, side dishes, and dessert? This provides a good starting point.

Don't overlook simple dishes when planning the menu. Everything doesn't have to have a fancy sauce or elaborate name. Simple dishes with beautiful presentation often can be just as impressive as those with a high price tag.

Health Conscious Choices

With today's emphasis on a healthy lifestyle, pay attention to what your guests will be eating and provide health conscious food choices regardless of the type of event.

In the movie *When Harry Met Sally*, one of Sally's mandatory dining rules was that accompanying sauces, butter and so forth, be served "on the side." We can take a lesson from this. To keep it light, we may want to offer our guests the option of adding sauces, salad dressings, or other condiments according to their own individual choice. It's even better if the sauces and dressings are low in fat but big on taste.

NOTES

Keep meals on the light side. You don't want the audience to go to sleep in the middle of the event. Another way to lighten up a dinner meal is to serve lunch-size portions.

Vegetarian and vegan options. An increasing number of people are vegetarians or vegans, and even those who aren't may enjoy vegetarian menu options. In addition to vegetables, some of the tastiest dishes can include such things as pasta, potatoes, tofu, or fruit. Rice is a staple of many cultures and is a considered an honored food. Always include a vegetarian option in the menu.

Take care to ensure that what claims to be vegetarian actually is. Rice prepared with chicken broth is not vegetarian. Dishes that include dairy products like milk or cheese are not vegan. Make sure to request an ingredients list for the dish to verify.

Beverages

In selecting beverages, consider those that best fit the event and the venue. Some sites do not allow alcoholic beverages or require special permits for alcohol service. Some do not allow donated wine or beer. A selection of both alcoholic and non-alcoholic beverages is the most common.

Non-Alcoholic Beverages

As a general rule, people drink more non-alcoholic beverages than alcoholic beverages. At the very least, water and other beverages such as coffee, tea, or soft drinks should be offered. If conducting beverage service outside a standard venue, don't forget the ice!

Coffee. Order coffee by the gallon rather than by the cup. It costs much less that way. One pound of ground coffee makes about 60 cups of brewed coffee. A gallon of brewed coffee equals about 20 6-ounce cups. Cream and sugar should be made available, as well as sugar substitute.

Bottled beverages. Ordering bottled beverages by consumption saves money by paying only for what is used as compared to the per-person price. Depending on the level of trust with the caterer, make sure to discuss with the staff how to account for how much as been consumed.

Punch. A gallon of prepared punch will serve about 24 people. Punch mix typically comes in powdered or concentrate form, or a custom mix is made. Add fruit or ice cream for a different taste. Remember that some people are allergic to strawberries, bananas, or other fruit!

Beverage deposits. Some states charge deposits on bottles and cans and this may be added to the bill. If purchasing a keg of beer, you will be required to pay a deposit to ensure the safe return of the keg if it is not provided by the caterer.

Alcoholic Beverages

The serving of alcoholic beverages is serious. If you haven't already done so, please read the Liability, Permit, and Security section of this book, taking special note of the section relating to alcohol service. Since alcoholic beverages are considered to be controlled substances, events must conform to laws which basically state that those who provide alcoholic beverages may be held liable for incidents relating to intoxicated patrons.

The legal drinking age for most states in the U.S. is 21 years old. If minors attend, make sure that alcohol is monitored. For events held on college campuses, you should be especially careful. Adults can also be held liable for serving alcohol to minors at private parties.

Alcoholic beverages should not be the only activity. Know your clientele and understand that people behave differently when drinking. Use trained servers who know what to watch for and make sure food is available.

NOTES

151

Wine. For events on a tight budget, even a relatively inexpensive wine can be a luxury item if it needs to be purchased in large quantities. Serving a wine punch can stretch the servings for a bottle of wine by adding juice, sparkling soda, or other ingredients.

Wine comes in 750 milliliter bottles and often in magnums (1.5 liter) bottles which are the equivalent of 2 bottles. A standard wine pour is 5 ounces which equates to 4-5 glasses of wine per 750 ml bottle. A magnum provides 8-10 glasses depending on the pour.

Matching wine with food is another consideration. While serving the proper wine with the proper food is no longer so relevant, you should plan to offer both white and red wine for a sit-down meal.

Wine stewards at wine shops or restaurants can offer excellent and cost-effective selections. There is a significant mark up on wine purchased through wine shops or restaurants, so for large quantities try to work with a local distributor or directly with a winery for the best price. If you want a specific brand of wine, you'll need to make inquiries about which local retailer or distributor handles that brand.

Beer. The serving of beer lends itself extremely well to outdoor events, but is also a good choice for indoor events, especially those that are sports related. Another popular trend is food and beer pairing because beer goes surprisingly well with many foods.

A standard beer pour is 12 ounces. Bottled beer comes in 12-ounce bottles which eliminates the need to measure. A full keg of beer is 15 gallons (half-barrel). A quarter-barrel, or "pony keg" is half that.

For large groups, it's cheaper to buy kegs than bottles but kegs are more difficult to handle than bottled beer. Kegs are hard to maneuver if you're trying to wrestle them yourself. They are bulky and very heavy! Kegs are a good choice if they can remain stationary on a table, barrel, or other solid surface. Once the event is over, due to liquor laws, the keg needs to be emptied before transporting.

NOTES

NOTES

Be sure to monitor guests if the keg is set up as a serve-yourself affair. At the very least, a trained volunteer should be stationed at the service area, both to provide assistance and to monitor alcohol consumption. For large groups of people, you'll need more than one keg to avoid long lines waiting to be served.

Keep the keg service on a "by-the-glass" basis. We don't advocate allowing guests to have pitchers of beer because they tend to over-consume at the event's expense. The by-the-glass approach helps in monitoring guests and their behavior.

Distilled spirits. Most distilled spirits (a.k.a. hard liquor) are 80-proof or more in alcoholic content. Proof is a measurement used in determining the strength of distilled spirits based on a number that is twice the percent by volume of alcohol present. In other words, a bottle of 90-proof liquor is actually 45% alcohol by volume. The higher the proof, the more potent the liquor. By comparison, most beer and wine runs from 7-13% in alcohol content.

A standard pour of hard liquor is 1.5-2 ounces. Most distilled spirits come in bottles called "fifths" but some come in quarts. A fifth is 25.6 ounces (or a fifth of a gallon) while a quart is 32 ounces. The number of pours in the bottle is determined by the number of ounces used in the pour. It is a good idea to set a policy that only one standard drink at a time will be served.

No-host cash bars are recommended. This means that guests pay for their own drinks. *Hosted* bars feature drinks made at the customer's request for which the event pays the tab. This invites both over-consumption and abuse of privilege in our experience. If the event is hosting, you will be charged for each drink, plus the gratuity.

One way to control liquor consumption is to provide each guest with a set number of "drink tickets," and allow only a limited number of choices on drink selections. Once the allocated tickets have been used, guests must purchase their own drinks.

Other Comments in Regard to Alcohol

Mark ups. Hotels, bars, restaurants, and venues that provide alcoholic beverages take a large markup on sales of these beverages. In fact, there is a far larger mark up on alcohol (around 85%+) than on food. In some cases, like wine for instance, the mark up can be 300% or more from what the restaurant paid for the bottle.

Corkage fees. Whether the event purchases wine through the venue or caterer, or whether the wine is donated, there may be a corkage fee charged ranging from $7-$15+ *per bottle*. This means that you will be charged a corkage fee on every single bottle of wine opened. For a $10 bottle of wine that adds a $15 corkage fee, the price is now up to $25 a bottle.

The good news is that an event can often negotiate a lesser (or waived) corkage fee in the price package, especially for nonprofit organizations, or events with multiple meals. Corkage is one of the things venues and caterers expect to negotiate on, so don't miss the opportunity or you may get a very big surprise on the bill!

Inebriated guests. Under no circumstances should an intoxicated person be allowed to drive. Send the guest home in a taxi, even if the event has to pay for it. It's much less expensive than a lawsuit.

Understand the Contract Terms

Before signing a food and beverage contract, be sure you understand what is—or what is not—included and the level of service provided

Guarantees. You'll be required to give a guarantee on the number of meals ordered anywhere from 48 hours to 30 days in advance. Once the guarantee has been given, the event will be charged for that number of meals regardless of whether they are used or not. *You are allowed to increase the guarantee number but not to decrease it.*

When giving the guarantee, it's better to give a number slightly less than what you expect (which you can later increase) than to be charged for unused meals. There are always no-shows, and if the attendance increases, you can always up the guarantee. For events holding multi-meal functions, a guarantee is required for each meal.

Guarantees give the caterer or banquet department time to order food, schedule staff, and do advance preparation. If the event has a customized menu, this is very important because the standard food preparation procedure has been altered.

Overset. Most caterers or banquet departments factor in an "overset" amount which is a percentage of the guarantee number, but don't assume this is true unless you have verified this. You'll need to keep this in mind in regard to the guarantee as well.

The current average for overset is 3-5%. This means that if a guarantee for 100 meals is given, the caterer will prepare 3-5 extra meals to cover unexpected guests. You will not be charged for these meals unless they are used.

If overset meals go unused, this is obviously a financial loss to the caterer, so try to accurately forecast the guarantee number. On the other hand, if the guarantee is too low and more guests are present than the overset can cover, some guests may have to dine on alternate courses or wait for additional meals to be prepared.

NOTE: This is not always the case with overset. There may be exceptions with special orders or split menus since they are outside the standardized procedure.

Attrition clauses. Most venues and caterers include attrition clauses in contracts. This means the venue (or caterer) pre-determines (based on your attendance estimate) the space and meal requirements for the event. This may be tricky if you're trying to book a venue a year or more in advance since attendance figures are strictly estimates at that point.

NOTES

Pay attention to—and negotiate terms for—attrition clauses because the event is essentially agreeing to an estimated guaranteed attendance long before the actual date, and for which you may be required to pay. Be realistic, but cautious. *The downside is that if another event comes in with larger attendance (hence more profit), your event may get bumped from the date.*

To calculate the attrition factor, the venue or caterer looks at the type and size of the functions planned and puts a price tag on each one. The numbers are then totaled and a factor of about 80-85% is applied (which allows for less than estimated). The revised number indicates to the venue or caterer the space requirements and amount of revenue anticipated to be generated by your event.

What this all boils down to is that the attrition clause is a projected amount on which a hotel, venue, or caterer can base their ability to accommodate other events in addition to (or instead of) yours.

Gratuities. Tips, or gratuities, used to be given for good service. These days, gratuities are automatically added to the bill (whether the service was good or lousy). When it comes time to pay the bill, if you feel the service was poor, renegotiate the gratuity charge *before* payment. If you must pay that night and can't talk to someone in authority, hold back part of the payment until it is resolved.

Currently, the gratuity rate is plus or minus 20%. This means that at a 20% rate, for every $100 the event spends on items subject to gratuity, and additional $20 will be added to the bill.

Clarify which items in the contract are subject to gratuity charges. These normally include food and beverage, but make sure to ask about room rental, parking, audio and visual, or other items are subject to the charge. Ask to have gratuity charges itemized in the bill to avoid any surprises.

The Budget

Food and beverage costs are one of the largest expenses in an event budget. Food focused events typically spend 60-75% of their total budget on food and beverage. In comparing this to minimal (or no) cost for events in which food and beverage are not predominant factors, you can readily see the budget impact.

The average margin of profit for catered food functions is 25-40%. The good news is that while occupying a big chunk of the budget, food costs are often some of the most flexible.

The average profit for beverage functions is 80-85%. This explains why liquor sales generate such tremendous revenue. This also applies to soft drinks, coffee, etc. For example, movie houses make more on soft drinks than any other food item or the movie ticket.

Here are a few ways to save money on food and beverage costs:

Provide smaller portions	Less quantity, less expensive
Serve cultural cuisine	Many inexpensive choices and tasty
Substitute menu items	Serve fish or chicken instead of beef, pasta instead of meat
Alcoholic beverages	Use Italian Prosecco instead of champagne – cheaper, tastes same
Beverage purchases	Coffee by the gallon, bottled beverages by consumption
Eliminate courses	Soup *or* salad instead of soup *and* salad, or a similar choice
Bar service	No-host cash bar instead of hosted
Keep it light	Serve lunch size portions for dinner
Accurate guarantees	Develop the art of estimation
Smart negotiating	Know how costs are calculated and which are flexible for negotiation
Underwriting	Find a sponsor to cover the cost

Contract Negotiation

Many considerations regarding food and beverage contracts have been discussed in this chapter. The best advice still remains—know what's involved, and understand it, before signing a catering contract.

The catering contract is a legally binding document. Don't hesitate to ask about any paragraph, sentence, or word that you don't understand *before* signing.

Negotiate. Then negotiate some more. Most caterers or facilities are willing to negotiate for food and beverage functions, especially if large numbers are involved, because it benefits them to do so. You may be able to get the best deals on functions involving liquor sales because the profit margin is greater than on food, and the venue/caterer has more negotiating room.

Don't a sign a contact with a guaranteed minimum in revenue. Know how much you have to spend (including gratuity). Juggle the menu to include less expensive options. If hotel rooms are involved, leverage those against food and beverage prices. Being creative can save money!

Be specific. Clarify the timeframe for guarantees as well as the percentage of overset. Ask that the service ratio of wait staff to guests be spelled out. Clarify on which items the gratuity will be charged. Are there corkage fees or taxes? Specify whether liquor sales are to be conducted on a "bottle" or "per drink" basis.

Cancellation. To negotiate cancellation clauses, try to negotiate the "lost profit" as opposed to "lost revenue" scenario. Profit is defined as 25-40% of anticipated food and beverage revenue. They would technically only lose the profit, not the total revenue, because they didn't have to pay out expenses for staff, food costs, and the like. Another method is to use a "per person" basis to calculate lost profit (e.g. $5 per person for breakfast, $7.50 for lunch, etc.).

Miscellaneous items. Don't assume that table linens, décor, votive candles, upgraded china, centerpieces, or like items are included in the package price. Ask what is included and what isn't. Based on the revenue the event brings, you may be able to obtain some of these things at no charge.

Banquet Event Orders. Hotels or venues such as convention centers use banquet event orders (BEOs) in addition to the original contract. Banquet event orders are usually broken out by date and time and present a very detailed schedule of what happens when, how many, and other pertinent information. You will be required to review and sign off on these documents approximately 1-2 weeks in advance. Examine each BEO carefully. These documents may contain mistakes such as original pricing when you've negotiated for less, wrong room numbers, or other considerations.

Do-It-Yourself Catering

Some events may opt to do their own catering. With this choice come various needs that may or may not be available at the event site. Outdoor events are particularly subject to these variables and present their own unique challenges.

It may seem like a superhuman effort to produce great volumes of food but if adequate facilities and volunteers are available it may be extremely cost efficient. Working in the kitchen or helping to serve the food are often jobs highly prized by volunteers.

Check into legal requirements or permits. You may need to obtain a permit from the local health department (especially for outdoor events). Check into food service requirements in advance. It may save much time and frustration at a later time trying to obtain needed permits at the last minute. It may also be necessary for those involved to hold current food and beverage handler cards which are obtained by attending training conducted by the health department or liquor commission.

Getting Organized

Develop a menu. Determine the foods to be served. Strive for a balance of color, nutrition, and food groups. Don't forget the vegetarians in the crowd!

Be creative in naming menu dishes but use understandable terms. If it's really meat and potatoes, don't describe it in a way that no one understands. When using titles, you may want to list the main ingredients in parentheses—Surf & Turf (lobster and sirloin steak).

Develop the recipes and ingredients lists. Use recipes with as few ingredients and steps for preparation as possible. Make sure they can be easily understood. The object is for the food to look and taste good with as little fuss as possible. Recipes with many steps for complicated sauces or desserts take too much time, slow down food service, and are more trouble than they are worth.

Avoid labor intensive foods. Some recipes do not lend themselves well to quantity cooking because of the labor involved. "Stirring constantly" means someone must devote their complete attention to the dish rather than being free to do other tasks. Carving vegetables into fancy shapes may be fun, but julienne or diagonal cuts may look just as nice and take a fraction of the time.

Increasing the quantity increases the cooking and preparation time. Bringing five gallons of liquid to a boil in an institutional sized kettle takes more than five times longer than boiling a gallon of liquid in a pan at home. It takes much more time and oven space to bake a casserole for 50 people than a casserole for the family. Frosting a dozen cookies is much different than frosting a thousand. Cracking dozens of eggs for omelets for 100 people takes far more time than breakfast at home, let alone preparing them. You will want to allow for plenty of time, and probably more than you think, for quantity cooking, preparation, plating, and service.

Time saving hints. Use convenience foods or prepared ingredients when possible. These can save hours of preparation time and free up helping hands needed elsewhere. Use frozen vegetables, commercial butter pats, pre-sliced meats, frozen pie crust or dough, fresh or dried pasta, concentrates, etc.

Warehouse food suppliers often have many pre-packaged (and surprisingly tasty) foods that can be unthawed or warmed up with minimal effort. Weigh the time, inconvenience, and cost of having to do everything yourself against the slightly higher cost for the convenience of using prepared foods.

Prepare or freeze as much of the food in advance as possible. Fresh foods should be prepared the day before and kept in the refrigerator. Choose foods that hold up well. Label and package everything with the preparation instructions so when the food is transported to the event site it ends up in its proper place and is easy to use. The more detailed the instruction, the better (e.g. chopped vegetables for beef stew recipe).

Check equipment needs. If the kitchen facilities consist of a four-burner stove with two working burners and one oven, don't expect to prepare dinner for 100 people. Be sure there is enough cooking equipment, counter space, refrigerator/freezer capacity, sinks, small appliances, cooking utensils, dishes, glassware, etc. You may need to rent or borrow much of this equipment.

Identify jobs and schedules. Divide the entire process into individual areas such as menu development, shopping, kitchen management, service, clean up, etc. Then break down each component into individual jobs to be performed.

For example, kitchen management could be divided into ordering equipment, organizing supplies, hot or cold food preparation, dishwashing, or other functions. These functions would then be further refined into individual jobs and shifts.

NOTES

161

It also helps to think through the step-by-step process of food preparation and service. For example, foods with longer prep times need to be started first, followed in descending order of time required for other dishes.

Dinner tables can be set with dishes and condiments in advance of the time food is served. How many wine glasses will be needed? How long will it take to reheat the baked beans or grill the steaks? This planning is a lot like preparing dinner for the family, but on a much larger scale.

Shopping concerns. If purchasing large quantities, don't take a Volkswagen if you'll need a moving truck to haul the groceries. Don't go alone to buy supplies to feed an army. You'll need all the help (not to mention extra hands and strong backs) you can get.

Supplies for a recipe that calls for 4 cups of flour, 4 cups of sugar, and 4 cups of milk takes on a whole new meaning when multiplied a hundredfold.

Don't forget about cleaning and other supplies such as paper towels, dish soap, plastic products, and the like which may need to be purchased in bulk.

High dollar amounts resulting from your purchases may be a concern if you want to write a check or use a credit card. Some warehouse foods suppliers don't accept credit cards. Always ask about volume discounts or use other means (such as going through an affiliated sponsor or vendor) to save money.

Estimating amounts. Recipe amounts usually specify "serves XX number of people." You'll need to divide the recipe by the number of people it serves to obtain a "per serving" amount for each ingredient. The per serving amount can then be multiplied by the total number of persons expected to consume the dish to come up with the total amount needed of that particular ingredient.

NOTES

162

NOTES

Don't forget about the need to use the ingredient in other capacities. For example, if four of the recipes need salt, combine the total for each of the recipes, plus the amount needed to fill salt shakers for dinner tables, to come up with the amount to purchase.

Make calculations before going to the store! Don't attempt to figure it out while shopping. Know how many, what size, how much, and so on. If ordering supplies, be very specific (and have them read it back to verify) or you may not wind up with what you ordered.

Food Preparation

Do as much in advance as possible. Maintain order in transporting foods and assembling them at the event site. Keep things together that belong together. Pre-measure and label ingredients, dishes or pans so they don't get used for something else.

Use an assembly-line approach to avoid congestion in the kitchen. Bring itemized lists for each recipe (ingredients, how to, who is preparing, cooking time, required equipment, etc.). Be sure to make multiple copies of the recipes.

Prepare each recipe and conduct a taste test in advance. Determine how complicated the dish is or how much time it takes to prepare; then factor the multiple preparation times. Is there a simpler or healthier way to prepare the dish? Does it taste good? Is it too sweet or too salty? Answer these questions in advance. If the recipe is too complicated, do something else.

Post and distribute numerous copies of schedules, floor plans, or seating charts. Schedules help everyone to know in what order and at what time things happen, and who is doing what. Floor plans help to identify traffic flow and locations of important event elements (bars, buffet tables, stage, etc.). Seating charts help to identify table numbers and who sits where, but can also be color coded to identify "special attention" tables such as sponsors.

After the Guests Depart

Leftovers. Be careful in packaging up leftover foods. Some events like to deliver surplus food to nursing homes or to organizations that feed the homeless. Determine *in advance* what will be done with any leftover food and ask about how it should be packaged for safety and what the organization's procedure is for delivery. You don't want to arrive with a bunch of food and have no one there to receive it!

Be sure that foods needing refrigeration are kept cold and that hot foods don't sit around in containers for long periods of time. The local health department can provide guidelines regarding food storage and safety.

Clean as you go. Clean to whatever degree possible during food preparation and service time. This provides for clean dishes or work space and will save time at the end of the event when everyone is tired and wants to go home. It's a good idea to hire dishwashers for the evening because the task of washing a lot of dishes and pans can be daunting. Especially when you think about glassware, china, flatware and about a million other things needing to be washed.

If doing your own clean up, be sure to leave the venue in the same (or better) condition than you found it—clean kitchen, floors mopped or swept, trash removed, restrooms clean, etc. Those involved will feel good about the job they have done and the venue will have no trouble with future use requests.

Use the Food & Beverage worksheet to help in your planning.

Food & Beverage Worksheet

Use this worksheet to outline the event's food and beverage needs.

General Items

1. Have you identified the audience?
2. What types of food and beverage would they prefer?
3. Do ethnic backgrounds, religious beliefs, or holidays need to be considered?
4. How will vegetarians and/or vegans be accommodated?
5. Will volunteers or contractors need to be fed?
6. _____
7. _____
8. _____

Financial Considerations

1. What is the budgeted per-person allocation? _____
2. Is there a cancellation clause in the contract and what are the terms? _____
3. Is there an attrition clause? _____
4. Will a corkage fee or other charges be applicable? _____
5. What is the gratuity percentage? _____
6. On which items is the gratuity charged? _____
7. _____
8. _____

Outside Caterers

1. What methods will be used to select the caterer? _____
2. Have you developed a list of potential caterers? _____
3. Who are the top candidates? _____
4. Have you conducted a visit or a food tasting? _____
5. Does the caterer offer other services? _____
6. Is wait staff included in the quoted price? _____
7. Will the caterer do the clean up? _____
8. Have you inquired about "additional" costs? _____
9. _____
10. _____

Food & Beverage Worksheet

Use this worksheet to outline the event's food and beverage needs.

In-House Catering
1. Does the facility allow outside food or beverage? _____
2. What services are included in the base price? _____
3. On what items are additional charges incurred? _____
4. What style of service will be used? _____
5. What type of seating will be provided for guests? _____
6. Is a seating chart or floor plan available? _____
7. What is the ratio of service personnel to guests? _____
8. Are linens, candles, or minimal décor included? _____

Food & Beverage
1. What are the portion sizes? _____
2. Will alcoholic beverages be served, and what? _____
3. What means of accounting will be used to track beverage charges? _____
4. What is the procedure to deal with inebriated guests? _____
5. When is the guarantee required? _____
6. What is the overset percentage? _____
7. Have you carefully reviewed the contract? _____
8. Have you reviewed the banquet event orders? _____

Do-It-Yourself Catering
1. Are there permits or other legal considerations? _____
2. Have menu items been selected for ease of preparation? _____
3. Have you tested and tasted the recipes? _____
4. Are kitchen facilities and equipment adequate? _____
5. Is there enough time to prepare all the food and get it out on schedule? _____
6. Have jobs been identified and enough help recruited? _____
7. Is there a schedule of duties, times, and equipment needed? _____
8. Who will do the shopping, and what is the payment method? _____
9. Have copies of schedules, floor plans, and/or seating charts been provided? _____
10. What will be done with leftover food? _____
11. Who will do the clean up? _____

Chapter 11 – Exhibitors

Showcase It!

Incorporating exhibitors into an event can serve a number of purposes—generate additional revenue, provide for sponsorships and/or add interest for attendees. The involvement of exhibitors equates to increased opportunities.

Exhibitor fees add to event revenue. Depending on the event, attendees can enjoy a variety of foods, beverages, games, crafts, information, and other activities offered by exhibitors.

This chapter covers interactions with exhibitors:

➢ Developing a list of potential exhibitors
➢ Recruiting exhibitors
➢ Developing recruitment and confirmation materials
➢ Determining types of exhibitor booths and fee structures
➢ Processing exhibitor registrations and payments
➢ Marketing for maximum exposure

"Hit the ball over the fence and you can take your time going around the bases."

John W. Raper

For our purposes, exhibitors have been categorized into two groups—indoor trade shows or exhibitions, and exhibitors at outdoor events such as festivals, fairs, and the like.

Trade shows and exhibitions are typically held indoors in large venues and may or may not be linked to events like conventions. They may also be conducted as independent industry-related events like trade or technology shows.

General Motors is a good example of a trade show exhibitor who annually participates in a circuit of automotive-related events where a variety of GM car brands are displayed and/or sold—Chevrolet, Buick, Pontiac, GMC, Cadillac, and others.

A food products show is an example of a trade related event. In many cases, retailers and/or specialty food providers feature product brands (e.g. soft drinks or snack foods) that help them underwrite the cost of the exhibitor fees. At these types of shows, most booths would offer sample tastes of the products being featured.

Outdoor venues like festivals and fairs have many exhibitors offering a wide variety of food, products, and services.

General Comments

Ask some basic questions. Should the event have exhibitors? Who is the audience? Does the event site have sufficient space? How many and what kinds of exhibitors are you hoping to attract?

If possible, designate one staff member or key volunteer to work with exhibitors. The reasoning is simply that it provides for one contact person with whom to communicate. The contact in turn becomes familiar with each exhibitor's needs and what they hope to achieve by participating in the event. If using an exhibition services company, the staff member can also work with the contractor. Working with exhibitors is very time consuming and an event manager often does not have time to devote to this function.

Help exhibitors succeed. Success is based on generating interest in what exhibitors have to offer and on the amount of opportunities for exhibitors to make sales or contacts. How well the exhibitor does at your event will have great impact on whether they repeat their involvement in future years. Exhibitors should be a good fit with the event and enhance the experience for attendees.

Another way to help exhibitors succeed is to limit the number of exhibitors in any one category (e.g. number of hot dog concessions, number of jewelry booths, artists, etc.). It's always a good idea to jury artists, jewelry, and crafts so you don't end up with a bunch of junky stuff, because it may affect the event's reputation or attendance.

NOTES

Market the exhibitors as well as the event. When exhibitors participate in the event—and especially if they have paid to be there—you have an obligation to make sure an audience is in attendance. The reason exhibitors participate is to sell or promote their products and services. If the event fails to provide an audience, the exhibitor has wasted their money and time. Use all marketing and promotion methods at your disposal and promote the exhibitors in conjunction with the event. This can be done through marketing materials, newspaper ads, Web site listings, and more. Ask the exhibitor to market your event in their promotions as well.

Information, Please! Clear, concise, and complete information is essential in recruiting and communicating with exhibitors. They need as much information as possible presented in an easily understood format. The two major forms of communication used by most events are exhibitor recruitment and confirmation materials, both of which are discussed in this chapter.

Avoid frustrations. Good communication and planning are essential to working with exhibitors. All too often exhibitors, contractors, and event managers become stressed during load-in, set up, and tear down when clear communication and diligent planning could have prevented most problems.

Tempers become short when people are frustrated. Exhibitors get upset when things they have ordered are incorrect or missing in their booth. Contractors get cranky when exhibitors haven't ordered the proper utility hookups or booth amenities. Event managers are stressed with exhibitors and contractors complain.

Since a substantial amount of equipment, materials, and supplies must be coordinated the communication in regard to logistics is critical to helping everyone work together and perform well.

Choose the site carefully. During the site selection process, carefully consider what exhibitors need in the way of space, access to utilities, ease of load-in and load-out, and other requirements.

Be sure to find out whether you must use the venue's authorized contractors or union workers. This can make a big difference when calculating rates the event needs to charge exhibitors to cover costs.

Conduct a post-event survey. Following the event, send out a survey asking exhibitors for their comments. You'll obtain both positive and negative feedback that can be of great use in planning future events. *An Exhibitor Survey worksheet is located at the end of this chapter.*

Exhibitor Recruitment

Don't expect exhibitors to come knocking on the door asking to participate unless your event is highly successful and/or one that has been a winner for them in the past. If it's a first-time event, you'll have to conduct an aggressive recruitment campaign.

This process is similar to prospecting for sponsors. Exhibitors will want to know why they should participate in your event as opposed to someone else's and you'll need to have ready answers to questions. Develop a comprehensive packet of exhibitor recruitment materials similar to that of creating the sponsor packet. You may even use some of the same elements like fact sheets or copies of news articles.

Exhibitors rely on leads or contacts they make at the event for on-site sales and/or as a way to promote their company or products to potential customers. It is also an excellent means to test market new products and gain contact names for a mailing list. For conventions or conferences, a list of the event's registered attendees could be provided to exhibitors as an added incentive to participate.

It is up to management whether exhibitors will be allowed to sell their products and services, or whether they only may conduct promotional activities. You will recruit many more exhibitors if they are allowed to make money from their participation which helps to offset the exhibitor fees.

How To Find Exhibitors

Look for exhibitors that are a natural fit. Certain kinds of companies, products or services, and/or those they are related to, will immediately come to mind. A solid marketing plan will also help in recruiting exhibitors to come on board.

If the event has previously worked with exhibitors, invite them to repeat their involvement and add new ones to keep the event fresh. Depending on the type of event, there may already be a list of possibilities, especially if the event involves a professional association with an extensive membership.

HINT: Call some potential exhibitors in advance to inform them about the event and obtain feedback about what would motivate them to become involved. Then build those suggestions into your exhibitor recruitment materials!

Events often publish lists of participating exhibitors or they are posted on the event's Web site. Pay attention to these, especially if the event is similar to yours, for ideas. You can also download their application materials or regulations to formulate your own ideas.

You can also attend events similar to yours and check out the exhibitors. If you see some that interest you, ask for a business card and a contact name, address, or phone number (to whom you can later send exhibitor materials). *Never hand out your materials at someone else's event!* This is ambush marketing and you wouldn't want someone to do this to your event.

Another option is to obtain a mailing list from a commercial service that sells lists of names and addresses for virtually any type of business or interest group. This can save many hours of research in trying to develop a list on your own, but you may get a lot of names you don't feel are appropriate for recruitment purposes. However, the time saved may be worth the expense of obtaining mailing lists and scanning them to weed out the unlikely candidates.

Exhibitor Recruitment Materials

Exhibitors need lead time! They may need up to 12 months in advance to schedule their participation. Start the recruitment effort as soon as possible after you have locked in the basic event elements.

The "packet" should contain the following information (as applicable to your event):

- Basic event information, fact sheet or background
- Marketing pitch letter
- Contact person's name, phone, e-mail address
- List of sponsors' names
- Exhibitor schedule
- Exhibitor regulations
- Security information
- Booth location assignment process
- Set up/tear down schedule
- Exhibitor fees and payment schedule
- Application form
- Contractor information, if any
- Equipment, services, or utilities order form
- Shipping and receiving information
- Floor plan or site plan
- Confirmation process
- Related hotel or lodging information, if any

Basic event information. The who-what-when-where-why-and how of the event including venue, dates, schedule, and more.

Marketing pitch. Use positive action statements that sell the exhibitor on why they should participate and what benefits are to be gained. The pitch is contained in a cover letter which makes it more personal, or it can be placed at the beginning of event information.

Contact information. Provide the name, e-mail address, phone number, and mailing address of whom to contact for questions or to make arrangements relating to involvement. This would ideally be a staff member or key volunteer who is familiar with the event and whose main focus is to act as a liaison.

Sponsor information. Be sure to mention sponsors (if you can) in the recruitment materials. To an exhibitor, the event merits consideration if sponsors have already come on board. Conversely, sponsors could receive an exhibitor booth as a benefit of sponsorship and would have to submit completed application materials and conform to exhibitor guidelines.

Exhibitor schedule. Provide a listing of dates and times during which the audience will be present and exhibitors can promote or sell their products and services. Most conference or convention exhibitors prefer to operate during blocks of time that do not conflict with other major activities. It makes the job of staffing the booth a little easier and allows them to attend other activities. For outdoor events such as fairs or festivals, exhibitors will need to staff their booths during all hours the event is open to the public.

Exhibitor regulations. Guidelines and regulations are necessary for equal treatment of all exhibitors. Be warned that without them havoc will reign! Exhibitors must agree to operate under the event's regulations in order to participate. Most expect to conform to these rules of operation and understand why they are needed.

Exhibitor regulations should include general guidelines as well as specific references to liability, permitted activities, security arrangements, etc. *Samples of Exhibitor Guidelines appear at the end of the chapter.*

Security Information. Provide a description of security measures that will/will not be in force relating to exhibitors, and the event as a whole.

173

Booth location assignments. The method by which exhibitor spaces are assigned (first-come, first-served, previous exhibitor priority, etc.) should be outlined.

Set up/tear down schedule. Exhibitors need dates and times of exhibitor load-in/set up as well as the schedule for tear down/move-out so that these activities are conducted in an orderly fashion.

Stagger the arrival, set up and tear down times so that "traffic jams" are less likely to occur and be realistic about how long each of these various elements takes to complete.

Application form. The form should be as complete and concise as possible to avoid staff having to spend time gathering needed information. The form should include the exhibitor's name, address, phone, fax, e-mail, type of booth desired, related fees and payment schedule, how to pay, where to send the payment, cancellation policy, liability/hold harmless statement and signature line.

Contractor information. If the event requires exhibitors to use an authorized contractor, this should be indicated. For the sake of uniformity, one contractor is often used for all exhibitors and this is especially true of trade shows or exhibitions. For outdoor events, this may not be so critical but helps to lessen the logistical burden.

If exhibitors have the option of choosing their own contractors, they still need to conform to event regulations in regard to colors, sizes, signage, etc. It helps if the event can provide a list of preferred service providers with a disclaimer that the event does not endorse one over another.

Contractors need to also be familiar with event regulations *prior to* exhibitors placing orders. It is recommended to use one or two contractors to avoid confusion, unless it is a big event where mass quantities of equipment are needed from numerous vendors.

Services and utilities order form. Exhibitors use this form to order specific services and/or utilities. The event may opt to include basic items in the booth fee and have the exhibitor use an "ala carte" checklist for additional items. The exhibitor pays any additional optional costs that were pre-determined when developing the exhibitor packet (e.g. extra electricity, ice, tables and chairs, etc.).

If the event collects the exhibitor forms, keep a master list (which can be sorted by booth name or booth number) as to which booths need what services. If forms are handed over to an exhibition services contractor, keep a copy in case there is a dispute about what the exhibitor did, or didn't, order. The other option is to require the exhibitor to mail forms directly to the contractor, but the downside is that you won't see them and will miss the opportunity to cross-check for accuracy.

If you go with an exhibition services company, meet with them ahead of time to discuss the best method for your event and various ways this can be handled. It is really simpler than it sounds.

Shipping and receiving information. Some exhibitors will want to ship their supplies in advance of the event, especially trade shows. Very specific shipping and receiving (a.k.a. drayage) information should be included in both the recruitment and confirmation materials. Some venues will not accept shipments in advance, so make sure to check before publishing the information.

Site plan or floor plan. These drawings show the pre-numbered layout of exhibitor booths within the site area or floor space. They are done to scale so that the number and locations of exhibitor spaces shown on the drawing are accurate. The plans should include aisles between major traffic lanes that are wide enough to accommodate attendees, registration areas, entry or access points, restrooms, pillars or other obstacles, food and beverage locations, stage, and other event elements.

NOTES

If possible, the plan should show the numerical location of exhibitor booths which provide a reference point for requests for specific booth locations (e.g. near the stage, on a corner, close to an entry).

If exhibitor booths are located at a convention center, it is helpful to show the layout of the exhibit space in relation to the rest of the convention space for that floor. An outdoor venue may locate the exhibitor booths in the center of a park, but without a drawing of the overall site, this would not be easily understood.

Examples of site plans are located in the Site Plans & Logistics chapter.

Confirmation process. Recruitment materials include information about confirmation processes for application approval, when they can expect to receive it, and what other actions may be required.

Confirmation materials should include general information, booth number, equipment and/or services ordered, load-in and set up schedules, event schedule, parking information, site map, registration procedures, and so on. *This information should go out a minimum of **30-45 days** in advance so exhibitors can pass the information on to their staff or suppliers who will facilitate their involvement.*

Hotel or lodging information. Exhibitors often need hotel accommodations or other lodging to facilitate their involvement. If the event has negotiated hotel room rates for attendees or exhibitors, information to help facilitate their planning should be included.

Determining Exhibitor Fees

Add together the cost of the exhibit facility rental, contracted services, insurance, security, or other related items. You may want to factor in a percentage (say 10-20%) of the overall expense budget to cover staff time, marketing, or other items from which the exhibitor indirectly receives benefit. Then divide this total by the total number of booth spaces to come up with a "cost per space" factor.

NOTES

Exhibitors requesting outside corner booths, food and beverage concessions, those located at entries or in highly visible locations should have to pay more than exhibitors placed in out-of-the-way locations or along back walls.

The number of complimentary booth spaces given to sponsors or in trade to service providers need to be considered. These booths do not directly generate revenue through exhibitor fees but the event must still bear the cost of providing the space and related amenities.

For example, if the event can take 100 exhibitors but 10 of the booth spaces are sponsors or trades, the event has 90 exhibitor spaces which can be sold to other parties. However, expenses to provide the exhibit spaces will apply for the full 100.

At the very least, the total revenue generated from exhibitor fees should more than cover the cost of having them there. Some events require a percentage of sales, in addition to an exhibitor fee, especially for food and beverage concessions that traditionally make the lion's share of sales.

Taking a percentage of sales is very difficult to track unless you have electronic registers. It also brings up a number of other questions that have to be dealt with. How will sales be monitored—honor system (doesn't work), duplicate cash register tapes, or by other means? Who will provide the equipment? Will food and beverage prices be capped to avoid price wars between food vendors? It's basically just opening Pandora's Box, so we recommend charging those exhibitors a larger fee to start with and avoid all the hassle.

Some events opt to use scrip or tickets as payment methods to track exhibitor sales, but this isn't very desirable because it creates "another line to stand in" before attendees can obtain their food, beverage, or entertainment. An exception would be a concert within a fair or festival that required a separate ticket purchase.

Exhibition Services Contractors

The use of a designated service contractor can be of great help when working with exhibitors. These are companies whose business is to work with exhibitors and they can be tremendous sources of information. Most have an assortment of exhibitor forms which can be used as-is or easily adapted.

These contractors can provide pipe and drape, equipment, install, dismantle, decorating, lighting, staging, drayage, tents, canopies, carpeting, booth construction, rigging, special effects, custom displays, sets and props, signs and graphics, personnel, and more.

The "shopping list" provided to exhibitors should include the price for each of the items that are outside those included in the standard booth fee. Stick to "normal" things as additions and if they want something fancy, the exhibitor can find it on their own.

Collect competitive bids and obtain references from several service providers before making a choice. Venues are often willing to provide the names of reputable companies. Include the service company's name, address, phone number, and other information in the exhibitor materials. The names of the contact persons for both the service company and the event should be provided.

Another thing to consider is the cut the service company will take if they handle the exhibitor interactions and you'll have to factor this into the exhibitor fee. Remember that the event will be in the middle of any dispute between the exhibitor and the service provider, so choose carefully who you work with.

Union Labor

Some venues require using union labor for set up, construction, tear down, or other services. Union requirements vary from city to city and venue to venue, so be sure to check on this since it adds costs.

Exhibitor Booth Structures

The industry standard on which service providers base their rates is a 10' x 10' exhibitor space (10' wide, 10' deep with an 8' back wall). Any variables are combinations of the 10' x 10' standard (e.g. 20' x 20' equals four 10' x 10' spaces). Back wall height is sometimes increased to a maximum of 16' depending on the event and/or venue. Side walls normally range 3' or 4' to 8'.

The main driver of the industry standard is the International Association for Exposition Management. They have created guidelines, rules, and regulations for continuity among exhibitions in North America and to comply with ADA, fire, safety, and other government requirements.

The most common booth types used for events are:

- **In-line or linear booth**—One side open to the aisle and arranged in a series along a straight line; standard 10' x 10' with an 8' back wall
- **Corner booth**—An in-line/linear booth that is exposed to aisles on two sides
- **Perimeter booth**—An in-line/linear booth that backs up to the wall of a facility rather than to another exhibit booth; maximum back wall height is 12'.
- **End cap booth**—Exposed to aisles on three sides; generally composed of two booths totaling 10' x 20'
- **Island booth**—Any size booth exposed to aisles on all four sides; a free-standing booth not abutted to linear booths or a fixed wall; typically 20' x 20' or larger in size
- **Peninsula booth**—Exposed to aisles on three sides; composed of a minimum of four 10' x 10' booths; usually backed up to linear booths

All booth types have height and distance restrictions that apply to display elements or signage, as well as to the booth itself.

Use the Exhibitor Worksheet at the end of the chapter to help framework exhibitor involvement.

Exhibitor Survey Worksheet

Use this worksheet to conduct a post-event survey of your exhibitors.

ALTER THE FORM TO FIT YOUR EVENT.

1. How did you learn about this event? _____
2. What motivated you to participate as an exhibitor? _____
3. What was your perception of the event as a whole? _____
4. Were you easily able to reach designated contact persons? _____
5. Was your booth request and confirmation handled in a timely manner? _____
6. Did you receive all the information you needed in advance of the event? _____
7. Where was your booth located? _____
8. Did you receive the booth amenities designated on your form? _____
9. Was there a good amount of traffic past your booth location? _____
10. How do you feel about the site layout in regard to the exhibitor booths? _____
11. Do you feel that event marketing was well targeted and produced results? _____
12. Do you feel that the participation of exhibitors is beneficial to the event? _____
13. Was the exhibition services contractor easy to work with and responsive? _____
14. Was the security adequate for exhibitors? _____
15. Were venue personnel helpful? _____
16. Did you have any problems with load-in or set up of your space? _____
17. Were personnel available to help you check in upon arrival? _____
18. Were electrical power, equipment, labor, or other support available if needed? _____
19. Did you require overnight lodging? If so, where did you stay? _____
20. What forms of transportation were needed to participate? _____
21. Was exhibitor parking available? _____
22. Were the shipping and receiving functions adequate? _____
23. How did you market your booth? _____
24. What parts of your exhibitor experience did you feel were best? _____
25. What things do you feel could have been done differently? _____
26. How would you rate your exhibitor experience (1 being poor, 5 being best)? _____
27. Would you be willing to participate again in the future? _____
28. _____
29. _____
30. _____

Good Neighbor Days Festival

2008 EXHIBITOR INFORMATION

Previous Exhibitor Deadline – August 9

New Applicant Deadline – August 16

PLEASE READ THE FOLLOWING CAREFULLY! Previous vendors not returning application forms by the deadline forfeit priority for location or inclusion. **NO EXCEPTIONS.**

Exhibitors agree to abide by these rules and regulations as a condition of participation. All persons working in booths are expected to know and conform to these regulations.

EVENT INFORMATION

What: **Good Neighbor Days Festival**

When: Friday, September 13 6-10pm
Saturday, September 14 11am-10pm
Sunday, September 15 11am-6pm

Where: Schiffler Park - Beaverton, Oregon

Event Management: Power Productions
503.332.5000

EXHIBITOR CATEGORIES

- **NONPROFIT**: Those applying in nonprofit categories **must show** legal verification of nonprofit status. A photocopy must be included with the application. **No proof, no participation, no exceptions.** Food, beverage and game booths **must be nonprofit organizations.** Those linking with commercial enterprises **must use booth revenue to support the nonprofit.** The name of the nonprofit will be listed as the booth exhibitor.
- **PRIVATE ARTS & CRAFTS:** Handmade goods sold for profit by private individuals. Arts and crafts are juried.
- **POLITICAL:** Candidates, legislative or political.
- **BUSINESS PROMOTION:** Businesses may promote their products and/or services. No sales.
- **OTHER:** Booths not fitting above descriptions.

Exhibitors Must Show Proof of Insurance.

GENERAL GUIDELINES

1. Management reserves the right to judge the suitability of all exhibitor booths and categories.
2. All booths will sell ONLY those items, or conduct those activities, approved as listed on the application. You may not operate outside your booth or in aisleways.
3. Management reserves the exclusive authority to assign booth locations or reassign as deemed appropriate considering the needs of the event as a whole. **Attempts will be made to honor requests for booth locations however the festival is under NO obligation to do so.**
4. **A 10' x 10' booth** space and one (1) 110v **electrical plug in are included in the booth fee.** Exhibitors supply their own booth structures, tables, extension cords, displays and other items. No "visqueen" type structures are permitted. We have provided a list of rates and providers who are familiar with our requirements.
5. Booths must fit into the designated 10' x 10' space, keeping all tents, ropes, supplies and other items **within** the booth space and aisle markings. If more space is required, it must be paid for. If in doubt, rent two booth spaces. **DO NOT GUESS—If you take more space than you "guessed," your location will be forfeited and you will be moved elsewhere!**
   TRAILERS: Exhibitors using trailers must include tongue length and window awnings in the booth space measurement. If protruding into another vendor's space, you will be moved. You must set up prior to other vendors due to space requirements.
6. **ONLY** the organization or business name registered with event management may identify your booth.
7. The **nonprofit's name must be most prominently displayed** for organizations sponsored by commercial enterprise
8. No amplified activity–including loud speakers, radios, musical or other noise making devices–is allowed except by permission of event management.
9. Cleanup of each booth area is the responsibility of individual booth vendors.

10. Garbage cans and liners are provided for inside and outside each booth. These will be emptied by litter patrol. **Do not** dump refuse into the public trash containers. If you need to have trash picked up, please notify event staff.

11. Grey water disposal receptacles will be provided. **Do not** dump wastewater on the ground!

12. Neither the City of Beaverton, Tualatin Hills Park & Recreation District, the sponsors, sub-contractors, nor Power Productions will be responsible for any items which are lost, stolen or damaged.

13. Security is provided Thursday through Sunday night, however, exhibitors should not leave valuables unattended.

FOOD BOOTHS

1. **Food booths are limited to fundraisers for nonprofit organizations only.** No commercial enterprises are allowed to sell for themselves. Violators will be removed without a refund.

2. The number of food booths will be limited. Previous exhibitors submitting their applications by the deadline will receive priority over new applicants.

3. **No one vendor will be given an exclusive right to sell a particular food item.** We impose a limit of two (2) vendors selling identical foods, however, this is discouraged.

4. Food vendors **may not alter food items from what is listed on the application** without approval. Violations will result in closure of your booth without a refund. Booths will be monitored for compliance.

5. A sign showing price of meals, beverages and other items is to be posted according to what is listed on the application.

6. All cooking activity must take place within the designated booth space. Exhibitors needing to cook outside the booth structure must pay for additional space and block off the cooking area for public safety. **NO EXCEPTIONS.**

7. Enforcement of health safety will be conducted by the Washington County Health Department for all food booths. Food concessions are required to have a temporary restaurant license and booth workers must have a current food handler permit.

8. Exhibitors may sell any soft drink beverage, ice tea, lemonade, coffee, etc. No alcoholic beverages. All beverages must be listed on the application form. **No beverages in glass containers are allowed.**

9. Ice may be purchased from the City of Beaverton booth. Pay by cash or check at time of purchase. We need an estimate of how many 40# bags of cocktail ice you expect to use before we place the order. Please indicate this on your application.

POLITICAL BOOTHS

1. Political booths shall be informational or educational in keeping with the spirit of the event.

2. All activity must remain INSIDE the booth.

ARTS & CRAFTS BOOTHS

1. Products will be juried prior to application approval:
- Items must be made by the craftsperson.
- Handcrafted components must dominate any commercial components.
- Starting materials must be significantly altered or enhanced by the craftsperson.
- Items must meet basic expectations of product life, function and safety.

2. Management reserves the right to accept/refuse any item. **Items not reviewed may not be sold.**

3. Email or send a photo of your product(s) with the completed application form.

4. **Crafts persons assume responsibility for the honest representation of their work.**

FIRE REGULATIONS

1. The areas within and surrounding each booth shall be kept clear of unnecessary combustible material.

2. Cooking appliances shall be used in accordance with manufacturer's instructions. Fuel supplies shall be handled/stored properly to prevent accidents.

3. Charcoal or gas barbecues may be used. Ignition of barbecue fuels must be conducted in a safe manner

4. All cooking activity must take place in the designated booth space or according to food booth regulations.

5. Cooking appliances shall be on a sturdy base, stand or table to prevent being knocked over.

6. All electrical devices shall be approved. Distribution cables/cords must be adequate size and properly installed.

7. A fire extinguisher of not less than 2A-10BC UL rating shall be provided at all locations where cooking is done. A minimum of one 40BC size extinguisher is required where deep fat fryers are used.

8. Booth framework must be of flame retardant material or have flame spread of less than 200.

9. Structures in excess of 200 square feet must meet requirements of the Uniform Fire Code.

Good Neighbor Days Festival

September 13-15, 2008

2008 EXHIBITOR APPLICATION

Previous Exhibitor Deadline – August 9

New Applicant Deadline – August 16

PLEASE READ RULES AND REGULATIONS CAREFULLY BEFORE SUBMITTING APPLICATION.

Organization/Company Name _____ Contact _____

Mailing Address _____

City/State/Zip _____ Day Phone _____

E-Mail _____ Fax _____

Nonprofit Organizations Only

☐ Food $500
☐ Game $350
☐ Display Only $200
☐ Misc. Sales $350

Other Categories

☐ Arts & Crafts $250
☐ Political $200
☐ Business promo $250

Application Fee $ _____

Extra Electricity Fee $ _____

($75 if applicable)

Ice pre-pay ____ bags @ $4 $ _____

TOTAL $ _____

No Refunds Will Be Given After August 13 or for Inclement Weather

---

DESCRIBE ALL BOOTH ACTIVITIES. FOOD VENDORS MUST LIST ALL FOODS/BEVERAGES AND PRICING.

_____
_____
_____
_____

PAYMENT METHOD: ☐ Cash ☐ Check ☐ VISA ☐ MasterCard ☐ AmEx

Credit Card No. _____ Exp. Date _____ 3-digit Code _____

Name on Card _____ Signature _____

BY MAIL: Good Neighbor Days
Street Address
City/State/Zip

BY PHONE: 503.332.5000
BY FAX: 503.000.0000
BY EMAIL: powerproductions@comcast.net

HOLD HARMLESS: I, the undersigned applicant for exhibitor privileges, hereby agree to indemnify and hold harmless the Good Neighbor Days Festival, the City of Beaverton, Tualatin Hills Park & Recreation District, Power Productions, sponsors, promoters, subcontractors, their officials, employees and agents, from all liability, damage, loss, injury, cost or expense including, but not limited to attorney fees, arising from participation in this event by self, agents, employees, customers, invitees, or guests. I further agree to abide by the regulations set forth in the Exhibitor Guidelines and attest that I am duly authorized to sign this agreement on behalf of the organization or company listed above, or as a private party. This agreement is binding on inure of successors and assigns of the indemnities and the applicant.

Signature _____ Print Name _____ Date _____

HAVE YOU... Enclosed Payment? Signed the Application? Ordered Ice? Ordered Electricity?

OFFICE USE ONLY

Date Paid _____ Proof of Nonprofit Status ____ Insurance ____ Ice ____ Electrical ____ Permits ____

Good Neighbor Days Festival

ELECTRICAL INFORMATION

You must indicate whether or not your exhibitor space requires electricity. One 110 volt electrical outlet is provided for each exhibitor. Those requiring more than 1,000 watts are required to pay an additional $75 fee to cover the extra costs for electricity and to have a licensed electrician oversee electrical usage by exhibitors exceeding the 1,000 watt limit.

Contact Name for Your Booth's Electrical Requirements _____

Day Phone _____ Cell Phone _____ Email _____

Will this person be available during your booth set up? _____ What day? _____ What time? _____

LIST ALL ELECTRICAL ITEMS TO BE USED AND THE WATTAGE/AMPERAGE EACH REQUIRES.

Vendors are responsible for supplying their own UL approved electrical cords

Description of Appliance or Electrical Item	Watts	Amps
❏ We Do Not Require Electricity TOTAL		

✳ ICE ESTIMATE ✳

Please indicate the amount of ice—based on **40# bags of cocktail ice**—you ESTIMATE to use. **Pay only for what you actually use.** Order enough ice to cover your needs for ALL DAYS of the festival. The ice company is making only one delivery. We may have very limited quantities of extra ice available but only until it is gone. The weather is typically between 75-85° during the festival so plan accordingly.

FRIDAY ____ **40# bags**   **SATURDAY** ____ **40# bags**   **SUNDAY** ____ **40# bags**

The ice truck is located near the City of Beaverton booth. Your ice usage will be monitored
by a checklist kept by the volunteer manning the ice truck.
The best method is to pay for ice in advance with your application (over payments will be refunded).
You may also purchase ice on site at the City of Beaverton booth by cash or check at time of pick up. No credit sales.

THANK YOU.
Filling out this form in advance helps ensure there is enough electricity and ice for everyone.

Chocoholiday™ is a trade show opportunity for all chocolate-related businesses, products, or services. Chocoholiday exhibitors pay a flat fee and are not required to pay a percentage of sales. The event centers around chocolate, however, it is not mandatory that every item offered be chocolate.

The event has been designed to appeal to people of all ages and will be heavily publicized through an extensive marketing campaign courtesy of our media and print sponsors. Net proceeds from the event will benefit the XYZ Charity.

We encourage you to apply now due to limited space. This year's exhibitors will receive preference next year. **Please read the packet carefully.** Exhibitors are expected to comply with regulations set forth.

EVENT INFORMATION

What: Chocoholiday

When:

Friday, December 3	10am-9pm
Saturday, December 4	10am-9pm
Sunday, December 5	10am-5pm

Where: Red Lion Lloyd Center – Portland, OR

Event Management: Power Productions
503.332.5000

EXHIBITOR CATEGORIES

Standard Exhibitor entry fee is $500. This includes a 10' x 10' exhibit space, pipe and drape, one 8' topped and skirted table, vinyl lettered sign, waste basket and exhibitor listing in event advertising. Other equipment may be brought in or ordered through our exhibit services contractor, Imaginary Exposition Services.

Corner spaces are available for $950 on a first-come, first-served basis. Exhibitors may purchase more than one booth space. Special needs will be handled individually.

All fees must be paid at time of registration and proof of insurance is required.

EXHIBITOR REGULATIONS

1. **Liability**—Exhibitor is solely responsible for space leased and shall not deface the premises. This includes use of pins, tacks, hooks, nails, screws, or adhesive products. Exhibitor agrees to reimburse management or sub-contractor for any loss or damage occurring to equipment or premises due to exhibitor's participation.
2. **Exhibit Display**—No partitions, shelves, signs, etc. may extend more than eight (8) feet above the floor along the rear of the exhibit. Exhibitors may not obstruct the view, create safety hazards, or adversely affect displays of others.
3. **Exhibit Space**—Contracted space is for sole use by the registered exhibitor. Exhibitors may share space but no portion of the exhibitor's space may be assigned or sublet without permission of management. Exhibitor will forfeit right to space without refund for failure to comply.

   All exhibitor activity must be contained within the assigned space and may not be conducted in aisles or outside the booth space.
4. **Restrictions**—Management reserves the right to restrict or remove any exhibits without refund that have been falsely entered or are deemed to be unsuitable to the family-oriented purpose of Chocoholiday. This applies, but is not limited to, conduct, noise, public address systems, printed materials, or interfering with the conduct of business in other spaces.
5. **Compliance**—Exhibitors must comply with all event, health, fire, and safety regulations.
6. **Alcoholic Beverages**—The general public may consume wine at exhibitor tasting stations. Exhibitors conducting this activity must comply with Oregon Liquor Control Commission special event permit requirements and provide insurance.

   Exhibitors, employees, or their agents shall not consume alcoholic beverages on duty. Failure to comply will result in shutdown of your booth.
7. **Food & Beverage Sales**—Exhibitors may not sell or distribute food or beverage items not registered with event management. Multnomah County Health Department temporary restaurant license requirements apply. A copy of your approved license must be submitted to event management no less than one week in advance.

TERMS & CONDITIONS

1. **Indemnification**—Exhibitor agrees to indemnify and hold harmless event management, XYZ Charity, the Red Lion Lloyd Center, sponsors, volunteers, sub-contractors, and the their officers, assignees, guests, heirs, or visitors from and against any and all claims, damages, losses, and expenses including attorney fees arising from exhibitor's participation in the Chocoholiday event.

2. **Insurance**—Proof of insurance is required. If the exhibitor does not have insurance coverage, special event insurance is available through Gales Creek Insurance. Please contact management for details.

3. **Licenses**—Any and all city, county or state licenses, inspections or permits required by law of any exhibitor are to be obtained at exhibitor's expense. This includes temporary restaurant licenses from the Multnomah County Health Department, or special event permit through Oregon Liquor Control Commission. Copies of approved permits must be provided to management no less than one week in advance of event.

4. **Cancellation Policy**—If exhibitor withdraws, or participation is cancelled by management for any reason, fees paid shall be retained as follows:

    60 days or more in advance – 100% refund
    31 days or more in advance – 50% refund
    30 days or less – No refund

All cancellations must be in writing and must be received in event office by specified deadlines.

5. **Rights of Management**—Neither Chocoholiday, XYZ Charity, nor event management will be liable for damages or expenses incurred by the exhibitor in the circumstance the event is delayed, interrupted, or not held as scheduled due to acts of God, emergency, or for any other reason beyond management's control.

6. **Assignment**—Management may assign, sell, or transfer any or all of its rights, benefits, privileges, obligations, or duties under this agreement.

7. **Complete Agreement**—Exhibitor, by signing and submitting application, and upon acceptance, attests that exhibitor has read and agrees to abide by the rules and regulations set forth in these exhibitor materials and agrees to act in good faith in all circumstances relating to exhibitor's participation.

HOTEL ROOMS

Discounted hotel room rates are being offered by the Red Lion Lloyd Center for Chocoholiday exhibitors or guests. Please contact the Red Lion directly to make arrangements 503.333.0000.

MISCELLANEOUS

1. **Exhibitor Confirmations**—Initial confirmation will be sent upon receipt of application form, registration fee, and proper documentation. Exhibitors will receive final confirmation packets no less than 30 days in advance containing exhibit space number, set up/tear down schedules, site map, location map, event schedule, exhibitor identification badges, parking passes, and other supplemental information.

2. **Exhibition Services Contractor**—Basic exhibit space amenities are provided through our service contractor, Imaginary Exhibition Services. Exhibitors will receive order forms and information well in advance to enable them to take advantage of the 30% discount for this event on additional equipment or supplies. Please contact Name at IES 503.000.0000 for assistance.

Payment for equipment or supplies rented outside of the standard exhibitor benefits must be made a minimum of 14 days prior to the event to receive the discount. An IES representative will be on site during exhibitor set up on December 2 to fill last minute requests.

3. **Shipping**—*No shipments will be accepted by the Red Lion Lloyd Center prior to December 1.* Shipments must be clearly marked for Chocoholiday event and addressed to Red Lion Lloyd Center Receiving. Shipments may not exceed more than 2 boxes measuring 36" x 36" or no more than 72" x 36" total space per exhibitor.

4. **Set Up**—Exhibitor move in and set up begins Thursday, December 2 from 8:00 am until 8:00 pm. The loading dock will also be open at this time. Exhibitors are required to vacate the premises by 9:00 p.m. and no set up will be allowed past 9:00.

4. **Tear Down**—Move out and tear down will commence after the public has left the premises on Sunday, December 5 (approximately 5:30 pm.). The Exhibit Hall will remain open until 9:00 p.m. IES and event management will be on site from 7:00 am until 11:00 am on Monday. All exhibitor equipment or supplies must be removed no later than 10:00.

5. **Security**—Event security will be provided by Red Lion personnel. The Exhibit Hall will also be locked and monitored during non-event hours.

6. **Storage**—Fire regulations prohibit storage of boxes, crates, packing materials, and/or more than a one-day supply of literature in exhibitor's space.

EVENT MANAGEMENT
Power Productions - 503.332.5000
powerproductions@comcast.net

Exhibitor Worksheet

Use this worksheet to framework exhibitor participation.

ALTER THE FORM TO FIT YOUR EVENT.

Working With Exhibitors

1. What types of exhibitors will be included? _____
2. Does the event site have sufficient space for exhibitors, and attendees? _____
3. What is the maximum number of exhibitors that can be accommodated? _____
4. What is the maximum capacity for attendees after exhibitor space is deducted? _____
5. Have exhibitor fees for booth types/sizes been determined? _____
6. Are electrical power and other utilities available? _____
7. Who will be the contact person for exhibitors? _____
8. How will exhibitors be recruited? _____
9. What communications will exhibitors receive? _____
10. Will exhibitors be allowed to select their booth locations? _____
11. How will exhibitors receive marketing exposure through the event? _____
12. Is use of union labor required? _____
13. Is an exhibition services contractor involved? _____
14. What services will the exhibition services contractor provide? _____
15. Does the contractor handle exhibitor sign up and equipment orders? _____

Recruitment Materials

1. Does the "pitch" information motivate exhibitors to sign up? _____
2. Have exhibitor guidelines been developed? _____
3. Does the application form contain contact, cost, size, and payment information? _____
4. Have you communicated the assignment process for booth locations? _____
5. What are the exhibitor hours for the event? _____
6. Has a load-in, set up and tear-down schedule been developed? _____
7. Has the exhibitor service contractor's information been included? _____
8. Have you provided shipping and receiving information? _____
9. Is the floor or site plan accurate? _____
10. Is lodging or transportation information available for exhibitors? _____
11. Have you outlined the confirmation process and dates? _____
12. _____

Exhibitor Worksheet

Use this worksheet to framework exhibitor participation.

ALTER THE FORM TO FIT YOUR EVENT.

Confirmation Materials
1. Have you provided the exhibitor with the correct booth number? _____
2. Has the exhibitor received all information and schedules? _____
3. Have you explained about parking, load-in, and tear-down procedures? _____
4. What is the process for exhibitor check-in upon arrival? _____
5. _____
6. _____

After the Event
1. Have exhibitors been thanked for their participation? _____
2. Have they been apprised of the event results? _____
3. Have they received an Exhibitor Survey and postage-paid return envelope? _____
4. Have you evaluated the survey results to use in planning the next event? _____
5. Which things went well? _____
6. What things would you do differently? _____
7. _____
8. _____

Chapter 12 – Production & Entertainment

The "Dazzle" Is In The Details.

It takes many people working together to create the look and feel of a great event that makes people say "Wow, this is really amazing!" Ideally, we would all have big budgets to create show-stopping events but in actuality, it often takes a lot of creative planning.

Think about how the event can encompass the senses—sight, smell, hearing, touch, and taste—then strive to create a sensory experience.

There are a number of ways to create ambience as well—décor, staging, electronic visual media, lighting, sound, rental equipment, and other means—that fall into the production category.

"Tonight, we've got a Really Big show."

Ed Sullivan

Production and entertainment elements create energy and excitement because they set the tone for the event. They should build emotion, make people want to get into the theme, change the pace, add an element of surprise, and create those "magic moments" that your guests or audience will long remember.

The first section of this chapter is on *Production* and covers:

- ➢ Production elements and selection of contractors
- ➢ Decisions about décor
- ➢ Use of stages, sound, lighting and electronic visual media
- ➢ Time allocation for load-in, set up, and tear down
- ➢ Making choices in rental equipment

The second section of the chapter covers *Entertainment*:
- ➢ Determining what entertainment works best
- ➢ Using a talent agent or hiring it yourself
- ➢ Answering questions regarding contracting and pricing

Production

This chapter gives a broad introduction of what production entails. Since methods and technology are constantly changing, this information does not give minute details, and is general in nature.

The very best way to gain basic knowledge about production is to link up with reputable contractors who are happy to discuss how they can enhance your event and how what they do fits in with other production elements. Talk to several companies and decide which one is the best fit. It is to their benefit to spend time with you because they want the business, and you will learn a great deal.

Once you select production contractors, hold an initial group meeting to discuss your event. You'll find that most of these companies work together on a regular basis at various events and venues. They may already have worked out any logistical concerns and can easily make modifications for your event. The decorating company, contractors, and/or venue can assist in completing the site plan. Make sure all parties have the most recent version of the plan at all times so they are not operating from outdated information.

Another excellent source of ideas and articles is Special Events magazine, a publication of the International Special Events Society (ISES). There are many publications that are free for the asking, both printed and on-line that you can use for reference about events, trade shows, marketing, and more.

The Venue

No room or location was designed specifically for your event, so look for one that works from both a practical and aesthetic standpoint. Consider the ceiling height, available natural and artificial light, and the capacity to accommodate decorations, lighting, sound, or video equipment that may need to stand on the floor or be hung from the ceiling.

Electrical Power Supply

Lighting, sound, electronic visual media, and possibly décor providers all require electrical power. The availability of electrical service is a chief consideration when selecting a facility or venue. Not every event needs electrical service, but always ask about availability and cost. Certain venues charge a substantial fee for power usage, while some charge none.

Stage lighting alone can easily draw 600-1200 amps of electrical current. As a reference point, the electrical outlets in your home are 15 or 20 amps, so you can see why it is important to know capacity.

Working With Contractors

Allow plenty of time for production contractors to do their work. If there isn't enough time, they won't be able to do a quality job. It's incredibly difficult to transform a venue with staging, décor, sound, lighting, and visual media in a two or three hour time period, and the bigger the event, the more time is needed

Ask each vendor how much time they will require to load in, set up, and tear down, then reserve the venue for as much time as necessary to conduct these activities. Don't assume that the time needed will be available unless you have reserved it. Many venues are booked down to the hour with back-to-back events and will charge extra to reserve more time. This is critical if your event follows another one and they are late in getting out of the way because it significantly impacts the amount of time you have to load in and set up.

Coordinate schedules to be sure everything happens in the right order. You don't want to pay a crew to stand around and wait for something else to be done. Contractors can determine the proper order among themselves. Don't be afraid to rely on their expertise. You'll want to be sure to document the order in which things will occur in your logistics schedule.

NOTES

Dot the "I's" and cross the "T's." No matter what services are contracted, negotiate because package deals are more cost-effective for both the event and the contractor. Put all agreements in writing. *If it isn't documented, it technically doesn't exist and the contractor is under no obligation to provide it.*

Get references. Don't depend on a contractor that has nice equipment but is unreliable. If they show up an hour late for the set up, those who follow them won't be able to complete their obligations on time. And don't rely on appearances. Some of the most professional looking people can provide the poorest service.

Dress It With Décor

The décor industry is built around the creation of visual effect. This can include everything from table centerpieces to all kinds of props that add to the charm, whimsy, or classiness of an event.

The décor is one of the main drivers around which other production takes place—staging, visual media, lighting, sound—and contractors must work together to determine who will do what and when.

If the décor includes a ceiling treatment, the décor company needs to coordinate timing with the venue. They don't want to arrive to set the ceiling only to find the venue has already placed the dinner tables and chairs (which have to be moved). Also, the ceiling treatment needs to go up before other productions elements are able to set up.

It's definitely worth a visit to a local company to see what they can offer. See the equipment first-hand or look at photo albums of their work to determine quality. Look under event services, convention services, or party suppliers in the Yellow Pages or on-line.

If you live in a city that has an annual trade show for event planners, this is an excellent way to meet representatives of décor companies or other production contractors who are participating as exhibitors.

Theme or Mood?

Early in the event cycle, you may have adopted a theme. The theme should tie auction elements together—logos, invitations, brochures, decorations, signage, video, food, and others. The venue will also come into play, especially if it lends itself to the theme (e.g. a safari theme for an event held at the zoo).

It is sometimes tedious to come up with an event theme every year. Or, the theme may be an inappropriate fit. An example of this is an event that chose the theme "A Night To Remember." The problem was that it was an event for the Alzheimer's Foundation!

A traditional example of a "themed" event is a 1950s-1960s dinner dance for a demographic of Baby Boomers. Bring in classic cars, build a big jukebox with balloons and chaser lights, and hire entertainment that enhances the fun. The wait staff could wear blue jeans and white t-shirts. You'll create energy and excitement!

Another way to use décor is through creation of a "mood" as opposed to a formal theme. An example of this is a million-dollar charity auction formerly managed by the author held at a local hotel ballroom featuring luminaries of the wine and culinary worlds.

One year the desired "mood" was a classic, old-money feel. The décor consisted of tenting the ballroom ceiling and walls with sheer fabric in soft, earthy tones. An enormous chandelier was created with silk flowers, dangling crystals, and twinkling lights as the focal point for the ceiling. Tables were topped with a sheer gold-tone fabric over the hotel's wheat-colored linens. Centerpieces were bronze-colored roses in clay urns. Antique gold chair covers were placed over the hotel's banquet chairs.

The entire effect was breathtaking using a combination of décor and standard hotel banquet equipment. Volunteers helped perform some of the decorating activities which resulted in additional cost savings.

The point is that regardless of event size, type, or budget use what equipment is included in the facility rental and enhance it to whatever degree you are able.

Props

Renting props is a wise choice for cash-conscious events because it normally costs less to rent an existing prop than it does to make one. Prop houses have a wide range of items in stock for nearly any theme or budget. If what you need isn't readily available, they can often create props for your event which are then put into their inventory for future use by others.

Visit a local prop supplier and check out the inventory. It is lots of fun to wander the aisles and see how much there is to choose from, and it triggers ideas. Make sure the props are in good condition. It's better to pay a little more for well-maintained décor than to have it look shabby. To be fair, props do take a beating in multiple uses, so take that into account.

One drawback to using local prop houses is that guests who attend many events may find themselves seeing the same props over and over again. To avoid this, use props that can be easily customized to fit the theme and/or change their appearance.

As a general rule, unless you plan to use a prop many times, it's best to rent. If you opt to create your own props, you need to think about the time it will take, the labor involved, and where to store them.

Critical Décor Considerations

Set priorities. Focus on the major impact areas rather than spreading a lot of little things all over the place that no one will notice. The stage should be the number one priority, followed by entrances and food areas. Ceiling treatments have high visual impact but cost dearly because they are very labor intensive to create. Consider using volunteers for activities such as placing table linens, centerpieces, chair covers and like activities to save money.

Scale. Keep the scale of the venue and how the prop or décor will be used in mind when making your selections. Something that looks really huge in a showroom can look miniscule in a big ballroom or outdoors.

Staging

Stages come in many sizes and shapes from a single 4' x 8' or 6' x 8' riser to an elaborate outdoor stage with roofing. Most hotels and convention facilities have 6' x 8' portable riser sections with limited or no height adjustment. Rental companies typically have 4'x 4' or 4' x 8' riser sections that can be set at several heights with a maximum of 30"-36". A good staging company can create stages of any size, height, or combination.

The primary function of a stage at an event is to serve the speaker or entertainer. Stage requirements may also be listed in an entertainer's performance contract. Other factors include the size of the room and the size of the audience. Using a small stage in a large room will make the speaker appear small and unimportant. The size of the audience will also help in determining stage height.

The shape of the stage can create impact as well. Using a multi-layered stage with a thrust, runway, or island can help create a level of elegance or grandeur (e.g. a fashion show). Once the stage is set up, make sure to check that the surface is solid. You don't want anyone to trip on an uneven stage or to have it pull apart.

One person stage setups. A simple fold-out design, easily rolled into position, and set up by one person. They are made of plywood with a heavy gauge steel frame that folds out to form the stage floor.

Performance risers. Many sizes and leg heights for maximum options. Sections come in 3' or 4' widths and 4'-6'-8' lengths. Stage sections are attached to steel frames and folding heavy tubular steel legs with safety locks. Stairs or guard rail are optional.

Modular scaffolding and decking. Heavy-duty versions of the more simple forms featuring heavy gauge steel pipe and plywood decking, providing excellent versatility even in extremely challenging settings such as slopes or windy areas. Set up is time consuming and labor intensive.

Mobile stages. Basically, a large stage on a semi-truck trailer that folds out to create a roofed structure. These are cost effective because they can be set up by a 2-3 man crew within a couple of hours since everything is done by hydraulics. These are great for outdoor events or large indoor venues like arenas.

Regardless which kind of stage you need, talk to a professional company and they can steer you in the right direction.

Audio & Visual

It wasn't all that long ago that the audio and visual elements of an event meant a slide or overhead projector, a projection screen, and possibly a TV/VCR setup. Today, the role that audio and visual elements play in our events is anything but simple. Increasing demands for "larger than production and constantly changing technology, mean that our audiences will expect us to keep up with the times.

Technically, audio visual relates to three main areas—sound, lighting, and electronic visual media. In other words, equipment that is used to help people "hear" (audio) and "see" (visual).

Audio Reinforcement (Sound)

You can have the most expensive lighting, the greatest video, and unbelievable sets or decorations, but if your audience can't hear and understand the speaker or entertainer, the direct result is a loss of interest.

Audio systems can range from the built-in systems to full concert systems. The size and complexity of the system depends on the audience size, intended use, the type of space, and the type of sound that is being amplified. Sound systems usually involve the use of professional sound technicians, but smaller systems can be rented for individual use if you don't need sophisticated equipment.

In-house (built-in) audio systems. In-house audio systems are typically speakers mounted on the ceiling or wall of meeting rooms or large spaces like a ballroom. Multiple microphone jacks are spaced throughout the room with amplifiers, volume controls, and any signal processing located in another room. These are normally adequate for speaking with hand-held or podium microphones, but not for conducting an auction or a large event.

Small audio systems. The basic audio package consists of a small audio mixer (a.k.a. sound board), an amplifier, and speakers on floor stands. The mixer and amplifier may be combined in a single unit. These systems can be used for groups of up to 250-300 set in a theatre design depending on the quality of the system. A minimum of four speakers are needed to better cover the entire room. If music is an important element, sub (woofer) cabinets will help bring out the lower frequencies.

Large audio systems. For larger indoor and all outdoor events, more substantial systems are required. These systems will include several speaker cabinets, amplifier racks, mixer, and process racks. The speakers can be ground supported, usually at the same height as the stage and placed on speaker wings that are built on the sides of the stage. The sound technician and the sound board are typically located at the back of the room, or for outdoor events, are at least 50' out front and facing the stage.

Another option is to hang (fly) the speakers from the ceiling or stage roof. This requires more time to set up than ground support but increases system efficiency and frees up floor space.

Delay Systems. For large crowds, in large spaces, or in long and narrow rooms, it makes sense to add more audio speakers to help the people in the back hear as well as those in the front. Adding delay systems allows everyone to feel a sense of intimacy with what's happening on the stage. This is exactly the same rationale as why we need large video screens so the people in the back can see.

These sound systems are called delay systems because the audio is adjusted (delayed) through each added set of speakers so that the timing between the front and rear speakers is natural sounding.

Microphones. The most common audio source for voice is the microphone. Microphones may be used at a podium, on a stand, hand-held, or wireless. Wireless is by far the microphone of preference.

Wireless microphones give a speaker or entertainer the ability to walk the stage or go out into the audience and have their hands free to gesture or do other tasks. The most common wireless microphones come in hand-held, lavaliere or headset configuration.

Use of an audio equalizer is recommended. The sound technician will work with the individual frequencies to achieve the maximum effect without feedback.

Stage & Ambient Lighting

Lighting can play a key role in your success. Whether the event is large or small, well-planned lighting can help transform the stage and other visual elements from ordinary to outstanding.

When it comes to venues, most existing lighting is basic, utilitarian, minimal and unattractive. If you want something else, a professional lighting company is the best place to find what you need.

NOTES

NOTES

Costs. If you need a small lighting package, it's sometimes more cost-effective to rent the professional lighting equipment and set it up yourself, especially if the budget is less than $500. Even $800-$1,000 is considered reasonable for lighting rentals. If you need to spend more than $1,000 to obtain the desired effect, you'll probably need professional technicians.

Regardless of whether you just rent the lighting equipment, or contract for full lighting services, get quotes from several vendors and be honest about the budget. Lighting for the same event can cost from $500 to $5,000. The only difference is in the size of the lighting package and the budget.

When obtaining quotes from vendors, very rarely are you comparing identical products and/or services. Look the bids over carefully and don't be afraid to ask questions to clarify exactly what equipment and services are included.

Uses. Most of us tend to think of lighting the stage and/or the entertainment first, but even minimal lighting can enhance the event experience.

Up-lighting walls with a color wash (placing colored celluloid plastic sheets over a light source) softens the overall effect and adds color to the space. Projecting a gobo of a logo or design on the wall or ceiling adds interest or conveys messages. Lighting décor and props add a new dimension to their effectiveness. All events can benefit from enhanced lighting, no matter how simple.

Permissions. Some activities may require permits or special permissions from the venue, city, fire marshal, or other parties. These activities may include loading dock use, lasers, pyrotechnics, use of open flames, chemical fog or strobe lights, generator location, and use of property owned or maintained by municipal jurisdictions (e.g. streets, parks, etc.).

Electronic Visual Media

Electronic visual media refers to the use of electronic and software tools such as video and data/video projectors, PowerPoint, slides and other electronic communications.

The primary purpose of using visual media production is to broaden the total experience of event-goers. This simply means to more effectively provide information, create intimacy, extend the design, build the brand, and engage the visual senses.

Video/Image Magnification. The primary purpose of image magnification (I-MAG) is to create intimacy between a speaker or entertainer and the audience. Experts agree that while 7% of our communication is based on words and 38% is based on tone of voice, 55% of communication is based on body language.

The powerful intimate messages expressed by our eyes and facial expressions are often lost in large groups. By providing a conduit for personal experience, image magnification helps each guest to feel more like a participant than an observer. Even in groups of 20,000 or more people, larger-than-life screens strategically placed can allow someone in the very back row to make eye contact.

Depending on the site or room configuration, image magnification should be considered for an audience of 300 or more. The cost for electronic visual media varies, so if you opt to use this method, you'll want to obtain quotes from several companies who do this work.

Video. Video is also a powerful tool for playback of pre-produced programs and image magnification using live cameras.

Pre-produced video programs can set or enhance the mood of the event. Whether used as openers, lead-ins to subjects, speaker introductions, or informational segments, video (when used well) will amplify the total effectiveness of the event.

PowerPoint. The current version of the slide projector is the presentation graphics program, PowerPoint. Combined with a late-model laptop computer and LCD projector, this method is ideal for providing visual or text support and offers a high degree of flexibility for last minute updates.

Surprisingly, the greatest disadvantage to PowerPoint is its ease of use. Because building a PowerPoint presentation is relatively simple for people who are not trained professionals, presentations can be prone to design errors, misspellings, graphics that are too big, type that is too small, outlandish color combinations, and general feeling of haphazard construction.

There are fewer, more effective ways to undermine a message and add distractions than to use a high-tech tool to present an amateur low-tech image.

Slide projectors. With the advent of digital cameras and software programs like PowerPoint, slide projectors aren't used much in the current market. They can still be a great tool, but 35mm slides are expensive to produce and over time will decrease in visual quality.

If you have slides that are used for presentations, we recommend having them transferred onto a CD so that they can be used with computerized technology and the quality will not deteriorate.

The Right People

Nothing can replace the most important ingredient in effective sound, lighting, and visual communications—a top-quality professional team. These technically savvy team members will help your event to be polished and professional with a sense of timing and flow that will impress your audience. If you're not more than adequate in these disciplines, hire people who are.

Rental Equipment

Not only are equipment rental companies good sources of event needs, they are also great sources for ideas! By visiting their showroom, you'll gain lots of knowledge about what others have done. Most rental companies have promotional photographs and brochures in addition to what's on view in the showroom.

Work closely with a designated representative throughout the planning process. Based on the venue and theme, they can help make educated choices as to which items are needed and in what quantities. Rental items should complement other event elements and be in good condition.

Inventory. Rental companies carry an amazing array of inventory of nearly every kind of need. If they don't have what you're looking for, they know who does and can obtain it for you. Just like walking through a prop house, a trip through the warehouse will reveal many options from which to choose, some of which you may not have even considered.

Among the things you'll find are tents, tent liners, fencing, tables, scaffold-type staging, chairs, chair covers, arches, linens, flatware, glasses, dishes, flatware, catering equipment, and everything in between. These items can vary from plain to fancy depending on the rental company. Many also carry sound, lighting, or other equipment. *More information on equipment use is contained in the chapter on Site Planning.*

Communication rentals. There are rental companies who specialize in communication equipment such as portable radios, cellular phones or pagers. Check to make sure the equipment is well-maintained. Since communicating with each other during the event will depend on the proper functioning of this equipment, make sure someone is on call in case problems occur. It's always a good idea to ask for a quick lesson in operating the equipment prior to the event and to have extra batteries, as well as battery chargers on hand.

NOTES

Reserve equipment with a deposit. To ensure the rental equipment will be available when it is needed, a deposit will be required to secure the order. Each rental company has only a certain number of tents, chairs, tables, and other items available at any given point. This is especially true of the summer months when multiple events occurring simultaneously may stretch the company's inventory to the limit.

Reserve the rental equipment as far in advance as possible. Not only will you be assured of obtaining the equipment you need, you won't wind up with the "dregs" of what's left over after everyone else has gotten the really good stuff because they had the foresight to reserve in advance.

Rental items are reserved on a first-come, first-served basis. No matter how well-prepared you are, there are always additions or deletions to the original equipment order. Reserving the majority of the equipment in advance should keep these changes to a minimum.

The event will also be held responsible for repair or replacement of any items that are lost, stolen, damaged, or broken.

Delivery, set up and returns. A charge is usually assessed for delivery, set up and return of rental items if this is done by the rental company. Make sure these charges are included on the list of equipment ordered. Don't automatically assume everything is taken care of by the rental company unless it is listed in the rental contract.

Audio visual equipment. If you have rented sound, lighting, or visual equipment, be sure that it is in good working order prior to the event. Make note of anything out of the ordinary so that you don't get charged for damage you didn't cause. After the equipment has been set up, test it out to make sure it works properly. Nothing is more frustrating to someone who is trying to impress the audience than to have the tools that are supposed to help them become a hindrance. Spare bulbs or extension cords should be available.

Entertainment

Some events include live music and/or dancing, or the event may have other forms of entertainment. The entertainment is often one of the biggest audience draws and encompasses a vast array of talents and activities from which to choose.

Entertainment is much more than a band on a stage—it embraces everything from live music to disc jockeys, ceremonies to clowns, keynote speakers to parades, dancers to drama, casinos to carnivals, and everything in between. The audio and visual elements of an event might also be used as the entertainment (e.g. recorded music, PowerPoint, big screen projections, etc.).

Identify the Audience

If you have previously identified the audience demographic, you'll be one step ahead in choosing entertainment.

Matching the entertainment to the audience is critical. Failure to do so can result in spending a lot of money for entertainment that totally falls flat. This is not the entertainer's fault, because they did what they were hired to do; it is the event's fault for not identifying the demographics of the audience.

For example, entertainment featuring rap or heavy metal music may be fine for a younger crowd, but would not appeal to an audience of Baby Boomers who may prefer good old rock and roll, Motown, or 70s-80s music.

On the other hand, if you are hoping to draw a younger crowd, choose a type of entertainment that they will enjoy. Keep this in mind whether the entertainment consists of live music or other activities. Ask several people in the targeted age group what they like. This will give a cross-section of opinions on which to base the selection of entertainment.

NOTES

If the event features a range of activities for all ages, include something that appeals to everyone. Program the entertainment into logical timeframes that match when the greatest segment of that particular audience may be present (e.g. children, teenagers, young adults, older adults, senior citizens).

Match the entertainment to the venue. Double check to make sure that the entertainment is a good match with the venue as well as the audience. Certain types of entertainment may not be allowed within a venue (e.g. church), or may require special permits from local jurisdictions for things like noise, pyrotechnics, staging, or the like.

Avoid personal preferences. Many events make the mistake of selecting entertainment based on personal preference rather than what is the right fit for the audience. Just because the decision-maker may like rap music doesn't mean it will work for your event.

Using A Talent Agency

When you need bands or other entertainment consider using a professional talent agency. A common misconception is that the event will save money by directly booking the entertainment. While it may appear cheaper to "do it yourself," this is very often not true.

A reputable talent agent knows current entertainment market trends and should have a variety of suggestions from which to choose. They will provide, at no cost, a packet of information complete with photos, song lists and CDs for various acts you may wish to consider within the interest area you have specified. They can help with everything from a birthday party to a huge event with a variety of entertainment.

Musical entertainment can include national acts, bands, duos, singles, and even disc jockeys. Talent agents can provide access to other performers such as celebrity look-alikes, illusionists, clowns, balloon artists, jugglers, mimes, speakers, circus performers and more

Matching the entertainment to the budget. A good talent agent should voluntarily offer to help to save money by getting the most for the dollar. Reputable agents know how much entertainment should cost, can negotiate a better rate (especially if they book the entertainer on a regular basis) and may be able to obtain production needs (e.g. sound, lighting, etc.) at a discount. They also act as a buffer between the client and an entertainer during negotiations.

National acts. It's common knowledge that national acts hold out as long as they can before committing to a contract in case they may receive a better offer.

You can expect to pay a significant amount of money (usually with a 50% deposit) to lock in a band or individual entertainer who is enjoying a high level of national or international popularity. While the performance fee may seem exorbitant (and probably is), competition in the entertainment industry is fierce and the entertainer's "moment in the spotlight" can wane at any time.

Entertainers who are well-known names, yet are still "becoming famous" are much more affordable. This is also true of nostalgia-type bands or individual entertainers who are still on the performing circuit but have already peaked in their career. Many of these entertainers have had huge hits in their heyday and audiences still love to sing along or dance to their music.

Link dates. If booking national acts, a talent agent can research "link dates" to entertainers that are currently on tour. They can often obtain national acts for less than the standard rate if the entertainers are performing at another engagement within a reasonable timeframe and traveling distance.

Contract riders. Riders are addendums to performance contracts. These documents may be much more detailed than the contract itself. In fact, what is contained in the rider may significantly increase the entertainment cost over and above the performance fee.

Riders often contain specific requirements regarding stage size or structure, sound and lighting equipment, rental of musical equipment (such as pianos), electrical requirements, airfare, limousines or other ground transportation, security personnel, dressing rooms, vehicle parking, food and beverage, guest lists, and many other provisions.

"30 Day Out" Clauses. Watch for 30-day-out clauses in contracts. This means that an entertainer can cancel at any time up to 30 days in advance of the performance. If you see a contract with this provision, cross this section out and initial it. If the entertainer or entertainer's representative initials the change and signs the contract, this clause is null and void.

The reason this can be critical is that if the entertainer's name has been included in all of the event publicity surrounding the event and then backs out, it creates a financial and marketing hardship in motivating people to attend. Most entertainers do honor the contracts they have signed, but there are exceptions, so cover the event's backside.

Do-It-Yourself Selection

It is possible to contract the entertainment yourself, but be aware of potential pitfalls that come with this practice.

Don't underestimate the amount of time it will take. You'll need to do some scouting at other events or local nightclubs to conduct a firsthand observation of the entertainment. This will take a substantial amount of time, most of which will be outside normal working hours.

Try not to book entertainment without seeing it firsthand. Do not book entertainment based solely on a CD, video tape, photo, or other promotional materials. All of these can be easily doctored to make the entertainment sound or look great, when in fact, it may actually be terrible.

NOTES

NOTES

Make arrangements to see the entertainment in person (this also applies if working with a talent agency if the entertainer is local). Telephone numbers or contact information for entertainers is often hard to obtain without actually going to see them in person. Ask for a business card or contact information for their manager.

Other suggestions for making contacts are musicians associations, and events or clubs where the entertainers are slated to perform. For national acts, work with a local talent agent to contact the manager who represents the artist.

NOTE: Under no circumstances should you circumvent a talent agent who has made arrangements for you to view entertainment and try to book the entertainers yourself. This is totally unethical.

Guest lists. Entertainers often have a "guest list" which allows admission for select individuals who are not required to pay the ticket price or cover charge. This provides opportunity for you to see the entertainer in action.

Be considerate of the privilege extended by the entertainer. While a group outing for the entire entertainment committee may be great fun, do not ask entertainers to put more than two people on the guest list unless they outright offer to do so.

If there are more than two in your party, it's a good business practice to pay admission for the extra folks, order a drink or food, and leave a generous tip.

Go incognito. An excellent way to make a decision about local entertainment is to just "drop in," pay the cover charge or ticket price, and conduct an observation. This way, you'll base your decision on the "real" entertainer, and not just their "best behavior" because they know you're there if you're attending via guest list. You can check out how they sound, look, and behave to see if it's a good fit with the event.

Know what the market is charging. Don't agree to the first price quoted. It is very difficult for inexperienced entertainment buyers to know a fair price. If an entertainer thinks you aren't savvy about the market, you may be quoted a higher than normal performance fee. And, if you don't know the difference, you will end up paying more than you need to. In many cases, you'll find that a talent agent is able to obtain the entertainer for less, including the agent's commission.

Booking The Entertainment

It's always a good idea to place the entertainment on hold if they are available for the specific date and time you require. This should be done as far in advance as possible. Once the entertainment lineup is in place, release the entertainers that are not selected so they may pursue other opportunities.

Book early to lock in the entertainment. Don't assume the entertainer is still committed to your event if they haven't been contacted for several months and there is no signed contract. If they have another offer, they may take it without contacting you, especially if you are not working through an agency.

Deposits are required. The standard deposit amount is usually 50% of the performance fee, excluding the rider. This may be tricky if it's a national act and you're required to pay out a large sum of money well before you've collected sponsorships or ticket fees.

Read the performance contract very carefully before signing. Pay attention to the rider, cancellation clauses, or liability statements, and be aware of hidden costs. When adding the cost of the stage, sound, lighting, and electrical requirements, plus travel and lodging, security personnel, food and beverages, or other stipulations, you may find the true cost to be prohibitive.

Read every word in the contract. Is production included in the fee, or is it extra? How long are the sets (durations of time the entertainer performs)? How long are the breaks? Does the entertainer want to be able to sell souvenir merchandise? Are they willing to sign autographs or have photos taken with VIPs or fans? Would they do a backstage greeting with sponsors? These questions need to be answered in advance.

Always use a written contract. Whether the entertainment is paid or volunteer, amateur or professional, you should require a basic performance agreement even if you have to create one. Even the most amateur entertainer will take the commitment more seriously if they have a signed contract. If you program the entertainment into the schedule and they are a no-show, it leaves a gap in what attendees are expecting and can be incredibly embarrassing.

Other Entertainment

Passive entertainment. We tend to think of storytellers, slide shows, video presentations, movies, award ceremonies, and the like as passive entertainment because we can enjoy them without direct participation. Passive entertainment can also generate energy as in the case of concerts, comedy shows, and the like even though the audience mainly participates as viewers.

Active entertainment. Interactive games, dances, parties, and similar activities require our direct participation.

Exceptions. Entertainment such as parades, sports, and others can be passive or active depending on whether one has chosen to be a viewer or a participant.

Whether you use a talent agent or opt to hire the entertainment on your own, choose wisely and well and your guests will thank you.

Use the worksheet at the back of the chapter to help develop entertainment for your event.

NOTES

Production Worksheet

Use this worksheet to outline production elements and help select contractors.

ALTER THE FORM TO FIT YOUR EVENT.

Identify the Facets of Production

1. Have production elements been identified (stage, sound, lights, visual media? _____
2. Is electrical power adequate to support contractors and other activities? _____
3. Does the venue lend itself to décor, and other needs? _____
4. Have you interviewed and selected production contractors? _____
5. Have you negotiated for package deals on production needs? _____
6. Have contractors provided references and have they been verified? _____
7. How much time does each contractor need to complete their part? _____
8. Have you reserved enough time to cover load-in, set up, and tear down? _____
9. Will the décor be built around a theme, or around a mood? _____
10. Can the event save money by using volunteer labor? _____
11. Can the décor be used to enhance equipment included in venue use? _____
12. Will props be needed, and will you rent or make your own? _____
13. Are the decorations and props in scale with the venue? _____
14. What forms of audio and visual media will be used? _____
15. If using PowerPoint, does the presentation look professional? _____
16. Will a stage be required? _____ What type and size? _____
17. What will the stage be used for? _____
18. Will a professional lighting contractor be used? _____
19. What are the total lighting requirements for the stage and other needs? _____
20. Are you using lighting to enhance décor or other event elements? _____
21. Are any permits required for lighting or other production elements? _____
22. Is the in-house sound system adequate, or will it need to be supplemented? _____
23. What forms of audio enhancement are required? _____
24. If using microphones, what kind is needed? _____
25. Will sound speakers be free-standing or need to be hung from the ceiling? _____
26. Are communication tools such as portable radios or cell phones needed? _____
27. Are battery chargers and extra batteries available? _____
28. What other rental equipment is needed? _____
29. Does the price include delivery, set up and tear down? _____
30. _____

Entertainment Worksheet

Use this worksheet to outline entertainment needs.

ALTER THE FORM TO FIT YOUR EVENT.

Selecting Entertainment

1. What is the audience demographic? _____
2. Have you avoided personal preference? _____
3. What is the entertainment budget? _____
4. Will you use a professional talent agent or do it yourself? _____
5. If using national acts, have you been able to take advantage of link dates? _____
6. What events has the talent agent worked with? _____
7. Have you checked the talent agent's references? _____
8. Has the talent agent offered cost-effective suggestions? _____
9. Is the talent agent working in the event's best interests? _____
10. Has the contract rider been examined? _____
11. Will there be additional costs due to rider requirements? _____
12. If booking the entertainment yourself, how will you determine a fair price? _____
13. Do you know what the current rates are in the entertainment market? _____
14. Have you seen the entertainment, and what was your impression? _____
15. Have you compared prices quoted by the entertainer with the talent agent's price? _____
16. Have you booked the entertainment well in advance? _____
17. If a deposit is required, has it been paid to lock in the date? _____
18. Have several people read all performance contracts carefully? _____
19. Does the contract contain cancellation clauses or liability statements? _____
20. Have you checked the budget to ensure the entertainer's fee is covered? _____
21. Have all your questions been answered? _____
22. _____
23. _____
24. _____
25. _____

Chapter 13 – Site Planning & Logistics

Tying together the "where" and "how"

Whether the event is indoors or outdoors, a site plan will need to be developed—along with a logistics schedule—that can be shared with others for actual implementation.

These are two of the most important tools used to help execute the event. Site plans and logistics schedules, while time consuming to prepare, are one of the more creative aspects of the planning process. The Site Plan details "how it all looks" and the Logistics Schedule details "how it all happens."

The first section of this chapter on *Site Planning* shows how to:

➢ Determine space requirements
➢ Examine event elements and requirements
➢ Create a site plan
➢ Work with contractors and key personnel

The second section of the chapter covers *Logistics* which includes:
➢ Establish time allocations for event elements
➢ Create a logistics schedule
➢ Get a head start

Of General Note

On-site meetings. It helps to hold an on-site meeting with contractors in the early stages of planning and at least one more just prior to the event. At a minimum, the event manager and/or appropriate committee chair should be present. You may wish to include staff members, the volunteer coordinator, logistical personnel, and others who are key to the execution of the event.

"It's kind of fun to do the impossible."

Walt Disney

During the meeting, all parties will have an opportunity to view the site, ask questions, address logistical concerns, and problem-solve. It's much better to work out the details at these meetings than to find something has been overlooked during the actual event set up.

On-site meetings are an excellent way for those involved to get to know one another and to create a better understanding about how the event should look and how it should function. The meetings provide each person the opportunity to relate to the actual event site and see how their role fits into the plan.

Americans with Disabilities Act (ADA). Events and venues must conform to provisions of the Americans with Disabilities Act. Not only is it necessary for legal compliance, but our friends with physical or other challenges appreciate being able to participate in as many of the activities as possible.

The Site Plan

The site (or floor) plan is a detailed drawn-to-scale "footprint" of the event that is used by staff, contractors, the venue, and others. It shows the proper locations of utilities, entrances, exits, restrooms, equipment, exhibitors, activities, staging, dinner tables, and other event elements.

Commonly used forms of site plans show "named" locations as they appear on the plan while others may show "numbered" locations which are referenced by a "key." Numbered versions are often used when the amount of text involved in labeling the various parts of a plan would otherwise be prohibitive.

How To Get Started

Start with a blueprint, scale drawing, or aerial photo of the site (venues normally have these), then draw various elements of the event (also to scale, onto the plan in their proper locations.

One drawback to using an original blueprint is that changes occur during construction and the blueprint may not be accurate. This is of particular concern for outdoor events where locating utility hookups, underground cables, and the like can be critical. Aerial photos may not be accurate depending on how long ago the photo was taken.

Indoor venues. The majority of facilities have existing floor plans they are happy to provide. The plans show room configuration, entries, exits, restrooms, air walls, capacities, and more. Many venues have computer software programs that can generate drawn-to-scale plans with tables and chairs, stage placement, aisleways, and so on.

The plans probably won't show the location of electrical panels and outlets, thermostats, beams from which rigging can be hung, light fixtures that may protrude into décor, fire extinguishers that cannot be blocked, and other items of concern. These will need to be marked on the plan as necessary.

Outdoor venues. Events held outdoors are sometimes tricky. A basic blueprint can provide information regarding perimeter boundaries, location of constructed buildings, pathways, etc. It may be necessary to physically measure the property for the placement of activities that take up large areas or where spacing is tight. Outdoor venues look huge at first sight, but the space quickly shrinks when stages, tents, equipment, traffic lanes, and other elements are placed.

CAD Drawings. One way to develop a plan if one is not readily available is to obtain an aerial photo or diagram of the site and create a CAD (Computer Aided Drafting) drawing.

The CAD process is relatively simple. The aerial photo or diagram is scanned into computer using the scale at which it was created. The technician then creates an "overlay" drawing for property lines, boundaries, utilities, or the like onto the plan. The result is a base drawing of the site to which event elements can be added. These can also be created in color to color-code different parts of the plan.

NOTES

215

If you don't want to pay a professional and are good with software, a number of computerized programs are available that are relatively simple to use.

Graph paper. Before CAD and more sophisticated means came along, site plans were drawn to scale by hand using graph paper, and this method may work just fine.

Keep the master drawing for future use. Make *copies* of the master (original base drawing), and use them to create the site plan. They can be marked on or changed without altering the original drawing that you may have had to pay to obtain.

Once all the changes and additions have been made, a "secondary master" can be created on a clean copy. This way, if changes occur in the event layout from year to year, the original drawing containing the basic site elements has not been ruined.

Save the "annual" copies and mark the year they represent on each site plan so you don't get confused as time goes on.

Other Site Planning Considerations

Use common sense in developing the site plan. Allow for traffic patterns, aisleways, buffer zones, and other space that is not taken up by actual event activities.

Provide logical and adequate entry and exit points, remembering to take disabled individuals into account. For example, if 500 people attend the event, it's not advisable to have just one entry and exit, in case of emergency.

Meeting rooms should be separated from noisy or distracting areas. Many facilities have no smoking policies or require smokers to use designated areas. All of these suggestions and more should be taken into consideration.

The Command Post

A central location is needed to serve as a temporary office where key people can be contacted. A knowledgeable person should be present to answer questions or provide assistance. They should have a working radio, telephone, or other form of communication. Tables, chairs, and other equipment like computers and printers may be needed to efficiently function in this temporary space.

For indoor venues, a side room works well. For outdoor venues, travel trailers or motor homes provide an efficient and comfortable alternative. Tents can also be used, but it is difficult to secure equipment or valuables, and night-time dampness may be an issue.

Space Requirements

Each event element will require space. Some commonly used space allocations are listed however, *they do not include aisleways or space requirements dictated by the Fire Marshal and others.*

Tables and Chairs

Table Type	Accommodates	Space inc. chairs
42" rounds	6 people	10' x 10' floor space
48" rounds	6-8 people	12' x 12' floor space
54" rounds	8 people	12' x 12' floor space
60" rounds	8-10 people	14' x 14' floor space
72" rounds	10-12 people	16' x 16' floor space
5' x 30" banquet	4-6 people	10' x 8' floor space
6' x 30" banquet	6-8 people	12' x 8' floor space
8' x 30" banquet	8-10 people	14' x 8' floor space

The manner in which the tables are laid out in the plan determines the maximum number of tables the space can accommodate.

Each chair takes approximately 24" x 24" of floor space.

Consider the placement of guests. Just because there is space in the back corner doesn't mean you should place guests there. They won't be happy if they can't see, hear, or enjoy the experience they paid to obtain. If it's the staff or volunteers, that may be all right.

Tents

If the event is to be held outdoors, tent companies can offer a wide range of selections to fit every need. Survey the site to make sure it is safe to put a tent in the location you have chosen. This is best done with the tent company representative.

Some sites do not lend themselves well to tent placement because the tent cannot be safely anchored or the site may have sloping or rough terrain. Neither would you want to pitch a tent in low or uneven ground that could fill up with water runoff if it rains.

Take the position of the sun into consideration. You don't want to place the tent opening or transparent side in such a way that those inside will be blinded or baked by the sun.

Weather is always a factor. Connecting tents can be set up with rain gutters to avoid leaks and puddles at connection points. Sidewall can be used to help block out the elements.

Flooring is also an option. It's much easier to place tables and chairs on a level surface. A floor can also be carpeted to create a more finished look. If using dance floors outdoors, it's best to underlay with plywood to provide a more level surface and to protect from ground moisture.

Fencing

If temporary fencing is required, it can usually be rented through a party rental supplier, fencing company, or other source. Fencing is rented by the linear foot and can be used in numerous ways.

There are a number of fencing choices—plastic web fencing and cyclone panel fencing are two of the most common. Contact a supplier for pricing and selection.

Electrical Power

Events will need electrical hookups for lighting, sound, or other equipment. Power availability should have been identified in your initial site visits. If the venue simply doesn't have enough power, a generator can be rented for this purpose.

In checking out the electrical power, a common term you may hear is "tie-in" or "tail-in." This is when a licensed electrician attaches bare wires directly to an electrical panel. These may also be called "distribution panels." Tie-ins are often required for events with sizeable power requirements.

Portable Restrooms & Hand Washing Stations

Outdoor events often require portable restrooms and hand-washing stations to meet health and sanitation requirements. Even if the venue has existing restroom facilities, they may be inadequate for large groups of people.

Portable restrooms come in individual units, or in trailer units containing several stalls and may/may not include hand-washing facilities. Trailer units are available in plain or fancy versions.

Hand washing stations are individual or "dual sided" with foot pedals to pump water, soap, and paper towels for wiping hands.

At a minimum, you'll need one restroom for every 100 people and frequent servicing of the units if the event is more than one day in duration. Hand washing units are based on different allocations depending on the type of event. Check local health department requirements for ratios.

NOTES

219

Communications Equipment

All key people should be provided with communication tools. Since communications are only as good as the tools available, when using rented equipment such as portable radios, cell phones or pagers, make sure they are in good working order. You'll also need a central location for battery chargers, extra batteries, or extra radios for the duration of the event, including set up and tear down.

Signage

Think about how attendees will use signage to get around the event site. Pay particular attention to logical locations where people might look for directions or information. Be sure that there are enough signs and avoid placing them too far apart

Signage needs should be determined well in advance of their actual use, along with a list of their placement locations. The sign order, or portions thereof, should be given to the printer as far in advance as possible. Conduct another review about a month prior to the event. This allows enough time to have more signs printed if necessary.

Sign materials. All kinds of materials can be printed—vinyl, poster board, foam core, fabric, and more. Use contrasting colors that are easily read such as light backgrounds with dark lettering. Lettering should be sized in comparison to the distance from which the sign will need to be seen.

For example, lettering on a stage banner needs to be much larger than letter on a sign with a schedule of activities that will be read up close. Use common colors and type fonts for all signage to create continuity.

For outdoor events, signs need to be weatherproof. Plastic signs with vinyl lettering work well. Even if it doesn't rain, the overnight dew alone will ruin paper-based signs if they are not laminated.

NOTES

NOTES

Sign placement. Indoors, signs can be placed in sign stands or on easels, but make sure the legs don't stick out into the flow of traffic and cause a safety hazard. Outdoor signs can be hung with cable ties, clips or other means on any number of surfaces. Free-standing signs can be staked or placed on wire sign holders (like real estate signs).

Give the person who will place the signs a list of their locations. This same list will be used after the event to take the signs down.

Telephones

With nearly everyone having a cell phone these days, the need for pay phones should be minimal. However, temporary pay phone units can be provided by the local telephone company.

Trash Removal & Recycling

The staff for venues like hotels normally handles trash removal and recycling. But for outdoor events, you'll need to provide dumpsters and their location needs to be noted on the site plan.

Provide those who are collecting trash with latex or rubber gloves to prevent their hands from coming in direct contact with waste. It's also a good idea to provide individually wrapped antiseptic wipes that can be kept in a pocket and used as necessary.

Outdoor events need enough dumpsters and at least one daily trash pick up. Plenty of trash cans and liners need to be available, and don't forget about containers for sorting recyclables.

Location Maps

Location maps can contain as little or as much information as desired. These are commonly used to show the event location in relation to a city or other area, directions on how to get there, where to park, etc. They can also be included in confirmation packets for exhibitors, sponsors, or volunteers.

Emergency Plans & Safety Considerations

Emergency and security plans should have been developed in the early planning stages. Make sure that key personnel have copies and know what to do in case of emergency. If something critical happens, you don't want to have people panicking about what to do.

Go over the event with an eye to safety during and after set up. Check for obstacles. Anchor or tape down cables or cords crossing traffic lanes. Children are of special concern because they like to climb over or under things and to poke their fingers into holes.

Lost & Found Articles and Children

Identify a location where missing articles will be collected or can be retrieved. You'll also need to determine a post-event location where leftover items will be taken and whom to call.

If children become lost, make sure that staff and volunteers know where they are to be taken and cared for until their parents arrive.

Create A Photo and/or Video Record

Take lots of photographs or video—during the set up, event, tear down, and clean up. Take pictures of all event elements, key people, sponsors, the audience, contractors, displays, dining tables, food, centerpieces, volunteers, and more.

This task can be assigned to a photographer, volunteer, or staff member as long as they have a list of pictures that are needed. The event manager may want to carry a camera as well.

There are good reasons for all this photo documentation. You'll have a visual chronological accounting of what occurred before, during, and after, as well as know what everything looked like. Photos also make great thank you gifts for sponsors, contractors, and volunteers.

Have Supplies At Hand

Each activity or area needs its own supplies. It is counter-productive and frustrating to be constantly trying to find a woefully inadequate number of supplies that are being moved from place to place, person to person, left somewhere, or used up.

Box or bag the supplies and label them according to where they will be used (e.g. registration, temporary office, etc.). Check them off the list as they are placed in the box or bag. The supplies can then be distributed to the correct locations or people at the event site. Once they are no longer needed, they can be returned to a central location (such as the command post) and taken back to the office post-event.

Logistics

Webster's Dictionary defines logistics as "the managing of the details of an undertaking." Technically, we could use this term to encompass the entire process of event management, but for this purpose, the "undertaking" is defined as the set up, execution, and tear down of the event.

Logistics schedules show a chronological listing of "how things happen" and describe the order and action of "when-what-who-where." The schedule can be created ahead of time, added to, deleted from, or changed as the event progresses with a final tweaking just prior to the event date. **Do not wait until a couple of days before the event to do this!**

This day-by-day, hour-by-hour listing is given to key personnel and contractor to track event progress from the first moment of arrival to the last moment of clean up.

The important thing to remember is that if it's not on the schedule, don't expect it to get done or for anyone to remember. The schedule should indicate who is to do what by when.

Pocket sized info. It is really helpful to have a laminated pocket-sized list of cell phone numbers for key people, as well as a small version of the event schedule. These will prove invaluable, are easy to carry, and will be used many times by all involved. These should be distributed 3-7 days or more in advance.

The Order of Things

Developing a logistics schedule may be difficult for a first-time event manager because there are numerous factors starting and stopping within the timeframe.

Begin by loading the major activities into the logistics schedule to create a basic framework based on dates and times of actual occurrence. Remaining activities and tasks can then be inserted backward or forward from those points. By starting to format the schedule about a month before the event, and filling in details and times as they are developed during the event cycle, you save the frustration of trying to remember everything at crunch time.

As a general rule, the following is the order of set up—stage, lighting and décor, electronic visual media, sound, tables and chairs. For outdoor venues, the set up of tents, equipment, and other event elements can be taking place simultaneously. You'll also need to load the timing of contractors into the schedule.

Break the event and schedule into phases—load-in, set up, the event itself, tear down and clean up. Each day should be scheduled individually, and included to create a master schedule which is given to key individuals and contractors.

Let others have input by reviewing a draft of the schedule several times as it is developed to ensure the information is correct. A final version of the schedule should be distributed several days in advance. Any changes after that can be hand-marked on the schedule.

NOTES

224

This sounds much more complicated than it actually is. Just remember to think of it in the logical sequence things occur, log the main activities first, and fill in with the rest.

An example of a logistics schedule appears at the end of the chapter.

Timing the Set Up and Tear Down

Don't underestimate the amount of time it takes to perform the set up and tear down functions. Ask each vendor or contractor how much time they require for these activities, then add in your own requirements. In the case of a trade show, the schedule would contain set hours for exhibitors to set up prior to the event and to tear down following the event.

In general, evening events require all day to set up with an 8:00 a.m. start time and about 2-4 hours after the event to tear down. Larger or complex events may need to start the set up process a day or two in advance and may tear down the day after.

It may be possible to accommodate tight scheduling but what is saved in venue rental may cost more in paying the extra people required for a more expedient set up or tear down.

Bring Permits & The Event Notebook With You

You must have the original permit/s at the event for certain activities such as site use, liquor, raffle, or others. These permits are seldom required for presentation to authorities, but you must have them in case they ask. Keep them in a secure place in the command post.

Bring the event notebook with you as well. Make sure that you have copies of contracts or agreements in order to verify "who agreed to do what" if questions arise. This includes contracts with vendors, entertainers, rental companies, and more. You'll be surprised at how many times you'll need to refer to this information during the event.

Site Planning & Logistics Worksheet

Site Planning

1. What are the total space requirements? _____
2. Is there an existing site plan that can be altered for your event? _____
3. Has a detailed site plan been given to contractors and key people? _____
4. Has a Command Post or temporary office been established? _____
5. Is the power adequate? Will you need an electrician? _____
6. Will tents be used? If so, what kind and how big? _____
7. Do you need portable radios or cell phones? _____
8. Is there a comprehensive list of signage needed? _____
9. Does the signage look consistent and fit in with other event elements? _____
10. How will trash disposal and recycling be handled? _____
11. Has an emergency/security plan been distributed? _____
12. Who will take photos or video during the event? _____
13. _____
14. _____
15. _____

Logistics

1. Has the execution of the event been divided into days and hours? _____
2. Are all major activities, functions, and times of occurrence listed in the schedule? _____
3. Has there been enough time allocated for contractors to set up and tear down? _____
4. Who needs to receive copies of the logistics schedule? _____
5. _____
6. _____

Logistics Schedule Example

Auction Event with 5:00 p.m. Start Time

TIME	ACTIVITY	LOCATION	RESPONSIBLE
8:00 a.m.	Prepare for set up to begin – all areas	Exh. Hall/Foyer/Ballroom	Director, Assist.
8:30 a.m.	Team leaders/volunteers arrive for set up	Exhibit hall/ballroom	Teams #1, 2, 3
	Set up commences		
	Computer set up begins	Ballroom/foyer	Computer Man
9:00 a.m.	Continental breakfast for staff, volunteers	Foyer	Volunteer Coor.
	Registration/cashiering set up	Foyer	Team Leader #4
10:00 a.m.	Mtg. event director, chairmen, auctioneer	Catering conference room	All indicated
	Décor set up – use color coded plan	Ballroom	Team Leader #5
	Hotel set base linens, chairs	Ballroom	Banquet Dept.
	Chair covers on chairs	Ballroom	Décor Company
	China, glassware, menus	Ballroom	Banquet Dept.
	Sponsor gifts	Ballroom	Volunteers
11:00 a.m.	Floral delivery – centerpieces, other	Ballroom/foyer	Team Leader #5
12:00 p.m.	Lunch for volunteers, event staff	Volunteer room	Volunteer Coor.
1:00 p.m.	Auction lots verified, addendum to printer	Outside service	Auction Assist.
	Set up should be complete or close to done	Exhibit hall/ballroom	Team Leaders
2:00 p.m.	Media company crew arrives	Ballroom stage area	AV Crew
2:30 p.m.	Event Director changes clothes		Event Director
3:00 p.m.	Décor photos and pre-event photos	Ballroom/exh hall/foyer	Photographers
	Auction assistant changes clothes		Auction Assist.
3:30 p.m.	Dinner buffet for volunteers begins	Volunteer room	Volunteer Coor.
4:00 p.m.	Photos of VIPs, chefs, chairs, auctioneer	Ballroom stage area	Event Director
	Video of VIPs, chefs, chairmen, auctioneers		AV Crew
	Press opportunity, interviews		Event Director

(continued on next page)

Logistics Schedule Example (continued)

Auction Event with 5:00 p.m. Start Time

TIME		ACTIVITY	LOCATION	RESPONSIBLE
5:00 p.m.		DOORS OPEN	Foyer/ballroom/exh. hall	Everyone
		Registration, reception, live auction viewing,		All team leaders
		silent auctions, raffle ticket sales		
		Videotape until 6:00 p.m., edit until 7:00		Event Director
6:30 p.m.		Auctioneer/spotters meeting by stage		Auctioneer
7:00 p.m.		Silent auction closes (or 5 min. intervals)	Exhibit Hall	Team Leader
		Reception ends, lights flash, call to dinner	Exhibit Hall	Hotel Staff
		Conversion of silent auction to Item Pickup	Exhibit Hall	Team Leader
7:10 p.m.		"Please Be Seated" announcement	Ballroom stage	Emcee
7:15 p.m.		First dinner course served	Ballroom	Chefs/hotel staff
		Last chance for raffle tickets announced	Ballroom stage	Emcee
7:20 p.m.		Live camera work begins, official welcome	Ballroom	AV Crew, Emcee
		Raffle drawing, "Night Of" video shown	Ballroom stage	
7:30 p.m.		Follow script – chairmen, awards, auctioneer	Ballroom stage	Emcee, Chairmen
		First course cleared from tables		
7:40 p.m.		LIVE AUCTION BEGINS	Ballroom stage	Auctioneer
7:50 p.m.		Second dinner course served, then cleared	Ballroom	Chefs/hotel staff
8:30 p.m.		Third course served, then cleared	Ballroom	Chefs/hotel staff
9:15 p.m.		Dessert course served	Ballroom	Chefs/hotel staff
10:00 p.m.		LIVE AUCTION ENDS (estimated)	Ballroom	Team Leaders
		Guests pick up purchases and depart	Exhibit Hall	Team Leader
11:00 p.m.		Clean up of all areas	Ballroom/exh. hall, foyer	Teams/event staff
		Move items to transport/overnight storage		
12:30 p.m.		Limp to hotel room, many aspirin, sleep!		Good Job!

Chapter 14 – Volunteers

You Can Never Have Too Many Helping Hands

Every day men, women, and children around the world devote their time and energy to help others through volunteerism. Some of these people enthusiastically seek out volunteer opportunities while others need to be recruited and motivated. Events appeal to volunteers because they are fun and offer all sorts of opportunities to become involved.

People volunteer for many reasons—to have fun, help others, support a cause, spend time with friends, or serve their community. Volunteers help events save money and they can bring needed skills as well as energy and excitement.

Remember that volunteers have lives outside of the event—work, families, friends, and other interests—that require some of their time. We need to respect that the event may not be their top priority and that everyone contributes to the degree they are able.

"Volunteer. Sometimes the jobs no one wants conceal big opportunities."

Life's Little Instruction Book, Volume II

Every job that a volunteer can perform is one less that you may have to pay someone to do (or have to do yourself). It also means that one more person has a small stake in the event and will do their best to help ensure success.

This chapter will help to:

- Identify a volunteer coordinator
- Conduct a volunteer jobs inventory
- Develop job descriptions
- Recruit volunteers
- Create a master schedule
- Provide confirmation and communication

Volunteer Guidelines

While individual job descriptions address duties and responsibilities, some basic guidelines apply to all volunteers working on the event.

It is very important to create guidelines. These should be documented and presented to volunteers in their confirmation materials. Guidelines should provide basic information—event hours, where to park, location of the volunteer headquarters and more—as well as outline what is expected in regard to dress code and personal behavior. An encyclopedia of rules isn't required. Guidelines can be incorporated into the volunteer's confirmation letter and/or job description. *Keep it simple and keep it positive.*

Guidelines should contain clear statements about working around alcoholic beverages, dealing with contracted workers, chain of command, assisting persons with disabilities, risk management, money handling procedures, security and emergency provisions. This will be important should a criminal or legal situation ever arise.

A Rewarding Volunteer Experience

Strategy plays an important part in events—those chosen as chairmen or sponsors, how we structure activities—and yes, in selecting volunteers. The volunteer "family" that collectively comes together in support of the event is much like a real family. Some people get along well with others and some don't.

The personalities of various individuals tend to influence their own volunteer experience and that of others. Each individual has positive and negative characteristics and may be a better "fit" for some jobs depending on their own personal agenda.

You'll also want to take care that the people acting as team leaders will motivate, teach and encourage others to do their best, rather than just boss their team members around.

NOTES

Remember that a person volunteers because they have a positive expectation about helping on the event. If they have a negative experience, they won't be back. You obviously aren't going to be able to please everyone all the time, but treating volunteers with respect will ensure the majority feel appreciated for their help.

Give Volunteers the Information & Tools They Need

Nothing is more frustrating to a volunteer than to not know what is expected of them, how to do their job, or to be missing the tools needed. A volunteer will go the extra mile to help if they have a very clear understanding of their role and how it fits into the event.

Don't expect volunteers to read minds. They need information to effectively perform their role. Providing detailed job descriptions in advance helps to alleviate questions about what the job entails and the steps to achieve success.

Providing complete information also helps to alleviate problems down the road because if volunteers don't know the answer when asked questions about the event, they tend to make up answers which are not often correct.

A pre-event or on-site group orientation session often helps address questions or concerns volunteers may have. Or, you might want to train the team leaders and have them follow up separately with their teams. Equipment and supplies should be given to volunteers upon check-in for their shifts or should be provided at the proper location.

The Volunteer Coordinator's Role

The duties of the volunteer coordinator are not limited to the day of the event. This person is charged with the express purpose of recruiting and coordinating volunteer involvement, acting as the main contact for volunteers, and working directly with the event manager. They should be well organized and able to motivate others.

The volunteer coordinator helps to identify volunteer roles and helps to develop a clear, concise job description for each. The volunteer coordinator heads recruitment, screens volunteers, helps create and maintain the master schedule, and conveys necessary information to the volunteer force. They should take the lead in conducting training or orientation sessions in partnership with the event manager, either prior to the event, or on-site.

At the event, the coordinator monitors volunteers to ensure they are performing their duties and have the things they need to do their job. Following the event, every single person who volunteered should receive a thank you from the coordinator, and/or event manager.

What Kinds Of Jobs Can Volunteers Perform?

The list of functions that volunteers can perform is unlimited, but here are some typical things that volunteers might do in support of an event:

Leadership

Event manager	Manage all aspects of event
Event chairs	Lead event effort, work with event manager
Boards of directors	Highest level decision-making body
Committee chairs	Lead individual committee efforts
Committee members	Work with chair to accomplish goals
Volunteer coordinator	Oversee involvement of volunteers

Administrative

Catalog writer	Create descriptions for event program/catalog
Data entry (skilled)	Assist with entering reservations, donations
Errands	Pick up or deliver items
Gift wrapping	Wrap gifts for sponsors, VIPs, guests, others
Hospitality	Coordinate VIPs, guest lodging, etc.
Mailings	Assist with mailing printed collateral, other
Office/clerical	Phone, filing, computer work, more
Professional services	Legal, accounting, marketing, printing, etc.
Registration	Record reservations, sell tickets, obtain info

Event Set Up

Auction set up	Auction lots displayed in sequential order
Computer technician	Transport, set up, troubleshoot computers
Decorations	Décor, table linens, chair covers, centerpieces
Fluffer	Puts finishing touches on displayed items
Handyman	Basic assistance not provided by contractors
Set up assistant	Whatever is needed on-site
Signage coordinator	Place, retrieve signs at event site
Tactics coordinator	Transport, delivery, pick up of needed items
Volunteer room mgr.	Oversees volunteer room, check in

The Event

Audio/visual assistant	Help camera crew, run PowerPoint, etc.
Cashier	Assist at registration and check out
Clean up	Event tear down, prepare items for transport
Coat check	Assist guests with coats, use tag system
Delivery coordinator	Oversees next day delivery process
Greeters	Welcome guests, questions and directions
Photographer	Take pictures of people and event elements
Raffle ticket seller	Sell raffle tickets before or during event
Reader	Reads copy from pre-developed script
Recorder/clerk	Writes or records information in computer
Registrar	Assist guests at check in, verify info
Registration assistant	Assist registrar, retrieve guest files, etc.
Security	Guard items, observe behaviors
Site monitors	Observe for compliance, all event areas
Team leaders	Manage one or more volunteer groups
Timekeeper	Records actual time things occur during event

Post-Event

Delivery coordinator	Same person as event night, oversee deliveries
Transporters	Transports supplies and equipment
Office/clerical	Assist with post-event letters, mailings, etc.

Volunteer Job Descriptions

Each volunteer position should have a job description. Recruitment materials should contain summarized versions for quick reference. Confirmation materials contain a more detailed version.

NOTES

The volunteer coordinator and the event manager should think through every volunteer job and the steps that will be required from the time the volunteer arrives until they have finished.

Job descriptions should define exactly what the volunteer will be doing. Be honest about the job and the level of responsibility or authority the volunteer will have. Even simple positions should have job descriptions. Some positions need a good strong back or manual labor. Others will require individualized recruitment for special talents or skills. Staff who perform roles the day of the event should also have job descriptions for what they do during the event.

The detailed version of a job description should contain:

- Job title
- Team leader's name
- Time frame
- Duties and responsibilities
- Qualifications
- Special information (attire, physical requirements, etc.)
- Benefits (t-shirt, meal, parking, special privileges, etc.)

A listing with summarized versions of job descriptions should have been provided in recruitment materials, as well as a volunteer registration form.

A sample of both versions appears at the end of the chapter.

Where Can You Find Volunteers?

Recruitment of volunteers should occur from the day the event cycle begins through its conclusion. Large events need to start recruiting volunteers at the outset. If there are only a few positions to fill, the need is less critical. And, it's never too early to start recruiting volunteers for the future, especially if they will fill key roles like chairpersons or will provide needed services.

Diversity in the volunteer force is desirable. If possible, volunteers should be obtained from a number of sources to create an interesting mix of ages, ethnicity, backgrounds, and talents.

There are many resources to recruit volunteers:

Current volunteers	Professional associations
Community groups	Special interest groups
Press releases	Existing staff
Corporate sponsors	Committee members
Nonprofit organizations	Volunteer organizations
Service clubs	Local businesses
Senior citizens groups	General public
Churches	Neighborhood groups
Vendors and suppliers	Friends, family, and co-workers

The people directly affected through the event should be the first ones on the radar screen for potential volunteers. Once volunteers start to register, a quick assessment can match specific jobs to specific people, or you can use the "whoever wants to sign up" approach, though some volunteers may not be a good match.

Recruitment Materials

A recruitment packet of informational materials should be developed that can be easily distributed via mail, fax, or e-mail. Providing information about the event and its activities in advance gives volunteers a good picture of what's involved and generates interest.

A recruitment packet should contain the following:

- A recruitment cover letter including benefits and guidelines
- An event fact sheet
- A volunteer registration form
- A list of summarized job descriptions from which to choose
- A fact sheet about the benefiting charity, if any

The Screening Process

Depending on the level of responsibility, you may want to conduct a screening process using any number of methods for this purpose—the registration form, a personal interview, references from someone who knows them—or in some cases, a criminal background check.

Another method might be to hold a mandatory orientation for new volunteers. That way, the screening can be done on a group basis without the volunteers being aware that it is part of the purpose.

How Many Volunteers Are Needed?

Based on the duration of the event and the number of hours that need to be covered, the next step is to break the timeframes and volunteer positions into shifts.

Keep the volunteer shifts short. *A good rule of thumb is 3 hours per shift including check in and meal time.* By keeping the shifts short, the volunteer is free to enjoy the event before or after their shift. Some people will want to work a double shift or to work a shift every day. Some jobs may require longer shifts if changing personnel would be too disruptive.

To determine the timeframe that needs to be covered—Take the total event hours per day and add extra time to both the front and back end for set up and tear down.

EXAMPLE: If the event begins at 11:00 a.m. and ends at 10:00 p.m. that's an 11 hour timeframe. To that, you'll need to add 30-60 minutes at the front end for the first shift volunteers to check in, find their location, get set up, or do other activities prior to the time the event starts. Add 30 minutes or more at the end of the event for the last shift to wrap up, return supplies, or help clean up.

Adding the two together results in a TOTAL event timeframe of approximately 12 ½ hours for this example.

To determine how many shifts—Using an example of 3 ½ hours per shift, which includes 30 minutes at the beginning of the shift to get organized or have a meal, the breakout of volunteer shifts based on our 12 ½ hour example would look like this for an 11:00 a.m. to 10:00 p.m. event.

1st shift	10:00 a.m.-1:30 p.m.	2 ½ hours + 60 minutes at start
2nd shift	1:00 p.m.-4:30 p.m.	3 hours + 30 minutes at start
3rd shift	4:00 p.m.-7:30 p.m.	3 hours + 30 minutes at start
4th shift	7:00 p.m.-10:30 p.m.	2 ½ hrs + 30 min. <u>each</u> start/end

Notice how the times assigned for the shifts allow 30 minutes overlap from the time the replacement volunteer arrives before they have to begin their duties. The last shift would arrive early but remain after close to help end the day.

To determine how many volunteers are needed—Calculate the "position total" by multiplying the number of people needed per shift for each position times the number of shifts. Add the position totals for all days to obtain the total number of volunteers needed to fill that particular position.

To calculate the "daily total," add the number of volunteers needed to fill all positions for that day.

To calculate the "event total" for the number of volunteers needed to fill all positions, add the daily totals.

For example, if 4 registration people are needed per shift, and there are two shifts per day, you'll need 8 volunteers per day, or 16 total.

To lessen the number of volunteers needed—*Decrease* the number of volunteers in each position, or *decrease* the number of shifts (thereby *increasing* the number of hours in a shift).

The Master Schedule

The master schedule is basically a spreadsheet showing each day, each position, each shift, and each person who is scheduled to work during that shift. The volunteer coordinator can see at a glance which positions and which shifts still need to be filled.

This schedule is also used at volunteer headquarters during the event to check in volunteers as they arrive for their shifts. If questions or concerns arise, the schedule can also be used to determine who worked specific positions at specific times.

All of the volunteer registration forms are kept in alphabetical order in a separate binder in case the person needs to be contacted from the event site, or a separate spreadsheet or table can be kept with this information.

A sample Volunteer Master Schedule appears at the end of the chapter.

Confirmation & Communication

Volunteers need to receive confirmation materials in advance. There is no set timeframe, but about 2-3 weeks ahead seems to work well. This reminds the volunteer of their commitment so they can plan their personal schedule, but isn't so far in advance that they forget.

It's a good idea to include a statement in the recruitment letter or on the volunteer registration form that says, "Confirmation materials will be mailed to all volunteers the week of XX."

Confirmation packets should contain the following information:

- Confirmation letter including benefits and guidelines
- Detailed job description including dress code
- When to arrive, where to park, where to check in, location map
- Parking or admission pass if needed
- Event schedule

Regular communication is important. As the base of volunteers begins to build, be sure they receive newsletter mailings or other forms of event communications. They love to be "in the know" and it gives them a better understanding of how to do their job well.

At The Event

When volunteers arrive for their shifts, they should check in at a designated location. Some events have fun names like "Volunteer Villa" but "Volunteer Room" works just as well.

At check in, the volunteer should receive a name badge or identification, supplies and directions to their post, as well as other promised benefits like meal tickets, passes, t-shirts, or other items.

Depending on the event, volunteers may or may not be allowed to participate for free, or in certain activities. This should be made clear up front in the recruitment materials, and again in the confirmation, so there are no misunderstandings on the volunteer's part (.e.g. volunteers may obtain a bid number for the silent auction, volunteers are provided with a meal but not the same meal as the guests who have paid to be there, etc.)

Firing A Volunteer

There may be instances when a volunteer flagrantly violates event guidelines, does not perform their job, or deliberately causes problems with others. The first line of approach should always be to resolve the issue, coach them or move them to a different position. If met with hostility, or the problem persists, you may have to ask them to leave.

Most volunteers are honest and play by the rules. Occasionally, there are those who feel they are exceptions. They drink alcoholic beverages on duty, put a few dollars from the till in their own pocket, or take liberties assuming "no one will know."

NOTES

There should be a "no tolerance" policy for this type of behavior. Depending on the severity of the violation, relieve the volunteer of their duties and have authorized personnel escort them completely off the premises. Send them home in a taxi if inebriated. Call security or the police if a criminal act has occurred and let them handle the situation. Failure to act will just make the situation worse.

BE AWARE: If the event has not included guidelines in the recruitment and confirmation materials, the volunteer committing the violation can say they were never informed that the behavior was unacceptable.

After The Event

Thank you letters. At the very least, the volunteer coordinator and/or event manager should send every volunteer a personalized thank you. If you must send out a standardized thank you letter, at least make sure the name is spelled correctly and the address is correct, sign them personally, and add a little note.

Under no circumstances should the entire letter and signature be created on a copy machine! This gives a message to the volunteer that their participation wasn't important enough to even warrant a "real" signature.

Volunteer Party. Post-event gatherings are a great way to thank and honor volunteers. These parties often feature free pizza or other food and beverage, and may include a small gift or certificate. They also give volunteers the chance to meet others who worked on the event and to meet event leaders. The volunteer coordinator, the event manager, and (if possible) the chairperson/s should attend.

Plan ahead for the party. While taking photos or video throughout the course of the event—during set up, during the actual event, tear down and clean up—make sure to include volunteers. Edit the photos or video down to create a 5-minute presentation to show at the party. Volunteers love to see themselves having a good time and this adds to the joy of their involvement.

NOTES

The Value of Volunteers

For a real eye opener, take the number of hours worked for each position and for each shift times the number of people per shift to come up with total volunteer hours for each day. Add each day's total together to come up with the total number of hours worked by volunteers during the actual event.

To that total, add in the estimated number of hours contributed by chairmen, committees, or other volunteer hours contributed during the course of the event cycle.

Then multiply the total number of hours times a standardized rate (around $15 per hour if paying minimum wage and benefits).

What you'll get is the amount of expense the event would have had to pay out at just minimum wage for all the manpower that volunteers have provided.

And, if you have a lot of volunteers, the value of the contribution of volunteers will be very high!

Use the examples that follow to create your own volunteer materials.

Volunteer Jobs Inventory

Identify volunteer jobs first by group. Then list each individual job that will be performed under that heading (may include staff or a paid service for tracking purposes). Use the list to develop individual job descriptions.

LOCATION / JOB TITLE	LOCATION / JOB TITLE
Set Up	**Registration/Cashiering**
Handyman (works with/independent of contractors)	Team Leader (finance person)
Set Up Assistant (helps set up site/equipment)	Registrar (register guests, process transactions)
Tactics Coordinator (transport, set up)	Trouble Shooter (solves registration issues)
Signage Coordinator (place/pick up signage)	
Decorations (décor, linens, centerpieces, etc.)	**Photographer**
	Professional (photos for formal purposes)
Volunteers	Volunteer (candid shots of people/action)
Team Leader (oversees blocks of volunteers)	
Check In (checks in volunteers, etc.)	**Timekeeper**
	Timekeeper (times/records activity open to close)

Master Schedule Example

This document is best created in a spreadsheet (portrait format preferred if using clipboard).

JOB TITLE/NAME		LOCATION	SHIFT TIME	TEAM LEADER
Set Up		Ballroom	8:00 a.m.-1:00 p.m.	Joe Smith
1	Joe Smith			
2	Susan Smith			
3	Jack Russell			
4	Linda Jones			
Registrars		Foyer	4:30 p.m.-10:30 p.m.	Sherry Miller
1	Sherry Miller			
2	Jane Doe			
3	Chris Emery			
4				
Volunteer Room – Shift 1		Lower Level	3:00 p.m.-6:30 p.m.	Jenny Boone
1	Jessica Moore			
2				

Volunteer Job Description Example – Summary Version

Part of a running list of volunteer job descriptions included in Volunteer Registration materials.

Registrar

- Check in attendees as they arrive
- Provide informational assistance to guests
- Verify the attendee's name, spelling of name, and address
- Collect any monies owing at check in (for tickets, etc.)

Signage Coordinator

- Pick up signs from sign printer
- Place signs in appropriate locations according to list provided by event manager
- Pick up signs after event and return to designated storage

Volunteer Job Description Example – Detailed Version

Included in Volunteer's Confirmation materials.

ABC Auction
VOLUNTEER JOB DESCRIPTION

Volunteer Job Title:	REGISTRAR/CASHIER
Your Team Leader:	Sherry Miller
Job Location:	Foyer
Shift Time:	4:30 p.m. – 10:30 p.m.
Attire:	Business attire

Duties and Responsibilities
1. Familiarize yourself with job duties and volunteer guidelines in advance.
2. Arrive 30 minutes prior to shift start time for check in and meal
3. Check in at Volunteer Headquarters located on the lower level of the hotel
4. Check in with Team Leader for direction and enjoy your volunteer meal
5. Register guests as they arrive
6. Verify name, address, and other information against the registration list
7. Process credit card payments
8. Collect any fees owing
9. Assist guests with payments for purchases or questions at end of evening
10. Have fun and make some new friends

Special Qualifications
1. Must be able to remain calm during peak times of registration crush

---

Volunteer Recruitment Letter

Date

Name
Address
City/State/Zip

Dear Volunteer,

We'd like to invite you to join us as a volunteer for the ABC Auction. There are some great surprises in store for our volunteers and we'd like you to be part of the action on Saturday, February 20, 2008 at the Continental Hotel in Portland. We're hoping you will choose to participate and we have enclosed informational materials, summarized job descriptions, and a volunteer registration form.

Approximately 100 volunteers are needed to support the activities the event requires, including those who help with event set up, who work during the event itself, and those that help with event tear down and clean up.

All volunteers receive a complimentary meal and free parking. The hotel is also offering guest rooms at half-price ($65 plus tax) to volunteers if you wish to stay overnight. Please call the hotel directly at 503.000.0000 to make your room arrangements and mention that you are a volunteer with the ABC Auction to receive the discount. Room lists will be verified against the volunteer list prior to the event.

We recommend that you sign up soon because of the popularity of some volunteer positions. Assignments will be made on a first-come, first-served basis.

Please return your registration form no later than February 5. You may fax the form to 503.333.3333, e-mail the form to volunteers@abcauction.com, or mail it to ABC Auction, 1700 SW Busy Street, Portland, Oregon 97204. Please feel free to call us at 503.333.3330 if you have questions or send an email to info@abcauction.com.

We hope you will join us!

Sincerely,

Signature   *Signature*

Name of Volunteer Coordinator   Name of Event Manager (optional)

Volunteer Registration Form Example

ABC Auction – Saturday, February 20, 2008

Name_____   Day Phone_____

Address_____   Evening Phone_____

City/State/Zip_____   Email_____

Please fill out this form and return it by fax or mail. **PLEASE INDICATE YOUR FIRST SECOND AND THIRD CHOICE.** Assignments will be made on a first-come, first-served basis. A list of volunteer job descriptions has been attached for reference. *Number of volunteers needed for each position is indicated in italics.*

Volunteer Positions Available

□ **Day of Event Set Up**
  ___ Live Auction *(4)*   8:30 am until done
  ___ Silent Auction *(8)*   8:30 am until done
  ___ Table Decoration *(6)*   10:00 am until done

□ **Volunteer Room Host** *(1)*   3:30-8:30 pm

□ **Volunteer Check In** *(2)*   3:30-8:30 pm

□ **Coat Check** ___ Shift 1 *(2)*   4:00-7:30 pm
             ___ Shift 2 *(2)*   7:30 pm-End

□ **Registrar/Cashier** *(4)*   4:00-10:30 pm

□ **Greeter**   ___ Shift 1 *(8)*   4:00-8:00 pm
             ___ Shift 2 *(4)*   7:00-End

□ **Ballroom Usher** *(4)*   4:00–8:00 pm

□ **Live Auction Runner** *(3)*   6:30 pm-End

□ **Live Auction Spotter** *(8)*   6:30 pm-End

□ **Raffle Ticket Seller** *(6)*   4:00-8:00 pm

□ **Silent Auction Steward** *(8)* 4:00-7:30 pm

□ **Holding Room Attendant** *(6)* 6:30 pm-End

□ **Holding Room Runner** *(2)*   6:30 pm-End

□ **CLEAN UP CREW** *(10)*   10:00 pm-End

Thanks Everyone!
We Need & Appreciate You!

PLEASE RETURN THIS FORM NO LATER THAN FEBRUARY 1st TO:

Volunteer Coordinator Name
Address, City, State, Zip
Fax Number   Phone Number

Volunteer requests will be confirmed week of February 5.

Volunteer Confirmation Letter Example

Date

Name
Address
City/State/Zip

Dear Volunteer Name,

We're pleased that you will be joining us on February 20, 2008 at the Continental Hotel for the ABC Auction and we know that you will do a quality job on our behalf. A detailed job description and other information materials have been enclosed, as well as a parking pass that allows you to park in the hotel garage in the area designated for volunteers. Watch for directional signs. The volunteer parking area is indicated on the site map. You must use the Busy Street entrance to avoid being charged and the pass must be displayed on the dashboard of your vehicle.

Please check in at Volunteer Headquarters 30 minutes prior to the designated shift time, and before proceeding to your job location. This way we'll know you have arrived and you can receive your name badge, meal, and other items. Volunteer Headquarters is located on the lower level of the Continental Hotel.

The enclosed site map also provides information regarding questions you may be asked such as locations for restrooms, parking, event office, etc. Admission opens to our guests at 5:00 p.m. and we expect the event to end by approximately 10:00 p.m.

Please read all information in your packet. It is the responsibility of every volunteer working on the ABC Auction to be aware of their job duties and the guidelines the event has established. We would like to reiterate our policy that no volunteer may consume alcoholic beverages while on duty. This includes wine left over from the banquet dinner. Any extra sponsor gifts or unopened wine are to be returned to the temporary event office located in the foyer. We appreciate your adherence to our guidelines since violation can result in complete shutdown of the event by the Liquor Control Commission and/or a monetary fine for us and the hotel.

If you are unable to volunteer due to emergency or illness, please notify us at once so we can fill your position. Prior to February 20th, please call 503.333.3330. The day of the event, please call 503.333.3337 (coordinator's cell phone) or the hotel at 503.333.0000 and ask to have a message delivered to the ABC Auction Volunteer Coordinator.

Thank you again for volunteering. Enjoy the action, have some fun, and make some new friends!

Best regards,

Signature

ABC Auction Volunteer Coordinator

Chapter 15 – The Event

Countdown to Liftoff

The culmination of all efforts leads to the actual event. Here, all of the roads intersect, all of the strategy comes into play, and all of the hard work pays off. A great program or activities, enthusiastic and knowledgeable volunteers, wonderful food, beautiful décor, and good company combine to create an exciting atmosphere with the best possible results.

This chapter identifies activities that take place from four weeks in advance, up to and through the event. Some of these are explained in detail here because they are a more logical fit in this chapter than in preceding sections.

This chapter talks about:

➢ The Pre-Event Phase
➢ Administrative and logistical matters
➢ Audio visual preparation
➢ Timing of food service
➢ Training venue staff and volunteers
➢ Seating arrangements
➢ Transportation
➢ Registration and cashiering functions
➢ Guest confirmations
➢ Care and handling of VIPs
➢ End of the event clean up and deliveries

THE PRE-EVENT PHASE

Technically, everything that takes place from the event's inception up to the actual event is the "pre-event" phase, but for this purpose, we are starting four weeks out.

"Do not go where the path may lead; go instead where there is no path and leave a trail."

Ralph Waldo Emerson

Four+ Weeks In Advance

The following are things you can do four or more weeks in advance, as well as tasks that will continue up to the event.

Registration lists. Names and addresses for as many guests as possible should be entered into the database software. Print out a guest listing and cross-check for correct spelling, addresses, and zip codes. A volunteer or staff member can telephone contacts for missing information. You will repeat this process up to the ticket or catalog mailing (and up to the event for late registrations).

Having to provide guest names and addresses for a mailing deadline is a good incentive for sponsors or table hosts who haven't finished filling their tables. Though there are always changes in table guests, having the majority of the information obtained and recorded in advance will save time as guests arrive and go through registration.

Keep up on the registration list! It is a very time consuming process and is best done every day or you will get far, far behind. This task can also be delegated with specific instructions to a staff person or a skilled data entry volunteer.

Donor data entry. Double check all donation information and make sure correct values appear. Print reports and cross-check to make sure none are missing or incorrect. Review and make any corrections.

Print Raffle Tickets. By now, the raffle prize should have been identified. State laws stipulate what information must be printed on raffle tickets. You may want to limit the number of tickets so that the odds are better of winning, which will in turn motivate people to purchase them. If you are selling raffle tickets in advance of the event, they will need to be printed sooner than if the raffle is only being offered during the actual event.

Print the raffle ticket in two parts with the ticket number on both ends. The ticket should be perforated so that the smaller numbered end of the ticket can be split from the larger portion that the purchaser retains. Number the tickets sequentially but make sure both ends of the ticket have the same number.

If the event is simple, and all guests will be present during the drawing, using rolls of duplicate tickets purchased from a party or office supply store may suffice and you won't need to go to the expense of printing tickets.

Methods for selling tickets are discussed later in this chapter.

Order gifts. Gifts for sponsors, VIPs, and others should be ordered 4-6 weeks in advance and should be received no later than 2-3 weeks before the event. It's hard to get an accurate estimate as to quantities if you order too early. Order extras to cover new sponsor tables or other needs that occur at the last minute. Surplus gifts can be used for other purposes throughout the year.

VIPs appreciate gourmet food or wine baskets, chocolates, or similar simple gifts. Flowers may not be a good idea if the recipient is from out of town because it's difficult for them to take the flowers with them when they leave or to have to carry them from place to place. It's nice to have the gifts delivered to VIPs upon arrival (or the day before the event if they are local).

Another low-cost option for events that benefit schools or nonprofit organizations serving children is to have the children create thank you notes or color pictures that can used to create thank you notes. These simple gifts often mean more to a sponsor, donor or guest than something you bought that they probably don't need.

Prepare event Thank You Notes and Letters in advance. There's no rule that you have to wait until after the event is over to create thank you letters or personal notes.

You can begin hand-writing personal thank you notes weeks in advance. Keep the thank you notes vague enough that you don't have to include specific numbers or references to what happened at the event. If you want to include a statement like "Thank you for helping us raise $XXX," in your personal notes, as long as you use the same pen, the amount could be filled in after the event. Then all you need to do is seal a pre-addressed envelope and send them out.

The same can be done with creating a thank you letter that will be part of a merge mailing.

Three Weeks in Advance

Prepare for the ticket or program mailing. This mailing needs to go out no less than 10 working days in advance. Work with volunteers to prepare for the ticket or catalog mailing a day or two before these printed pieces are scheduled to be delivered. That way, you'll be ready to go when you receive them.

If sponsors haven't provided names and addresses of guests, all tickets or catalogs will need to be delivered to the sponsor for distribution to their guests.

You will need envelopes, registration lists, address labels printed in the order of the registration list, all materials to be mailed, packing tape, anything else you need, and *lots of postage* in the meter (or take the ready-to-mail packages to the post office and have them weighed and stamped there).

It is especially critical to mail out the catalogs in advance for an auction event. Guests need time to peruse the various items for sale and plan what they want to bid on. It also provides time for them to figure out how they will purchase big ticket items before they get there. Not having this information in advance will cost the auction thousands of dollars because guests do not come prepared, so make sure to send out catalogs in advance.

NOTES

Confirmations. Confirmations should be sent in advance of—or along with—the ticket mailing. Each guest should receive a confirmation for the activities in which they have chosen to participate. Some events do not require sending tickets or event programs in advance (e.g. a fair or festival with gate admission and no pre-sales). Or there may not be "formal" tickets and the guest receives a confirmation postcard, letter, or form instead and their name shows on the registration list at check-in.

Use a letter, or use a form for confirmation? This is a matter of choice based on what works best for your event.

Gift certificates. Fundraising events such as auctions may use two kinds of certificates—gift certificates from restaurants, hotels and the like, as well as generic certificates which are generated by the auction.

As gift certificates are received, *make a photocopy of the certificate and all needed supplemental information.* This practice is well worth the extra effort. If you haven't kept a copy and the purchaser loses the original certificate or has questions, you have no reference to certificate numbers or other information to resolve the situation.

Certificates generated by the auction are provided for things such as catered dinners in private homes, large parties with multiple individual purchasers, and many other things. These certificates do not need to be sent by registered mail (unless they are going out with more critical certificates) because they can be easily printed out again if needed. Keep a copy of these certificates for event records.

Bullet points from catalog copy can be used as the foundation for the generic certificates. *Make sure that any changes or corrections from the catalog addendum are included since they will differ from the original catalog copy.*

Rather than bidders taking original certificates home from the event, some auctions have adopted the practice of mailing certificate items to winning bidders within 10-14 days of the event.

251

Gift certificates with high dollar value (e.g. airline ticket vouchers), should be sent by a method that requires signing for the delivery such as registered mail, Fed/Ex/UPS or courier. Certificates received from restaurants, hotels, spas, and so on may be very difficult to replace if the buyer loses them.

The *Rules of Purchase* in the auction catalog should contain a section about certificates and the method of distribution, as well as a disclaimer that the auction will not be responsible for certificates that are lost or misplaced.

Two+ Weeks In Advance

The following are things that can be done two or more weeks prior to the event.

Administrative Tasks

Data Entry. Data entry in regard to donations or ticket sales should be nearly complete and cross-checked to make sure none have been left out.

Registration Lists. Names and addresses of guests should be as complete as possible by this time.

Ticket and/or catalog mailing. Tickets can be mailed as registration comes in for events like plays, dinners, etc. if guests won't need further information. Otherwise, you'll need to do a mass mailing in advance.

Mail tickets or catalogs first-class mail. You'll ensure that guests will have the information on time. You don't want your materials sitting in some post office's bulk mail processing.

Confirmations. Continue up until a few days before the event when everything will have to transition to Will Call, or needs to be delivered either in person or via courier.

Special deliveries to key players. Use a local courier service or overnight shipping to get the materials into their hands as soon as possible. It is well worth the extra cost and they will remember what great service you provided when they are asked to participate in the future.

Email, ship overnight, or courier notes about AV, order of the program, and other vital information to the main speaker, emcee, or auctioneer. These folks need time to review and become familiar with the event in order for them to do their best. They may also want to make changes or modifications and you need lead time as well. A final version can be sent to them the week prior to the event. This is a critical process, but is often overlooked.

Check requests for on-site payments to vendors and others. Checks may be required to pay entertainers, contractors, or others during the event. These should be requested in advance so that they will be available when needed.

Unless prior arrangements have been made for billing, the event will be expected to take care of catering and other charges at the end of the evening. Most venues or caterers will accept credit cards or may be willing to send an invoice since it may not be possible to determine the exact amount of the charges until the event is over.

Another method is to provide a credit card in advance which will be charged post-event. Or bring a blank check that can be filled out and signed when the bill is presented. If you do this, make sure the signatory is available, or if the check is pre-signed, keep it in a safe place. Make sure to obtain all paperwork to back up the charges.

Prepare a media advisory. You may want to send out a media advisory (similar to a press release) two to five days prior to the event. This provides the press with the opportunity to cover the event with a news crew or send a photographer to take pictures.

NOTES

253

Provide a set time (e.g. 3:00-4:00 p.m.) during set up or just prior to the event opening for photo or video opportunities and interviews with VIPs. The media may also arrive unannounced during the actual event and you'll have to handle it on the fly.

Final printing of forms and last minute signage. Forms needed for registration or other purposes can be finalized and printed during this time period. These include things like auction bid sheets, delivery forms, etc.

Sponsor recognition signs. All sponsors should have been identified by this time, so take advantage of the opportunity to have signage crediting sponsors prepared at this time.

Provide the information to the sign maker 7-10 days in advance of the event, or sooner if there will not be changes. Be sure you see a proof of the sign before it is printed to check for spelling and accuracy and have it printed 4-6 days in advance. Plan to pick up the sign or have it delivered a couple of days before the event, and check it again for accuracy.

Menu printing. Print the menu as a separate document or include it in a printed program. Make sure the menu looks as professional as possible since guests will refer to it numerous times.

Print one for each guest expected plus with some extras. Hold back at least 5 copies for your records.

Logistical Matters

Confirm, confirm, confirm. Check to ensure that entertainers, production contractors, lodging, and any other critical arrangements are confirmed. Pick up or delivery of specific items such as floral centerpieces, wine, equipment, and such should also be confirmed. You don't want any surprises on event day!

NOTES

Logistics schedule finalization. The logistics schedule should be further refined during the event countdown in regard to timing of the set up, execution, and tear down of event elements. You will most likely find there are a number of things that will need to be altered or added.

Scripts and speeches. If you don't write or outline the opening speeches, recognitions or awards yourself, make sure that you review what the chairman or other speaker plans to say. We certainly want to thank people, but keep it short and simple. One way to circumvent a windy speech is to acknowledge people in the written program for their contributions, rather than have a long list of names read from the stage.

Chairmen and others often take advantage of the opportunity to be the center of attention and can ramble on and on. This will create a ripple effect by throwing off the timing of the rest of the event. Giving them a firm amount of time they can speak often helps to alleviate this problem.

The script itself should have set time frames for opening remarks, speeches, or awards so the event stays on track. If a speaker sees they have only 2 minutes, they may run over but will keep their remarks shorter than if there is no set limit.

PLEASE… For fundraisers, banquets or awards dinners, limit the beginning program to no more than 10-15 minutes *including any videos*, before the main event begins. Remember, raising money is the focus, so get to the heart of the event as quickly as possible. If guests have to wait through a lengthy program, they tend to leave early.

Create the AV script. The AV script is a document used by contractors or others working with the visual media (live camera, video, Power Point) to know what is happening in regard to the event sequence, projection, notations of where key players are sitting, and so on.

Use the Logistics Schedule (or order of sale if an auction), and adapt it for this purpose. List things in the order they will occur and what is happening in regard to the audio and visual production.

It might look something like this:

Time	Detail	Live Camera	PowerPoint/Video
7:00 p.m.	Emcee welcome	Stage, emcee	Sponsor Logo
7:15 p.m.	Chairman's remarks	Stage, chairman	
7:30 p.m.	Introductory video		Show video

Timing the Food Service

Again, use the Logistics Schedule to time the food service. As a general rule, it takes about 15 minutes after the initial call to dinner for people to finish their socializing with friends or to use the restrooms before they take their seats.

Setting specific times for dinner courses to be served is one way to time the food service. However, this may not match with the progression of the event program. If you choose to use this method, factor in the time it takes for the speeches and other preliminaries and schedule the first dinner course to be served at the end of the first segment (allow for a 5-minute leeway).

Do not *pre-set the salads or desserts on dinner tables if you are having a fundraising event like an auction* because you want people to stay for the whole thing. Having these food items already on the table speeds up the dinner process. Once the dessert is served, it's a psychological signal that it's time to leave. If it's already on the table when the guests arrive, do you see what kind of a message you are sending?

It's perfectly acceptable to pre-set salad or dessert for events like banquet luncheons where the program is about 90 minutes long.

NOTES

Another way to facilitate the timing of food service is to do it by program sequence. For example, let's use a 3-course dinner (soup or salad, entrée, and dessert) at an awards banquet to demonstrate how this works.

The first course (salad or soup) is served at the completion of the opening remarks and as the actual program is commencing. This means there are two courses left, including dessert (served when there are approximately 30 minutes left of the evening.

If we begin with the soup/salad at the end of the general remarks, and the program consists of two awards being given with recipients giving their own remarks, this leaves two more courses to distribute between the first award and the last part of the program. For a two-hour event, this means the first course would be served at the 15-20 minute mark.

A benchmark is that it typically takes 15-20 minutes for everyone to be served for each course, and another 10-15 minutes for a course to be consumed and plates cleared. This should give a good perspective on when the courses should be served.

Do not send out one course immediately following another. You may want to allow an extra 10-20 minutes between courses. It may seem like the dinner is dragging, but as previously mentioned, once the dessert comes out it creates a psychological signal to your guests that the evening is over. If dessert is served too soon, you'll lose a sizeable number of guests before the evening ends.

You are the best judge of what will work for your event. Take the entire length of the "formal" evening where people will be seated for dining and the event program, and divide it into logical breaks for food service. It should be easy to see the most appropriate place in the Logistics Schedule to do this with as little disruption to the program as possible. If it's a short program, you may want to have people finish their meal before the program begins.

More Helpful Hints

Gift wrapping. Schedule volunteers to help wrap gifts for sponsors or guests approximately two weeks in advance. Provide an adequate supply of wrapping paper and plenty of ribbon. Give volunteers clear instructions about how the gifts should be wrapped and provide a completed sample. After the gifts are wrapped, they can be put into boxes for storage until it's time to transport them to the event site.

Create decorative table signage, and gather props and other items for display. Many events use information set in picture frames, cardboard signs with cardboard easel backs, or décor that will be set up by volunteers.

Think about who will do this. They should begin to gather materials and supplies well in advance. Displays should look classy, rather than "homemade" and the more lead time to create displays the better.

Orientation for Venue Staff & Volunteers

Meet with venue staff. You may want to hold a meeting with the staff of the venue at least two weeks in advance. Depending on the event size, there could be a few people or many at this meeting.

Most venues coordinate food service through the banquet or catering department whose team leaders should attend the meeting. If it's a small event, meeting with the banquet captain (and/or catering manager) is probably sufficient because they will pass the information down to their crew.

At the meeting, review the standards of service and make sure you are clear about how things will work, who does what, and so forth. On the other hand, they should understand how you'd like things to be done and to whom their questions should be addressed during the event.

Be sure to designate one (event manager) or two people to work with the banquet captain, chef, or caterer. What often happens is that numerous volunteers ask the staff or the caterer to do things when these requests should be channeled through the event manager. From the venue or caterer's perspective, it is confusing because though they may know you, their staff may not and they aren't familiar with whoever is authorized to give them direction.

This is especially critical if extra charges may be incurred as a result of what unauthorized people are asking the staff or caterer to do.

Hold a volunteer training. An orientation for volunteer team leaders (or open it to all volunteers) should be conducted about two weeks in advance to go over logistics and volunteer functions. This is especially important if things have changed from the previous year (new venue, new volunteer jobs, different leaders, etc.).

Volunteers feel uncomfortable if they don't understand how things work and they tend to take matters into their own hands or give out incorrect information. This may create problems that could have been avoided with the proper training and information.

Coach team leaders, go over logistics, and provide them with a site map or floor plan and other materials so they will be effective in working with volunteers under their supervision. They need to know the chain of command regarding food service, registration, and such so that it's not a free-for-all once the event commences.

The event manager and volunteer coordinator must attend the volunteer orientation/training because there will be questions that only they can answer.

Prepare supplies. Take advantage of the opportunity to gather supplies that volunteers or others will need in advance. A person other than the event manager or volunteer coordinator can perform this task as long as they have a list of what's required.

Create a checklist for each area (e.g. registration, silent auction, etc.) or job group (e.g. auction spotters need flashlights) and verify as supplies are gathered. Place supplies in a box or bag, and label them. You could also group supplies according to the area of the facility where they will be used.

For example, supplies needed to set up a silent auction such as special props, tape, scissors, and so on would be grouped together with other things needed and prepared for transport. Specific supplies or décor for individual auction lots can be bagged separately and labeled with their lot number so items designated for display will not be used elsewhere.

Do not put auction bid sheets with volunteer supplies. The event manager should hang on to them until they are ready to be placed next to auction lots. These are a critical component of the evening's financial success and you don't want them to be lost among the volunteer supplies or in the chaos of set up.

Regardless of what kind of event it is, if you are borrowing supplies, props, or decorating elements, mark them with the owner's name and phone number, and label them "Display Only." This way, if their owner doesn't get them back, this will help to track the items down. Otherwise, whoever takes down the display has no idea what to do with these things.

Supplies needed at volunteer check-in would be assembled in the same way. These include name tags, registration lists, parking passes, meal tickets, and things needed to facilitate volunteers as they arrive and throughout the event.

The more organized you can be, the easier the process will flow once event set up commences and you'll ensure that there will be enough supplies for everyone to use. It's frustrating to look for common tools that are floating around "someplace" when it would have been so much easier to have your own supplies.

One+ Week In Advance

The following are things you can do one week or more in advance, as well as tasks that will continue up to the event.

Administrative Tasks

Finalize registration lists. The names and addresses for as many guests as possible should be entered by now. Print out a guests listing and cross-check for correct spelling, address and zip code. A volunteer or staff member can telephone or email contacts for missing information.

Final data entry. Double check all donations and make sure correct values appear. Print reports to make sure none are missing or incorrect. Review and make any corrections.

Tickets and programs. If some of the guests have missed the ticket or program mailing, they can come to the office to pick these up, they can be couriered, or they can be placed at Will Call.

Logistical Matters

Seating arrangements. This can be done two weeks in advance and then be adjusted at the one week point. We often find that the whole thing gets changed if it's done too far ahead.

Print out the guest list and assign sponsor or corporate table locations and individual seating assignments using the floor plan. Use a highlighter to mark off the sponsor/corporate tables on the site plan as they are assigned and write the table number on the guest list for cross-reference. Once this has been done and completely finalized, enter the table assignments into the registration information in the computer.

Don't enter the table numbers until they have been finalized or you may end up having to change them all and it's confusing for whoever is doing it. Make sure the event chairmen, the CEO, the event manager, and other appropriate parties take part in the process, or at least review the seating assignments, before entering the information into the system. You can expect there will be a number of changes in individual seating, but full tables purchased by sponsors or others should remain as they are on the seating diagram once it is approved.

Site plan finalization. Once table assignments are complete, finalize the site plan. If using more than one area of a venue (e.g. using the lobby for registration), the site plan for those areas can be completed well in advance.

Wait until the day before moving to the event site to make copies of the seating chart (unless it has to be done further out), but site plans for other uses (e.g. reception areas, silent auction layout, etc.) can be readied ahead of time. Make enough copies for staff, key volunteers and team leaders to hand out at the event site, and email them in advance for others to review if possible.

Print table signs. Two or three days before the event, and once the table assignments are firm, print the table signs. If you are only using table numbers without names, you can skip this process.

It's a nice gesture to create personalized table signs with the table number and sponsor's name on them. It helps the AV crew if a large number is printed on the back of the table sign to help them locate people identified on the AV script.

Creating table signs is easy with today's computer printers and specialty papers. These can be found in the specialty or wedding paper sections of office supply stores. Wedding invitation stock makes great table signs, but you may have to purchase a "kit" containing envelopes along with the invitation paper. Make sure the paper will feed through the printer and is not too stiff.

NOTES

The 8 ½" x 11" paper folds to a half-page sign (5 ½" x 8 ½") that is inserted into a wire number holder on the table. Another method that works is to use the tall, clear plastic "forks" in the flower arrangement/centerpieces that would typically hold a gift card to hold the table sign, as long as it is anchored well so it doesn't tip.

Logistics schedule finalization. The logistics schedule should have been a work in progress for some time prior to this point. Make any final adjustments before copying and distributing to staff, venue representatives, volunteer coordinator, team leaders, and others. This document can be electronically mailed to appropriate parties for their input before printing the final version.

Scripts and speeches. Keep the program as short as possible. Review and cut out anything that is not necessary. People can be thanked in the written program rather than from the stage if they are not playing a major role. Time the sequencing in advance to make sure you are on target. Event chairpersons, the event manager, or speakers should review scripts prior to making copies for distribution. The speaker should provide an outline of his/her remarks, and receive a copy of the script of what others will say.

Finalize the AV script. Make any final adjustments to the AV script. Contractors and others involved in the production of audio visual elements should have input and should receive the final version a week in advance.

Any adjustments in table seating should be reflected in an updated version of the AV script and handed out the day of the event. This is critical if live camera operators will need to find key people seated at numbered dinner tables.

Prepare for transport. Try to assemble everything in one room that needs to be transported from the office. It is helpful if things are grouped according to where they should be taken upon arrival at the event site.

Confirm arrangement for transport of event supplies from office or storage locations to the event site. Delivery-size trucks are ideal because they hold a large amount of items. Assign an organized, hardy volunteer to oversee this process since they may need to lift or carry heavy items when loading and unloading.

Two+ Days in Advance

Final catering guarantee. A final guarantee on the number of meals is normally required 2-3 days or more in advance depending on the venue, caterer or complexity of the menu. By this time, you should have a good gauge on how many meals to order, both for guests and for volunteers.

Final confirmation with venue. Confirm load in, set up, move out, and other critical functions with the venue. Reviewing this a final time will help you to remember what is supposed to happen when and who's going to do it.

Training on computer software. If a volunteer who is not familiar with the computer software will be entering data at the event, they need to receive basic training in order to perform their duties efficiently. This should take no more than an hour and can be done a week or more ahead of time, but not so far in advance they will have forgotten what to do. Doing this closer to the event keeps it fresh in their mind.

Finalize the logistics schedule. Make only as many copies as you need, plus a few spares. The logistics schedule can be marked up by hand if changes are needed beyond this point. Write the name of each recipient of the schedule in the upper right hand corner so if any are left, you know who hasn't received their copy.

The event manager's copy should include all adjustments. If a change doesn't apply to everyone, only mark up the copy the appropriate person will receive.

NOTES

Deliveries. The venue may or may not accept deliveries ahead of time based on other events or activities occurring at the facility. Schedule any deliveries to the event site for either the day before, or morning of, the event. Make sure deliveries are labeled with the name of the event and the person who is to receive them.

Confirm that there is secure storage space available if you will not be present when the delivery arrives, or assign a person to oversee this function. This is tricky if it's an outdoor event because you'll need overnight security to ensure nothing goes missing.

Confirm transport volunteers. Confirm arrangement for vehicles and person who will transport items from the office or other locations to the event site. Make sure everything is labeled as to where it goes.

Ready event operation for transport. It's a good idea to gather everything needed from an operational standpoint two or more days in advance where possible. You may be too busy with other matters the day before the event.

With the exception of final lists and reports that need to be printed at the last possible moment, you can gather office supplies, printed materials, the event manager's needs, the operational notebook, permits, signs, check or financial paperwork, and so on in advance.

Don't forget to bring extra copies of event programs, menus, or other materials your guests may need.

One+ Day In Advance

Review meeting. Try to schedule this meeting for the morning or afternoon of the day before, not the day of, the event. Meeting participants include the event chairs, committee chairs (if performing a major role). Go over the program and the main logistical elements.

NOTES

A review meeting is critical for fundraising events. If the event is an auction, the auctioneer should also be present to establish opening bids and discuss details pertinent to specific lots in the live auction.

This meeting can be held at the event site, a restaurant, or at an office location. Go over each event element and make notes. If everyone feels a meeting is not needed, or you can do it a week ahead, it's one less thing to worry about.

Deliver VIP gifts. Gifts are delivered to the VIP's hotel room or residence either by courier service, or personally by a key volunteer such as a board member, event chair or staff person.

Contractor load in and set up. If time and the venue allow, try to set up staging, props, visual media, sound lighting, and such a day in advance if the facility is secure. This is to the contractor's advantage because it helps to avoid scheduling conflicts with other jobs or having to pay overtime to their crews to complete the job under a time crunch. It is also to the event's advantage because contractors can provide better service when they aren't being rushed.

Back up the computer data. Do this toward the end of the day when no more data will be entered until after computers are transported and set up at the event site. If using rental computers, make sure the computers have the proper configuration and software is loaded and tested so that all systems function correctly.

Computers and printers. One or more very efficient computers are required, especially for events like auctions that have data entry going on for the duration. Wireless connections between computers used on the stage and computers in the lobby work are ideal rather than many feet of cable.

A fast laser printer and plenty of paper, as well as extra toner cartridges are required. Ink jet printers are too slow to print out the reports, receipts, and other on-site paperwork that events require.

Review registration/cashiering procedure. Review how it's going to work as if you were the guest. Supplies needed for registration and cashiering should be gathered together. If possible, have a staff member handle any cash rather than a volunteer.

Finalize guest/registration lists. Just before the event operation moves to the event site, back up the system and print out two versions of the guest list—one by individual name and one by table name/number. Be sure you have copied the information to a computer disk in case there are problems.

Finalize site plan/seating chart. Make copies early in the afternoon the day before the event to assure there are no further changes in table or seating locations. Alterations in guests at tables are to be expected. If event chairmen and other key players have signed off on the seating locations, there should be no need to change the site plan for seating beyond this point.

Print new or revised table signs. Copy the table sign layout to a computer disk in a common software program (like MS Word) so you can use other computers and printers located on-site if last minute changes are needed. Bring extra blank sheets of the table sign paper. There always seem to be company name changes or misspellings that pop up at the event site and this makes it easy to print new versions without a lot of hassle.

All items transported to venue. If you can use the venue the day before, transport as much as possible ahead of time so that it will be available as needed. Try to keep items that go together in the same group. Upon arrival, items should be placed in a secure central storage area if they won't be used right away.

Transport your own supplies yourself. This means event records, permits, contracts, checks or financial documents, office supplies, and other items you need. You don't want to be waiting for someone else to bring supplies or critical information if you need them.

NOTES

THE SET UP PHASE

Administrative Tasks

Items transported to venue (if not done the day before). If you can't bring anything in until the day of the event, it is extremely critical to be as organized as possible on all fronts. Allow plenty of time for transport of everything to the event site so that set up can begin at the scheduled time.

Computer set up. The technician who handles the office computers is often a good person to perform this function. If your organization uses an outside contractor for computer maintenance or assistance, they may be willing to donate their services, or trade for tickets.

Depending on the sophistication level of the event, you'll need at least one computer (and ideally two that are networked together). Primary computers are typically located in the temporary office or registration area, and satellite computers can be located at the stage or in other locations depending on what's needed.

Again, you need a fast laser printer, lots of paper and extra print cartridges to process on-site paperwork. Ink jet printers are too slow.

Be cautious about who enters information into the computer, and make sure they know how to use it. Things can get messed up in a hurry if data is entered incorrectly and you are relying on it for critical information during the event.

Logistical Matters

Provide the AV crew with an updated script. Any changes that were made during set up or in seating arrangements for key guests need to be noted. Make sure that the director/producer, video assistant, and other key personnel have up-to-date information. You could also hold a quick group meeting and everyone can mark up their own copy with the changes.

268

Registration/cashiering area. Getting guests through registration is a critical component of the event. To keep the registration line moving, allow one registrar for every 75-100 guests expected.

The configuration of the registration area is the key to a smooth flow. Use standard 6' or 8' banquet tables which have been topped with linen and skirted, and set straight across for guests to access. If space is limited another option is to use a "U" shape with one or more tables across the front and one on each side.

One work space and one chair should be allowed for each registrar. This may be cramped if using the U-shaped configuration. Place a designated "troubleshooter" at one end so that those guests taking a longer time to register can move to the end and not impede the flow.

Behind the row of registration tables is a second row of narrower tables that holds needed materials and files.

We don't recommend guests be required to stand in a registration line based alphabetically on last name. This bogs down the entire process. Neither should guests be allowed to mob the registrars.

One solution that works well is to stanchion off a section about 8' to 10' out from the front of the registration tables in a "V" formation. One main line automatically feeds guests to the next available registrar especially if a volunteer is stationed at the entry point to point out who's available to help them.

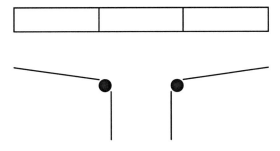

Another method would be to create several individual lines using rope stanchions similar to those used by banks, where guests would automatically be fed to a registrar based on what line they were in, not necessarily the next registrar who was available.

.The actual registration process is described in the Event Phase section which follows.

Registration supplies. These depend on the size and type of event.

Access to electrical power	Laser printer, print cartridge/s
Backup disks	Markers, erasers
Calculators	Paper, white 1-2 reams
Cash boxes	Paper, specialty
Computer, monitor, keyboard, mouse	Paper clips
Computer cables	Pens
Credit card machines	Petty cash
Credit card slips	Power strips
Envelopes for credit card receipts	Printed programs
Event software	Registration lists in alpha order
Extension cords, 3-prong	Registration lists by table name
Files and file holders	Stapler, staples
Highlighters	Tape

Volunteer area. Set up one or two skirted 8' banquet tables for volunteer check-in. The expected influx of volunteers for each shift should be the determining factor.

Provide banquet tables/dining rounds and chairs for volunteers to sit, eat a meal, or rest. If serving volunteer meals, the volunteer room is the best place to provide this service.

Name tags may be created in advance but some will change prior to the actual event. Bring extras to create name badges on site. It's a nice touch to add a small event logo or theme oriented graphic in the corner, rather than a plain name badge with only the person's name.

Signage. Signs should be placed in appropriate locations according to a list developed in advance. Signs or banners should be tasteful. Make sure that signage does not impact lines of vision to the stage or critical event elements. If using easels, make sure that the legs do not stick out into the traffic flow so people don't trip on them.

Decorations. This can include everything from floor to ceiling decorations, to things like tables, linens, chair covers, centerpieces, glassware, gifts, and more.

Floral arrangements. There are uses for floral arrangements other than table centerpieces. Consider entries, registration tables, display tables, and other locations. Make sure the flowers do not have an overpowering fragrance. This is especially critical for events where wine is a focus because it will interfere with the bouquet of the wine.

Centerpieces should not be so tall that they impact the line of sight to the stage, or so large they interfere with dining. One event created elaborate Eiffel Tower centerpieces for a Parisian theme that ended up on the floor because guests couldn't see each other across the dinner table, let alone see the stage.

THE EVENT PHASE

It's time for the show! The guests are coming, the place looks great, a delicious meal awaits and excitement is in the air.

Conduct a final sound, lighting, and visual media check. It's important to ensure that all systems are working properly well before the arrival of guests. You'll also need to do a check of any cameras, PowerPoint, and other AV elements.

Early arrival of chairmen, VIPs, or speaker. Ask them to arrive dressed for the evening approximately one hour before the event begins. This gives time to take professional photos or video and to allow these VIPs to go through registration before the doors open.

NOTES

The reason to set this activity for an hour ahead is that someone will invariably be late and you don't need too much to do in too little time right before guests start coming in. It also allows chairmen and VIPs to greet guests as they arrive and thank them for coming.

Photos and video. A photo and video record of the entire event is important. Ask the photographer to allow at least an hour in addition to formal photos to document every area of the event—the décor, the dinner table settings, the auction displays, the registration area, the volunteer room and more. Once the guests arrive, you'll lose the opportunity to take unobstructed photos.

Photo and video records can be used for many purposes. Create a record of how the event looked. Don't forget to take photos during the move in, set up and move out phases. These can be taken by a staff member or volunteer who is good at photography.

Photos of guests can be inserted in notes or cards to thank them for their participation. You'll also want an annual photo album of the event. Photos of volunteers can be used at a post-event thank you party or in many other ways.

On-site production of a "Happy Face" video allows guests to see themselves having a good time on event night. The Happy Face video can have a great introduction, be set over a music track, and is a tremendous marketing tool to show prospective sponsors or donors. The video should be 3 ½ - 4 ½ minutes in length (the same amount of time as the musical selection).

If using live cameras, make sure to record rough footage, with sound, of the entire live event from beginning to end. You'll be surprised at how many times you may need to refer to this later on. This is especially important for fundraising events like an auction to verify who sat where, who bid on certain items, to clarify bidder numbers (e.g. "19" sounds like "90" when spoken), to capture special or impromptu moments, and so on.

Registration and Cashiering. Registration is the first place that your guests have contact. Coach registration personnel on what to say when greeting guests. A good opener is *"Hello. Welcome to the Event Name. Could we verify your contact information?"*

For fundraising events, you might want to add something like *"How would you like to pay for your purchases this evening? If you like we can swipe your credit card or take a check now so that you can avoid the cashier line at the end of the evening. We'll only charge the card or fill in the check if you make purchases. You'll receive a credit card slip in the mail or a copy of the check that matches your receipt. If you don't make any purchases, we'll send you a voided credit card slip or check."*

Provide each registrar with copies of two reports—one lists guests by last name, and one is by table name with assigned guests. The event manager will need a set, and you'll need extra copies for use by registration assistants or others.

If corrections need to be made, use a postcard-size form and pass it to the data entry person for revisions, or save them to make the changes a little later in the evening.

One knowledgeable registrar should be designated as troubleshooter. If guests encounter problems during registration, they can move to a designated area for assistance and the rest of the registration line can keep moving.

Extra programs. Guests may have received their programs in advance, but a supply should be available at registration. Each registrar should have a few that can be replenished from a box placed under the table skirting. Events that don't require pre-event mailings could place the event program at each guest's seat.

Raffles. Sales of raffle tickets can be conducted in several ways as long as they comply with state regulations. Whatever method you use, keep it simple.

NOTES

Raffle tickets can be sold in advance of the event by numerous people and unsold tickets can be returned for sale during the event. Make sure that unsold tickets are accounted for so they cannot be used without payment. Roving ticket sellers can speak to anyone in any location at the event. A centralized raffle booth where the prize is displayed should also be used.

Give the larger part of the ticket with the prize information and other details to the ticket purchaser. Retain the end stub with the matching number for the drawing.

Try to offer a couple of options to potential ticket purchasers. One ticket for $X or 3 tickets for $X. You'll sell more tickets if you offer a price break incentive.

Cash only ticket sales tend to be tedious. If you allow credit card purchases of raffle tickets, you'll need enough volunteers to run back and forth to process purchases. If the event is an auction, you can allow guests to use their bidder numbers to buy raffle tickets. Keep a log of bidder number and amount which can be added to purchases made under each bidder's number.

Raffle ticket sellers need to actively solicit ticket sales, be assertive, and be pleasantly persuasive. Display the raffle item in one location (with a guardian!) where guests can see it. If raffle tickets are being sold in multiple locations and there is only one item, it complicates things if the prize is being carried around and no one knows where to find it.

Keep selling raffle tickets until just before the program begins. Make an announcement approximately 5-10 minutes before raffle sales close. Hold the raffle just before the opening speeches, or at the end of the evening. Incorporate the raffle drawing into the logistics schedule depending on when the drawing is to be held.

THE END OF THE EVENT

Tear down and clean up. Contractors will tear down and load out either the evening of the event or the following morning. Many contractors prefer to stay late and get this done rather than pay their crews to come back the next morning.

Don't start to tear down the event before the guests leave! Once they have departed, check all areas to make sure nothing is left behind. When tearing down the tables, stage or other displays, anything left on them or under them will be moved or thrown away.

Schedule enough manpower to take care of other needs either the night of the event, or the following morning.

Day-After deliveries. If you offer this service, plan carefully in advance. Don't offer this to everyone, just large dollar buyers or for heavy/bulky items, or it may get totally out of hand. You also might want to consider a small additional fee for this service.

Guests don't always give complete directions, so be sure you have a home telephone number and retain copies of the delivery forms. Delivery forms should be two-part NCR paper. One copy stays with the event and one goes with the items/driver.

It's always helpful to have printed directions from an Internet source such as MapQuest unless they have a GPS system in their vehicle.

Return everything else to the office. Schedule enough volunteers and vehicles for this purpose so that each only has to make one trip. Try to group things together rather than just dumping everything.

Congratulations! The hard part is over.

Program Script Example

ABC Auction

March 6, 2008

7:10 PM

Emcee Name   Good evening. We'd like to have you move to your tables so that we can get started. Please be seated.

Just a couple of items:

The raffle drawing for the **2-carat diamond pendant** will be held in just a few minutes. **THIS DIAMOND PENDANT IS VALUED AT $10,000 AND COMES WITH A CERTIFIED APPRAISAL.**

Please raise your bidder number if you'd like to purchase a ticket and one of our ticket sellers will come to your table.

7:15 PM

Emcee Name   Last chance to buy a raffle ticket!! Raise your bidder number if you still want to purchase a ticket.

7:20 PM   Welcome to the 20th Anniversary of the ABC Auction! I'm Emcee Name, news anchor for Northwest News Channel 5. This is our fourth year as the television media sponsor of this event.

We'd like to thank you for being with us this evening. We're here to have a great time and raise some money for charity, so hold those bidder paddles HIGH.

276

Confirmation Form Example

ABC Auction Confirmation

According to our records, you are registered for the following events.

Reservation Name _____

ABC Auction - Saturday, March 6, 2008
Continental Hotel Ballroom, 555 Main Street, Portland, Oregon

❑ ____ Individual seats   ❑ ____ Table/s of 10   ❑ Table guest of _____

Black Tie Optional. 5:00 p.m. – Registration, reception, silent auction   7:00 p.m. – Dinner and live auction

Preview Party – Friday, March 5, 2008
University Club, 222 Wide Street, Portland, Oregon

❑ ____ Individual seats   ❑ ____ Table/s of 10   ❑ Table guest of _____

Business Attire   6:00 p.m. - Reception   7:00 p.m. – Celebrity Dinner

Picnic In The Park – Sunday, March 7, 2008   ***(These confirmations were mailed separately)***
Cathedral Park, 111 Center Street, Portland, Oregon

PLEASE NOTE:
Due to heavy attendance on Saturday, and to keep the registration wait as short as possible, you may want to:
♦ Arrive Early   ♦Use Quick Check

PARKING & TAXIS: Parking is available at several garages and parking lots surrounding the Continental Hotel. Please be a responsible driver. Taxis are available at the curb.

DISCOUNTED HOTEL ROOMS: Rooms are offered by the Marriott Hotel for $XX, plus tax, on a space-available basis. Please make reservations directly with the hotel at 503.000.0000. Mention the ABC Auction to receive the discount.

CATALOGS will be mailed to registered guests on February 22nd. They may also be picked up on or after that date at the administration office, 456 NE Park, between 8:00 a.m. and 5:00 p.m. Monday through Friday.

QUESTIONS? Please call 503.111.2222

Confirmation Letter Example

Date

Name
Address
City/State/Zip

Dear Guest Name,

We're pleased you will be joining us for the ABC Auction on Saturday, March 6th at the Continental Hotel, 555 Main Street. At 5:00 p.m. the doors open for registration and the reception and silent auction will begin. This letter will serve as confirmation of your registration.

Parking is available at several garages and parking lots surrounding the hotel. Please carpool with others if possible. Please drive responsibly. If you are planning to drink alcoholic beverages, you may wish to assign a designated driver. Taxis will be available at the curb starting at 9:00 p.m.

If you'd like to stay overnight, the Marriott Hotel is offering a discounted room rate of $99. Please make reservations directly with the hotel at 503.000.0000 and mention the discounted rate for the ABC Auction.

If you have questions, please contact us at 503.111.2222 or via email at abcauction@serviceprovider.com.

Thank you again for your support of this annual fundraiser for XYZ Charity that serves children, families, and older adults in our community. We hope you have a wonderful time.

Warm regards,

Name
Chairman

(or Event Director, etc.)

Chapter 16 – Post-Event Activity

It's A Wrap

The event is over and it's been a big success. The guests have gone home and the clean up is done. As the event manager, you're probably ready for a tropical vacation or at the very least a well-deserved rest. But there are still some things that need to be done.

Post-event activities include such things as final press releases, budget recap, thank you notes and letters, gifts, volunteer parties, committee celebrations, staff recognition, evaluations, and a final report.

With good planning many of these tasks, or arrangements for them, can be handled well in advance of the event (and before you're tired and burned out). By making a few last minute adjustments to thank you letters, notes, or invitations to celebration parties, they can be sent out within a few days after the event.

This chapter talks about how to:

> ➤ Pre-plan for post-event activities
> ➤ Take care of yourself
> ➤ Prepare a final press release
> ➤ Conduct follow up with new contacts
> ➤ Prepare thank yous and letters
> ➤ Provide recognition to various people and/or sponsors
> ➤ Review and evaluate the budget
> ➤ Generate final reports
> ➤ Update work lists and records
> ➤ Conduct your own evaluation
> ➤ Create a plan for the next event

A Post-Event Worksheet and Event Manager's Evaluation are located at the end of the chapter.

"Everyone loves praise. Look for ways to give it to them"

Life's Little Instruction Book, Volume II

PRE-EVENT PREPARATION

Take care of yourself. Even with the best of intentions, it's hard to get enough rest, eat right, exercise, spend time with family and friends, or do other self-care activities during the "crunch."

There are ways to take care of yourself, even during stressful periods. Take vitamins and get as much rest as possible. Drink lots of water because this is one of the best ways to help your body. During the event, eat healthy foods (fresh fruit, trail mix, or organic energy bars are good because they contain natural sugar). Greasy foods or sugary drinks are taboo.

We're often too busy to eat right, or there isn't food available when we're starving, so bringing healthy "snacks" will ensure that you can keep going without eating a bunch of junk. You'll function better if your body has the right kind of fuel, even if you have to bring it from home.

If possible, schedule some time for a massage prior to or after the event. It will do wonders for a stressed-out, tense or aching body, and helps to calm your mind. Even better, plan to take a few days post-event at a peaceful place like the beach or mountains to relax.

You're not the Energizer Bunny! Don't expect to keep going, and going, and going… There is a physical letdown period about 3 days to a week after an event where your body says, "Time out!" This is normal. You may even get a cold or feel "wiped out" as things get back to their regular routine.

Event managers have to sustain high levels of concentration and energy for long periods prior to and during the event. Unless the event has been relatively stress-free, it's best to take a short break to give your mind and body a respite. This is especially true if the event is an extremely large one.

DURING THE EVENT

Take lots of notes. Use a small spiral bound notebook that you can keep in your pocket. You'll be amazed at how much this little "memory tool" will help.

Record your observations of things you want to remember throughout the event—not only the things you see that are wrong, but also things that are right. Do some polite eavesdropping. Write down comments that you hear as people move through the event.

If you see someone going the proverbial "extra mile," jot it down so you can remember to thank them. They will appreciate your remembering something personal that they did. Note things about the event itself that could have been done differently or ideas that come to you. Write them down for next year's planning because you're not likely to remember them otherwise.

Take photos or video for the same purposes. It's always nice to include a photo in a thank you note because it shows the recipient that their contribution did not go unnoticed.

Document statistics. These can be used to validate event goals. You'll need to collect this information to use in developing the final report.

AFTER THE EVENT

Final press release. A final press release can be prepared ahead of time and last minute details can be inserted prior to distribution. This is a good way to provide closure to the press and others. If envelopes or an e-mail list are readied in advance, it is relatively easy to insert the updated information and send it on its way.

If The Event is An Auction

Auction certificates. Some of this information is repeated from *The Event* chapter because it is important if your event is an auction.

We do not advocate sending actual certificates home with bidders the same day as the event. The reason for this is because if the purchaser's credit card is declined or there are other issues, you may have some difficulty getting the certificate back. It's best to make sure all is good to go and financial transactions have been completed. If you have a small event, and you feel comfortable sending original certificates home with bidders, then by all means do so.

Within 7-14 days of an auction, mail the "original" certificates received from restaurants, hotels and others to the winning bidders. These types of certificates need to be sent via registered mail so there is a record of receipt. Don't forget to keep a copy of all certificates and any pertinent supporting information for reference in case the certificate is lost or the buyer has questions.

"Generic" certificates, the second type, are created from auction software or in a word processing program. These are used for verification of the purchase of dinners in private homes, parties, stays at personal vacation properties, or activities that were sold in the auction but for which no formal certificate was provided.

Auction lots often contain both "original" gift certificates and "generic" certificates. In this instance, create the generic certificate for the applicable parts and create a list of the other certificates to make sure none are overlooked in the mail out.

If the auction is generating the certificate, make sure to identify the person to contact to make arrangements for using the certificate benefits. In some cases, it may be several contacts if the auction lot has multiple parts.

There are many specialty papers available that can be used to created "theme certificates or they can be produced on the event's letterhead. Use the bullet lists contained in the catalog copy to generate the certificate. If changes were made in the addendum from the original benefits, make sure those are incorporated into the certificate. Bulky narrative or a list of donors is not required. Include complete information, but keep it as simple as possible to avoid misunderstandings about what is (or isn't) included in the offering.

Keep a copy of every certificate in a file. Whether the certificate is an original or a generic version, keep a copy in numerical auction lot order. Live auction lots will have many more generic certificates than the silent auction will. It's also helpful to clip copies of certificates together with individual groups for live, super silent, or silent in order to find them easily.

The donor/s may also need a post-event letter. Depending on the auction lot, the donor may need to be notified who purchased their donation in case arrangements need to be made for use of vacation properties, private dinners, etc. Keep a copy of the letter sent to the donor with the copies pertaining to that auction lot.

Post-auction coordination of auction packages. It often falls to the auction director to coordinate larger parties, trips, dinners, or other activities sold through the auction. This has a secondary benefit because it takes the burden off the donor and/or purchaser in having to coordinate numerous elements to facilitate the activity.

Donors who are repeatedly called by a purchaser trying to work out the logistics of the activity are less likely to donate in the future than if they know the auction director will take care of the arrangements. If the trip, dinner or other activity is date specific, and is sold as such in the auction, many of these issues will already be resolved and it makes for a less stressful experience for both the donor and purchaser.

FINANCIAL MATTERS

Numerous financial matters need to be taken care of the week following the event and beyond.

Process credit card transactions. Using a service like Auctionpay simplifies the processing of credit cards through batching. Multiple credit card machines are used at the event which feed into one master terminal. Following the event, the transactions captured in the master terminal are sent to the bank in a "batch" rather than having to process each transaction separately. If you don't have this kind of service, credit card transactions will need to be processed individually through standard procedure.

Invoice those who haven't paid. Some event sponsors or guests will ask to be invoiced post-event so their purchases can be paid for through their company or employer. Send out invoices as soon as possible since this is uncollected revenue until it is received. You may need to invoice some people more than once. Don't let too much time pass before aggressively pursuing payment.

Review the budget. Everyone will want to know how the event did financially. This information will be of special interest to the chairmen and sponsors.

Compare the event revenues and expenses against the original projections. If data has been entered correctly, the software should be able to print out an accurate report that lists both revenue and expense breakout. Pay special attention to items that could be eliminated, obtained at less cost, or were added because they were overlooked in the initial budgeting process.

Pay the bills. Most of the bills should be received within 30 days or less after the event. Likewise, contracts and other payables should have been processed. While final financial figures may not yet be available, you should have a fairly accurate picture.

Charitable disbursements and procedures. If the event benefits a charity or multiple charities, disbursements need to be made before the end of the fiscal year (if possible) based on pre-established formulas. Disbursements should not be made until all revenue has been collected and all bills have been paid. If there are still payments to be made on items like elements contained in auction packages, make sure to hold those amounts in reserve as well as holding back enough for seed money for the next event.

Setting rules and requirements for participation, processes for receiving benefits, and methods for disbursement of funds are the responsibility of the event's governing body.

REPORTS

Financial reports. Event chairmen, committee chairs, and/or management will want to see financial reports. Do this as soon as possible after the event when all or most of the financial transactions or adjustments have been sorted out.

Guest listing. If your event had formal registration, print a report listing all guests in alphabetical order by last name, as well as their contact information. This aids in mailing certificates, receipts, invoices and so on and gives a written reference. If a guest has no information in the system, it can be obtained and added to the database. This report may also indicate at whose table the guest sat. This information is handy to have for events that produce Save the Date and invitation mailings for the next event.

SAY THANK YOU

Everyone will want to know how well the event did, especially for events that are fundraisers. All those who sponsored, attended, volunteered, or the like should receive a thank you letter or card. Emphasize the importance of their contributions and how what they did helped the event.

NOTES

NOTES

Except for the people who should receive hand-written notes, thank yous can be prepared ahead of time and mailed within a few days of the event. If using a merge mailing, be sure to add a little personal hand-written "Thank You!" or something to that effect on the letter when signing to make it more personalized.

You can create several versions of the same thank you that have been altered according to the role the person played in the event. For example, "Thank you so much for being a volunteer (sponsor, exhibitor, etc.) for the ABC Auction."

Never, Never photocopy a signature onto letterhead! Letters should have personal signatures (not electronic signatures). Nothing makes a person feel that you are insincere more than to receive a computer generated (or photocopied) letter that no one could bother to personally sign. It's like a double insult. Merge mailings are fine, but sign the letter, preferably in a contrasting ink color (like blue). If there are a lot of letters, sign them over a period of a few days.

Thank you lists. Create a list of "who will thank who" in advance to avoid confusion and duplication. Personal, hand-written notes should be sent by the chairperson or executive director to committee chairs and key players. The event manager may want to add a comment or have the note bear dual signatures. Committee chairmen may wish to thank their committee members. The event manager will also have their own personal list to thank.

Thank you gifts. Chairmen, select sponsors, and other high-level affiliates should receive a modest gift in addition to a thank you letter or note. Try to deliver gifts in person by setting an appointment ahead of time. Include "who will deliver what" on the list of "who's thanking who." The recipient will be doubly impressed if their gift is personally delivered by the event manager, management, chairman, or board member. Yes, it takes extra time, but it means so much more than receiving the gift through a messenger service or via mail.

The gift should be in good taste and relate in some way to the event or to the recipient's interests (e.g. bottle of wine, quality chocolates, a good cigar, etc.). Or the gift can relate directly to the event. For example, if the event benefits a children's charity, framed original children's art would be a good choice for a thank you gift and only cost might be a pre-fabricated frame from a craft store.

Schedule the "After" Party. Depending on the extent of the invitation list and budget, there should be a get-together with those who played key roles. The celebration can be used to recognize chairmen, committee members, staff, or volunteers. Invitations can be extended separately or included in the text of the thank you letter.

Whatever you do, make it fun! Arrangements should be made in advance even though the invitations will be mailed following the event. Decorate or make it festive. Have wine or beer and food. This creates energy and motivation for the next time.

If you don't want to have a separate party after the fact, you can use the debriefing meeting for this purpose and make it festive.

Recognitions. Share the glory. Very few people can claim to be solely responsible for the success of an event. Team effort requires that others share the limelight. At the wrap-up party, publicly acknowledge the contributions of others with framed photographs, certificates, or other small gifts.

Debrief & Evaluate

Evaluation meetings. Within two or three weeks after the event, you'll want to hold a final wrap-up meeting to summarize and evaluate. The meeting date can be set and announced in advance, with reminders sent out following the event. People's memories begin to fade about details and they move on to other activities so don't wait too long to do this.

Create the agenda in the chronological order of the event. Set a time limit to avoid getting stuck on one or two things. You may want to include committee reports or list specific topics. Be prepared to report on financial outcomes and key areas of success.

Note: Debriefing meetings tend to focus on "what we could have done better." Too often we forget to acknowledge all the things we did well. Make sure the helping of "praise" is equal to the helping of "suggestions."

Another way to handle the evaluation would be to include "individual reports" on the agenda where each person gives their input during the meeting. Those who are unable to attend could submit comments via e-mail or by other means to be shared.

Even though it's a "meeting," it's also a celebration. A nice gesture is to hold this gathering at someone's home, or in a relaxing location with special food or beverage.

Final report. Chairmen and decision makers will want a final report. It should be concise and include a summary, comparison of goals to results, budget recap, results of publicity efforts, etc. It's also good to include backup information such as copies of press releases, press clippings, and other supporting documents of interest.

Miscellaneous Follow Up

Personal evaluation. How do you personally feel about the event? Was it successful in your opinion? What part did you like best? What did you dislike most? Which people were easy to work with and which were difficult? Foremost question, would you do this again?

Decide on a course of action for the next event. After the event, a significant amount of information will be available on which to base any decisions about future changes. You'll need to create an updated plan that is a composite of the original plan and all the things that went well, what could have been done differently, what was learned, and whether the event was financially feasible.

The decision to implement changes. Don't make decisions based solely on whether the event made money. There are other important factors that contribute to success and create buy-in. A clear, well-defined plan with sound reasoning is essential.

Changes occur both internally and externally. Internal factors that may effect change include boards of directors or chairmen, personnel, lack of resources, and the like. External factors include things that indirectly affect the event like economic fluctuations, outgrowing a venue, timing, or ebb and flow in the event's life cycle.

Don't just look at tomorrow. There should be a plan for the event of where you want to be 1, 3, and 5 years down the road. Successful events need direction beyond what is happening in the moment. Older events experiencing a decline may not need to be totally reinvented, but need a fresh new look at what works or doesn't.

Update the timeline and work lists. Incorporate changes and adjustments while they are still fresh in your memory. With just a little tweaking, you'll have a good start on the next event and a clear path will be left to follow for whoever is the event manager.

Update records. Update sponsor, volunteer, donor, and attendee records. Clean out file folders and computer files but don't delete old documents unless they won't be used again.

That's It!

NOTES

Post Event Worksheet

Post-Event Activity

1. Did you take notes and record your observations? _____
2. Were there people who should receive special thanks or recognition? _____
3. Did you plan for some personal relaxation following the event? _____
4. Was a final press release sent out? _____
5. Have you followed up on new contacts? _____
6. Did you thank every person who volunteered? _____
7. Have chairmen, committee members, sponsors, donors, exhibitors, been thanked? _____
8. Will chairmen, sponsors, or high-level supporters receive thank you gifts? _____
9. Who will deliver thank you gifts? _____
10. Will a party be held for volunteers? _____
11. Has a staff party or one for key people been scheduled? _____
12. What forms of acknowledgement will be used? _____
13. Has a debriefing meeting been held? _____
14. Were the event goals realized? _____
15. Were strategies used the same as originally thought, or did they change? _____
16. Has input from sponsors, volunteers, and others been collected? _____
17. Have borrowed items been returned? _____
18. Have you reviewed the budget and paid all bills? _____
19. Has the final report been developed? _____
20. What is the course of action? _____
21. Have the timelines and work lists been updated? _____
22. Have the records and files been cleaned up and finalized? _____
23. Have computer files been cleaned up or updated? _____
24. Has the event plan been updated? _____
25. _____
26. _____
27. _____
28. _____
29. _____
30. _____

Event Manager's Personal Evaluation

1. Is the Event Manager's job description accurate? _____
2. Would better skills in certain areas have made your job easier? _____
3. Would you personally be willing to manage this event again? _____
4. Who did you most and least enjoy working with? _____
5. Did you have enough administrative support? Who provided it? _____
6. Did you use a notebook system or a different means? _____
7. Did the creative planning process include what the event needed? _____
8. Was the right mix of people invited to participate in the creative planning? _____
9. If not, who else should have been invited? _____
10. How long did the creative planning meeting take? _____
11. Was the General Timeline for the event fairly accurate? _____
12. What could have been done sooner, or done later? _____
13. Did you make notes or changes to Work Lists for future reference? _____
14. Was the forecasted budget realistic or were major adjustments needed? _____
15. Was the committee structure as it needed to be? Too many? Too few? _____
16. Did committee job descriptions accurately reflect the job performed? _____
17. Were there too many committee meetings or too few? Were they productive? _____
18. Were there enough sponsors? Too many? Too few? _____
19. Were sponsor benefits appropriate or do they need to change? _____
20. Were there media partners? What was their involvement? _____
21. Did the event have a marketing plan? Did it work? _____
22. What marketing methods were used? _____
23. Did you prepare a media kit? Who received it? _____
24. Did the event spend money on advertising? What kind? Did it work? _____
25. What forms of publicity worked best? _____
26. Was the media present at the event? What was the result? _____
27. Did you use a graphic designer? Did the materials enhance the event? _____
28. Were printed materials effective? Which ones? _____
29. What forms of printing were used? Should quantities increase/decrease? _____
30. Were enough photos available? Who took the photos? _____
31. What permits were required? _____
32. Was insurance coverage adequate? _____
33. Was security needed? Who provided it? _____

Event Manager's Personal Evaluation (continued)

34. Did contractors, entertainers, and others honor their contracts? _____

35. Was the venue a good location or were there issues? _____

36. Would you use the venue again? Why or why not? _____

37. Were needed amenities available, or were they obtained separately? _____

38. If an outdoor venue, was the space adequate and utilities available? _____

39. If a hotel or convention facility was used, were the prices fair? _____

40. What kinds of services were included in the cost? _____

41. What type of food service was used and did it work well? _____

42. Did you use the venue's catering, or bring in outside catering? _____

43. Were you presented with catering charges you weren't expecting? _____

44. How did the food look? Was it as hot or cold as it should have been? _____

45. Were there enough choices to accommodate everyone including vegetarians? _____

46. What types of beverages were served? _____

47. How far in advance was the guarantee required? _____

48. If the event used self-catering, did this work well or not? Why? _____

49. Were the food estimates accurate? Too much? Too little? _____

50. Was there enough equipment? _____

51. How would you do things differently next time regarding the food? _____

52. Was there enough staff or volunteers to prepare and serve the food? _____

53. Would it have been as cost effective to hire catering rather than do it yourself? _____

54. Did the event have exhibitors? What kind? _____

55. Did the site plan layout work well? _____

56. Was an exhibition services company used? Were they effective? _____

57. Did the event use production contractors? What kind? _____

58. Did contractor have enough time to load in, set up, and tear down? _____

59. What kind of décor was used? _____

60. Was the décor just right, too little, too much? _____

61. Would you work with the decorating company again? _____

62. Was visual media used? What kind? Was it effective? _____

63. Was there a stage? How big? Did it work well? _____

64. Was professional lighting needed? How was it used? _____

65. Did you use a sound system? Did it work well, or need changes? _____

Event Manager's Personal Evaluation (continued)

66. Did you rent equipment such as tables, chairs, etc.? _____

67. Was the rental equipment in good condition? _____

68. Did the rental company set up and take down the equipment? _____

69. Did you use rented communication equipment such as radios? Any problems? _____

70. What types of entertainment were there? Would you change anything? _____

71. Were entertainers on time and cooperative? _____

72. Did you use a talent agency or book entertainment yourself? _____

73. Were there ways that money could have been saved on entertainment? _____

74. Who received the site plans and logistics schedules? Was anyone forgotten? _____

75. Was the site plan accurate? How much detail was provided? _____

76. Did the venue site accommodate disabled persons? _____

77. Did locations for staging, tents, or other equipment work well? _____

78. Was electrical power, water, or other utilities readily available? _____

79. Were there enough restrooms? Too many? Too few? _____

80. How well did signage work? Did you need more, less? _____

81. Did you leave the event site clean and in good condition? _____

82. Were there safety concerns or emergencies? How were they handled? _____

83. Were there enough supplies, tools, or equipment available to cover all activities? _____

84. Was the logistics schedule accurate? Was anything major left out? _____

85. Did the timing work for all parties to load in, set up, and tear down? _____

86. How long did it take to tear down and clean up once guests departed? _____

87. Were there enough volunteers? Too many? Too few? _____

88. What provisions were made for volunteers regarding headquarters, food, etc.? _____

89. Did volunteers stay busy during their shifts, or do shifts need to be altered? _____

90. Do volunteer positions need to be added, changed, or deleted? _____

91. Were communications to volunteers adequate for recruitment and confirmation? _____

92. What did volunteers receive for their participation? _____

93. Has everyone been thanked? _____

94. Has a final report been developed? _____

95. _____

96. _____

97. _____

98. _____

Exhibitor's Evaluation Worksheet

1. How did you learn about the event? _____

2. What motivated you to participate as an exhibitor? _____

3. What was your perception of the event as a whole? _____

4. Was your booth request and confirmation handled in a timely manner? _____

5. Did you receive all the information you needed in advance of the event? _____

6. Where was your booth located? _____

7. Did you receive the amenities designated? _____

8. Was there a good amount of traffic past your booth location? _____

9. How do you feel about the way the exhibitor booths were arranged? _____

10. Do you feel that the event marketing was well targeted and produced results? _____

11. Do you feel that the participation of exhibitors enhances the event? _____

12. Was the exhibition services contractor easy to work with? _____

13. Was the security adequate? _____

14. Were venue representatives helpful? _____

15. Did you have any problems with load in and set up of your space? _____

16. Were event personnel available to help when needed? _____

17. Were electrical power, equipment, labor, or other support available if needed? _____

18. Did you require overnight lodging in the area? Where did you stay? _____

19. How was your lodging experience? _____

20. What forms of transportation were needed? _____

21. Was adequate parking available? _____

22. Were shipping and receiving functions adequate? _____

23. How did you market your booth? _____

24. What parts of your exhibitor experience were best? _____

25. What do you feel could have been done differently? _____

26. How would you rate your experience overall (1 through 5, 5 being best) _____

27. Would you be willing to participate as an exhibitor in the future? _____

28. _____

29. _____

30. _____

LaVergne, TN USA
02 April 2010
178050LV00001B/1/P

9 781449 075514